FREE & INEXPENSIVE CAREER MATERIALS

A Resource Directory

Second Edition

EDITED BY
ELIZABETH H. OAKES

ACKNOWLEDGMENTS

Special thanks to Ruth Oldenburg and Carolyn Schultz,
whose work contributed to the development of this directory.

```
              Library of Congress Cataloging-in-Publication Data

Free and inexpensive career materials : a resource directory /
   Elizabeth H. Oakes, editor. -- 2nd ed.
        p.      cm.
        First published : Garrett Park, MD : Garrett Park Press, 1995.
        Previous ed. edited by Cheryl S. Hecht.
        Includes bibliographical references.
        ISBN 0-89434-221-5
        1. Vocational guidance--United States--Information services-
   -Directories.   I. Oakes, Elizabeth H., 1964-
        HF5382.5.U5F72   1997
        016.3317'02'0973--dc21                                    97-26167
                                                                     CIP
```

Copyright © 1998 by Ferguson Publishing Company
Published and Distributed by
Ferguson Publishing Company
200 West Madison Street, Suite 300
Chicago, Illinois 60606

All rights reserved. This book may not be duplicated in any way without the express permission of the publisher, except in the form of brief excerpts or quotations for the purposes of review. The information contained herein is for the personal use of the reader and may not be incorporated in any commercial programs, other books, databases, or any kind of software without written consent of the publisher. Making copies of this book or any portion for any purpose other than your own is a violation of United States copyright laws.

Printed in the United States of America

TABLE OF CONTENTS

SECTION I
Introduction

SECTION II
How to Use This Book

SECTION III
Index and Guide to Resources

SECTION IV
Sources of Free and Inexpensive Career Materials

SECTION V
Career Sites on the World Wide Web

SECTION VI
Related Reference Books

(Note: Pages are not numbered in order to avoid confusion with the sequence numbers used to identify entries in section IV.)

Section I

INTRODUCTION

Ferguson's *Free & Inexpensive Career Materials* offers contact information for more than 700 organizations and associations that provide free or inexpensive ($10 or less) career information. The directory is designed to help individuals planning careers as well as those who guide them. It may also be useful to librarians who wish to expand their resources and to organizations interested in developing career materials.

To update the information published in the previous edition, we contacted every organization. If we were unable to verify the organization's contact information, we deleted its listing from the book. Ten percent of the listings are new to this edition. In addition we collected web site and e-mail addresses for 62 percent of the organizations listed in the book. We also added fax numbers to more than 400 listings.

This revised edition includes trade associations, professional associations, state occupational information committees, academic membership groups, foundations, college departments, government agencies, and commercial publishers. These groups are organized alphabetically by name, and each listing includes the following information, when available:

Name of organization
Mailing address
Telephone number
Fax number
Web site address
E-mail address
Name of publication(s)
Price for a single copy, if there is a charge
Number of pages in publication
Description of publication

Organizations in this directory that have a web site often offer a wealth of information that can be printed right off your computer screen. In some cases, the full text of publications listed in the entry is available at the web site. We encourage you to visit the web sites when possible.

When organizations such as commercial publishers and government agencies distribute dozens of items on careers, only illustrative titles are listed. You may want to contact these organizations to request a catalog listing all their available publications.

We invite readers to notify us of additional free and inexpensive career resources. Just send your suggestions to Editor, Free and Inexpensive, Ferguson Publishing Company, 200 West Madison Street, Chicago, Illinois 60606. Your assistance will be very much appreciated.

SECTION II

HOW TO USE THIS BOOK

The listings in this directory are organized alphabetically by name and numbered consecutively. If you are looking for a specific organization, just look for its name in alphabetical order in section IV of the directory. If you have a particular career field in mind or just want to browse for ideas, start with the index, which is located in section III. It lists career fields, such as nursing and public relations, and job topics, such as overseas work, and provides a reference to the entry numbers of associated listings. Because the directory is organized around the listings' entry numbers, the book does not have page numbers. All numbers you see refer to entry numbers.

Please respect the contribution these organizations make in providing free and inexpensive career material by doing the following:

> Request only a single copy of the material cited unless you are willing to reimburse the organization for the cost of multiple copies.
>
> Send a self-addressed, stamped business-size envelope to help cover the mailing costs. For items available from Canadian sources, be sure to add the required postage.
>
> Contact only those organizations whose materials are of specific interest to you. Excessive requests for free and inexpensive material may force some groups to discontinue its availability.
>
> Include the item number, if given, when requesting information.
>
> Send a check or money order for the proper amount along with your request for publications that specify a charge. Single copies of publications that do not list a charge are free.

Section III

INDEX AND GUIDE TO RESOURCES

Here's a quick guide to the resources cited in this directory. Each number refers to an organization offering free and inexpensive career materials, as listed in section IV.

Accounting and auditing, 129, 284, 336, 418, 420, 596, 671
Acoustics, 11
Actuarial science, 295, 691
Acupuncture, 68, 491
Advertising, 13, 35, 56
Aerospace, 16
Agriculture, 17, 36, 106, 256, 318, 377, 479, 495, 496, 498, 573, 647, 659, 730, 736, 756, 766
Agronomy, 180
Air conditioning and refrigeration, 21, 189, 669
Allergy and immunology, 26
Anesthesiology, 181
Anthropology, 39, 71, 753
Apprenticeships, 225, 275
Archaeology, 223, 682, 684, 692
Architecture, 127, 194, 251, 499
Art, 43, 255, 346, 395, 500, 529, 545, 592
Art therapy, 42
Astronomy and meteorology, 77, 144, 494
Athletic training, 78, 539
Auctioneering, 540
Automotive services, 79, 265, 384, 541, 542, 695
Aviation, 16, 19, 20, 22, 253, 366, 367, 374, 383, 752

Banking, 80
Beekeeping, 82, 334
Biological sciences, 128, 167, 168, 176, 260, 268, 269, 507, 579, 670, 693
Blind, 112, 238, 572
Blood banking, 57
Botany, 58, 159, 270
Broadcasting, 320, 508, 544, 666
Business, 44, 358, 370, 382, 427, 543, 645, 741, 750, 751

Camping, 84
Cardiovascular technology, 452
Career information, 1, 23, 220, 224, 293, 294, 301, 319, 353, 354, 360, 365, 371, 396, 454, 630, 643, 722, 744, 748, 759, 762, 764, 771
Ceramics, 85

Chemistry, 46, 59, 86, 130, 350, 696
Child care, 95, 300, 548
Chiropractic medicine, 87, 327, 428
College admissions and testing, 325, 348, 364, 394, 466, 510, 653, 728, 737
College study, 232, 305, 316, 468, 517, 657
Communications, 558, 690
Community education, 559
Computer science, 254, 313, 713
Conservation, 126, 356, 511, 583, 590, 605, 689, 711, 717, 743, 770
Construction
    Employment, 233, 234, 272, 273, 409, 434, 435, 439, 729
    Training, 94
Cooperative education, 556, 623
Cosmetology, 245, 321, 492, 562
Court reporting, 569
Credit services, 332
Culinary arts, 99, 299
Cytology, 186

Dance, 292, 335
Dance therapy, 100
Dental fields, 64, 100, 101, 103, 512, 513
Design, 104, 411
Disabled
    Employment of, 303, 393, 399, 651, 678
    Therapists, 222
    Training for, 4, 264, 462, 681
Drama and theatre, 38, 349, 531, 758

Ecology, 344
Editing, 196
Education and teaching
    Elementary, 75, 109, 244, 250, 290, 362, 514, 563, 668, 746
    Postsecondary, 297, 302, 361, 440, 536
    Preschool, 237, 323, 488, 504
    Secondary, 109, 145, 244, 250, 290, 362, 518, 533, 565, 738, 760
EEG technology, 187
EKG technology, 183
Electronics, 351, 352, 415, 438, 608
Energy, 252, 739
Engineering
    Agricultural, 179
    Biomedical, 267
    Civil, 184
    Cost, 3, 640
    Fire protection, 699
    Industrial, 417
    Mechanical, 198
    Mining, 482

All fields, 124, 171, 453, 493, 709, 720
Entomology, 357
Environment, 27, 622
Equine science, 397, 449
Extracorporeal technology, 188

Facility management, 431
Farrier science, 107
Fashion, 40
Financial aid, 12, 76, 108, 123, 135, 231, 285, 286, 304, 312, 369, 372, 609, 624, 626, 635, 719, 724, 725
Financial planning, 426, 609, 719
Fishing, 110
Flooring, 227, 375
Food sciences, 140, 416, 456
Forestry, 111, 694
Foundry, 113
Fringe benefits, 306, 432
Funeral service, 83, 574

Gemology, 447, 471
Genetics, 191, 385, 597
Geography, 246, 247, 386
Geological sciences, 70, 114, 132, 387, 388, 698
Gerontology, 65, 240
Government, 162, 166, 373, 408, 530, 576
Guidance and counseling, 98, 322, 331, 587

Health administration, 8, 89, 90, 262, 400
Health education, 6, 47
Health sciences, 97, 116, 398, 429, 575, 723
History and collecting, 54, 88, 549, 580, 638
Home economics, 402
Home study, 340, 672
Horticulture, 120
Hotel and restaurant management, 121, 329, 347
Human factors and resources, 404, 405, 437, 685
Hygiene, industrial, 125

Imaging science, 686
Industrial relations, 412
Information science, 173
Instrumentation, 423
Insurance, 25, 410, 522, 526
Interior design, 193, 381
Internships, 315, 719
Iron and steel industry, 134

Job Corps, 577, 628

Job search, 24, 45, 280, 289, 291, 298, 310, 316, 333, 342, 354, 363, 445, 448, 457, 461, 464, 475, 610, 611, 616, 617, 633, 662, 731, 740, 754
Journalism and communications, 10, 239, 343, 345, 621, 718

Labor relations, 41
Languages, 155, 390, 465, 485, 551
Law, 81, 309, 380, 441, 460, 463, 749, 757
Law enforcement, 502
Legal assisting, 519
Library science, 136, 282, 477, 714
Logistics, 326

Machined products, 648
Management, 137, 407, 414, 578
Manufacturing, 700
Marine science, 195, 283, 436, 446, 467, 472, 473, 474, 484, 497, 579, 581, 625, 629, 636, 676, 675, 677, 702, 755
Marketing and sales, 338, 339, 378, 470, 589, 673
Massage, 138
Mathematics, 139, 243, 314, 476, 566, 687
Medical assisting, 66
Medical recording, 50
Medical research, 170, 175, 177, 242
Medical sciences, 28, 32, 33, 60, 72, 133, 141, 142, 170, 235, 248, 443, 505
Medical technology, 143, 478, 515
Metallurgy, 688
Military, 18, 228, 229, 230, 480, 734, 747
Mining and minerals, 481, 483
Minority information
    African American, 459
    Hispanic, 564, 763
    Native American, 276, 624
    All minorities, 368, 561, 735
Minority programs
    Education, 588, 733, 763
    Employment, 368, 557
Motion pictures, 701
Municipal clerking, 433
Museums, 680
Music, 210, 486, 571, 683
Music therapy, 51, 503
Musical instrument repair, 525
Mycology, 489

Navy, 606, 607
Neurology, 29
Nonprofit employment, 5
Nuclear science, 146, 703
Nursing and midwifery, 30, 67, 91, 147, 257, 307, 523, 570, 599, 663, 632

Nutrition, 105

Occupational outlook, 226, 277, 278, 281, 341, 376, 406, 444, 458, 612, 613, 614, 615, 618, 631, 642, 761, 767, 768, 772
Occupational therapy, 148
Ophthalmology, 31, 450
Opticianry, 308, 490
Optometry, 149, 258, 715
Ornithology, 150
Orthodontics, 69
Orthotics and prosthetics, 30
Osteopathy, 152, 153
Overseas work, 317, 424, 742

Paralegal, 52, 582
Pathology, 185
Peace Corps, 641
Pedorthics, 650
Pest control, 584
Petroleum, 704
Pharmacy, 61, 96, 154, 190, 379, 442, 509
Photogrammetry, 178
Photography, 199, 266, 585, 644
Physical therapy, 157
Physician assisting, 34
Physics, 131, 156, 287
Physiology, 158
Planning, 160
Plastics, 705
Plumbing, 201, 524
Podiatry, 62, 161
Polygraph, 163
Postal service, 521
Psychiatry, 164
Psychology, 165, 236
Public health, 328
Public relations, 664
Publishing, 249, 469, 619, 620, 656
Purchasing, 527

Radiology, 117, 118, 202, 667
Real estate, 221, 421, 528
Recreation, 586, 601
Religion, 261, 554, 567, 649, 652, 732
Respiratory care, 53, 451
Retirement planning, 73

Safety, 37, 591
School administration, 74

Science, 55, 115, 594, 595, 600, 674
Scouting, 271
Secretarial science, 516, 520, 660
Security fields, 172
Sheet metal, 603
Shoe service, 679
Social services, 14, 49, 122, 534
Sociology, 205
Solar energy, 712
Sonography, 697
Special education, 552, 553
Speech and hearing, 206
Speleology, 598
Sports, 92, 151, 207, 208, 501, 535, 538, 550, 555, 627, 639, 658, 716, 775, 776
Statistical science, 209
Study abroad, 63, 241, 330, 745
Surgical technology, 259
Survey research, 324, 646
Surveying, 93

Temporary employment, 537
Textiles, 211, 430
Tool and dye, 726
Toxicology, 708
Training, 7
Translation, 212, 389
Transportation and travel management, 422, 593
Trapping, 604
Travel and tourism, 204, 602
Trucking, 213, 413, 661, 727

Utilities, 163

Veterinary medicine, 214, 288
Vocational training, 215, 547

Wage and salary information, 279, 280
Watchmaking, 216
Water industry, 217, 765
Welding, 218, 401
Women's programs
    Education, 774
    Employment, 2, 296, 309, 359, 391, 637, 769, 773
Wood science, 710
Writing, 532, 560, 654

Youth, 274, 311, 665

Zoology, 48, 119, 174, 182, 192, 197, 219, 506

Section IV

Sources of Free and Inexpensive Career Materials

1
50 PLUS PRE-RETIREMENT SERVICES
28 West 23rd Street
New York, NY 10010

- *Working in Retirement.*

2
9 TO 5, NATIONAL ASSOCIATION OF WORKING WOMEN
1430 West Peachtree Street
Atlanta, GA 30309
404-876-1604

- *Job Problem Hotline: 800-522-0925.* Provides information about workplace rights and links women with 9 to 5 members in their area.

- *The 9 to 5 Guide to Combating Sexual Harassment.* ($9.95) Contains step-by-step advice on what to do if you are being sexually harassed; information on how companies can adopt a policy against sexual harassment; suggestions for managers, unions, policy makers, attorneys, and advocates; and useful materials, including interactive exercises and resource lists.

- *Family and Medical Leave: Understanding Your New Rights.* 2 pages. Answers questions regarding the Family and Medical Leave Act.

- *Expanding Family Leave Policies at Your Workplace.* 2 pages. Provides information on the Family Medical Leave Act and how to apply it to your workplace.

- *Sources for Further Information on Family Friendly Policies.* 1 page. Lists organizations offering information on work/family issues.

3
AACE INTERNATIONAL: THE ASSOCIATION FOR TOTAL COST MANAGEMENT
Administrator, Certification and Education
209 Prairie Avenue
PO Box 1557
Morgantown, WV 26507-1557
800-858-COST or 304-296-8444
Fax: 304-291-5728

- *Careers in Cost Engineering and Related Industry Specialties.* 1 page.

- *Contacts for Engineering and Construction Programs Related to Cost Engineering.* 2 pages. SASE. Lists colleges and universities in the United States and Canada offering coursework related to cost engineering.

4
ACADEMIC THERAPY PUBLICATIONS
20 Commercial Boulevard
Novato, CA 94949-6191
800-422-7249 or 415-883-3314

Fax: 415-883-3720
http://www.atpub.com

- *Directory of Facilities and Services for the Learning Disabled.* ($5) 192 pages. Contains information on how to choose a facility or service for the learning disabled, as well as a state-by-state listing of programs; a bibliography of college-related publications; allied organizations and agencies serving learning disabled children, adults, and their families; educational journals and magazines; special education software publishers; and educational clearinghouses. Updated annually.

5
ACCESS: NETWORKING IN THE PUBLIC INTEREST
1001 Connecticut Avenue NW
Suite 838
Washington, DC 20036
202-785-4233
Fax: 202-785-4212
ACCESSCNTR@aol.com
http://www.essential.org/access/

- *Washington Gift Giving Guide.* ($4) 115 pages. Lists hundreds of nonprofit organizations in the Washington, DC, area by subject.

- *Community Jobs.* ($4 for back issues) Provides job listings from nonprofit organizations.

6
ACCREDITING BUREAU OF HEALTH EDUCATION SCHOOLS
2700 South Quincy Avenue
Suite 210
Arlington, VA 22206
703-998-1200
Fax: 703-998-2550
abhes@erols.com

- *Accrediting Bureau of Health Education Schools/Programs.* 31 pages. Lists by state the ABHES-accredited programs for medical laboratory technicians and medical assistants.

7
ACCREDITING COMMISSION OF CAREER SCHOOLS AND COLLEGES OF TECHNOLOGY
2101 Wilson Boulevard
Suite 302
Arlington, VA 22201
703-247-4212
Fax: 703-247-4533

- *Directory of Private Accredited Career Schools and Colleges of Technology.* 158 pages.

8
ACCREDITING COMMISSION ON EDUCATION FOR HEALTH SERVICES ADMINISTRATION
1911 North Fort Myer Drive
Suite 503
Arlington, VA 22209
703-524-0511

- *The Official List of Accredited Programs in Health Services Administration in Canada and the United States.* 8 pages. Includes the program name, date of initial accreditation action, and the degree(s) granted by the accredited program.

- *What is ACEHSA?* 6 pages. Includes a historical overview of ACEHSA, information on the accreditation program, and the ASPA Code of Good Practice.

9
ACCREDITING COUNCIL FOR INDEPENDENT COLLEGES AND SCHOOLS
750 First Street NE
Suite 980
Washington, DC 20002-4241
202-336-6780

Fax: 202-842-2593
acics@acics.org

- *Directory of Accredited Institutions.* 72 pages. Lists colleges and schools that offer specific programs, such as accounting and phlebotomy; and provides a state-by-state and international listing of private, postsecondary career colleges and schools. For educational institutions and businesses only (limited supply). Updated annually.

10
ACCREDITING COUNCIL ON EDUCATION IN JOURNALISM AND MASS COMMUNICATIONS
School of Journalism, Stauffer-Flint Hall
University of Kansas
Lawrence, KS 66045
913-864-3973
Fax: 913-864-5225
cklug@eagle.cc.ukans.edu
http://www.ukans.edu/~acejmc

- *Accredited Journalism and Mass Communications Education.* 72 pages. Lists accrediting standards, accredited programs at both the bachelor's and master's levels, and member associations. Published annually.

11
ACOUSTICAL SOCIETY OF AMERICA
500 Sunnyside Boulevard
Woodbury, NY 11797-2999
516-576-2360
Fax: 516-576-2377
elaine@aip.org

- *Acoustics and You.* 12 pages. Discusses career opportunities in the field of acoustics.

- *Directory of Graduate Education in Acoustics.* 24 pages. Lists the schools offering graduate programs in specific acoustical fields, such as architectural, physiological, psychological, and musical acoustics; acoustical instrumentation; noise and noise control; speech communication; ultrasonics; radiation and scattering; structural acoustics and vibration; underwater sound; nonlinear acoustics and aeroacoustics; acoustical signal processing; and bioacoustics. Contact information is also given.

12
ACT PUBLICATIONS
2201 North Dodge Street
PO Box 168
Iowa City, IA 52243-0168
319-337-1429

- *Preparing for the ACT Assessment.* 62 pages. Available in high school guidance offices or directly from the ACT.

13
ADVERTISING EDUCATION PUBLICATIONS
623 Meadow Bend Drive
Baton Rouge, LA 70820
504-767-0988

- *Where Shall I Go to Study Advertising and Public Relations?* ($5/$4 for students) 36 pages. Profiles 186 colleges and universities, with information on financial assistance, entrance requirements, tuition, programs and degrees offered, number of students and faculty, number of scholarships available, and student organizations. Updated annually.

14
ADVOCACY INSTITUTE
Publications Department
1707 L Street NW
Suite 400
Washington, DC 20036
202-659-8475

- *Why Not Work for a Change: An Introduction to Careers in Social Change.* ($1) 16 pages.

15

AEROBICS AND FITNESS ASSOCIATION OF AMERICA
15250 Ventura Boulevard
Suite 200
Sherman Oaks, CA 91403-3297
818-905-0040 or 800-446-2322
Fax: 818-990-5468

Write to them for details of their many workshops and training programs, including home study.

16

AEROSPACE EDUCATION FOUNDATION
1501 Lee Highway
Arlington, VA 22209-1198
703-247-5839
Fax: 703-247-5853
lswan@aes.org

- *Aerospace Technology Careers: The Opportunity to Soar.* 7 pages. Covers careers in aerospace, as well as job requirements and how to apply for employment with NASA.

- *Careers in Space: An Education and Career Guide for America's Space Program.* 22 pages. Lists degree programs in aerospace/aeronautical engineering, aeronautical technology, astronomy, astrophysics, planetary science, and aerospace/aeronautical science; information on NASA scholarship program, engineering research centers, and the job market; and aerospace companies and their programs.

- *Directory of Transportation Education: College Level.* 75 pages.

- *Aviation Careers: The Sky's the Limit.* 84 pages. Covers pilots, flight attendants, airline nonflying careers, flight engineers, aircraft manufacturing, aircraft maintenance, airport careers, government careers, and women in aviation.

- *Living and Working on the New Frontier* (PMS-017-C-KSC). Describes how the astronauts live while in space.

17

AGRICULTURAL RESEARCH SERVICE
U.S. Department of Agriculture
Human Resources Division
6305 Ivy Lane
Room 117
Greenbelt, MD 20770-1435
301-344-0134
Fax: 301-344-2962
http://www.ars.usda.gov

- *Science in Your Shopping Cart.* 34 pages. Describes in print and photos the research on consumer products developed at the ARS. Discusses ways that agricultural research touches and improves daily life. Applicable to middle school through college students and beyond.

- *A Scientific Career with the Agricultural Research Service.* 16 pages. Discusses the types of work available, salary, advancement, and where to learn about job openings.

- *An Employment Guide for Students.* 6 pages. Lists ARS student programs and how to apply for them.

18

AIR FORCE ROTC
United States Air Force Recruiting Service
551 East Maxwell Boulevard
Maxwell AFB, AL 36112-6663
334-953-2091

- *Air Force ROTC and Your Future.* 24 pages. Describes the opportunities available through the Air Force ROTC, the qualifications and scholarships, and Air Force career opportunities. Lists colleges and universities offering Air Force ROTC and those with cross-town enrollment agreements.

19
AIR LINE PILOTS ASSOCIATION INTERNATIONAL
535 Herndon Parkway
PO Box 1169
Herndon, VA 20172-1169
703-481-4440

- *Air Line Pilot Career Information.* 20 pages. Designed for students interested in a career in aviation. Provides an introduction to aviation; describes the three pilot positions and how to prepare for an air line pilot career; discusses licensing requirements; and provides sources of additional information.

- *Directory of Collegiate Aviation Programs and Options.*

- *Flight School Directory.*

20
AIR TRANSPORT ASSOCIATION OF AMERICA
1301 Pennsylvania Avenue NW
Suite 1100
Washington, DC 20004-1707
202-626-4000
Fax: 202-626-4181
http://www.air-transport.org

- *The People of the Airlines.* 8 pages. Details the necessary skills, education, and types of careers in the field. Contains a list of ATA member airlines.

- *Where to Find an Aviation Degree.* 4 pages. Contains contact information on schools offering aviation degrees, as well as a list of aviation scholarships.

21
AIR-CONDITIONING AND REFRIGERATION INSTITUTE
Education Department
4301 North Fairfax Drive
Suite 425
Arlington, VA 22203
703-524-8800
Fax: 703-528-3816
ari@dgsys.com

- *Career Opportunities in Heating, Air Conditioning and Refrigeration.* 8 pages. Describes job opportunities and required education and training for a career in the HVACR industry.

- *What You Should Know about ARI/GAMA Competency Examinations for Vo-Tech Students/Graduates of HVACR Programs.* 8 pages. Provides details about the competency exam program.

22
AIRCRAFT OWNERS AND PILOTS ASSOCIATION
421 Aviation Way
Frederick, MD 21701-4798
301-695-2000
Fax: 301-695-2375

- *Help Wanted! Careers in Aviation.* 2 pages. Includes career fields and educational requirements. Describes employers in the aviation industry in an easy-to-read chart format.

23
ALASKA DEPARTMENT OF LABOR
Research and Analysis
PO Box 25501
Juneau, AK 99802-5501
907-465-4500
Fax: 907-465-2101
http://www.state.ak.us/local/akpages/LABOR/research

- *Alaska Industry-Occupation Outlook from 1994 to 2005.* 44 pages. Includes statewide and regional occupational estimates and projections, as well as a narrative of the current industry status and outlook.

- *Alaska Wage Rates.* 36 pages. Presents the results of a statewide wage survey of nearly 1,500 employers for nearly 160 occupations.

24
ALBERTA ADVANCED EDUCATION AND CAREER DEVELOPMENT
Customer Sales and Service
Learning Resources Distributing Centre
12360-142 Street
Edmonton, Alberta T5L 4X9
Canada
403-427-5775

- *The Adult Back-to-School Book.* ($9.50) 56 pages. Offers practical, comprehensive information about going back to school, including budgeting, child care, and time management hints.

- *The Career Planner.* ($7.50) 94 pages. A basic guide to career planning featuring self-assessment check lists which help the user create a self-portrait. Written at a sixth-grade level, it is perfect for those who prefer a simple, direct style of writing or for those whose first language is not English.

- *Changing Course Midstream.* ($5) 45 pages. This reader-friendly workbook helps users through career transitions with exercises, tips, and profiles of those who have successfully managed transitions.

- *The Career Shop.* 31 pages. A catalog listing a variety of career information resources, many of which are $10 or under.

- The above materials are free to residents of Alberta and the Northwest Territories. Prices listed are in Canadian dollars and do not include government sales tax or postage; please call Customer Sales and Service for full details.

25
ALLIANCE OF AMERICAN INSURERS
Customer Service Department
1501 Woodfield Road
Suite 400 West
Schaumburg, IL 60173-4980
847-517-7474
Fax: 847-330-8602
http://www.allianceai.org

- *Careers in Insurance.* 22 pages. Provides an overview of career opportunities in the insurance industry, as well as educational requirements and sources for more information.

26
AMERICAN ACADEMY OF ALLERGY, ASTHMA & IMMUNOLOGY
611 East Wells Street
Milwaukee, WI 53202-3889
414-272-6071
Fax: 414-272-6970
news@aaaai.org

- *Academy News.* Includes classified ads for positions available in the allergy, asthma, and immunology field, plus other relevant articles regarding the field. Bimonthly.

27
AMERICAN ACADEMY OF ENVIRONMENTAL ENGINEERS
130 Holiday Court
Suite 100
Annapolis, MD 21401
410-266-3311
Fax: 410-266-7653
aaee@ea.net
http://www.enviro-engrs.org

- *A Crisis in Human Resources in Engineering? Yes, No, Maybe.* 7 pages.

- *Environmental Engineering Selection Guide: A Directory to Board Certified Specialists in Consulting & Education.* 115 pages. Lists institutions with professionally accredited environmental engineering or engineering technology programs.

- *Future Trends in Environmental Engineering.* 5 pages.

28
AMERICAN ACADEMY OF FAMILY PHYSICIANS
8880 Ward Parkway
Kansas City, MO 64114-2797
800-944-0000 (orders) or 816-333-9700
Fax: 816-822-0580
http://www.aafp.org

- *Activity in Family Medicine at the 126 United States Medical Schools and 11 Geographically Separated Campuses.* (Item no. 119) 27 pages. Provides names and telephone numbers of the medical school deans and the coordinators of the family practice predoctoral programs. Also includes a description of the family medicine administration structure of each medical school and the AAFP medical school code.

- *Medicine: Consider a Career in Family Practice.* (Item no. 146) 6 pages. Describes what family practice is, how to prepare in college for it, and how to choose an undergraduate college.

- *Careers in Family Practice.* (Item no. 205) Discusses for middle school and high school students careers in medicine, educational preparation, and choosing an undergraduate college. Lists college programs, financial planning, and sources of additional information.

- *The One Doctor Who Specializes in You: Premedical Packet.* (Item no. 206) Includes information on undergraduate academic programs, medical school admission selection factors, and a reprint of *Responses to Questions about Family Practice as a Career.*

29
AMERICAN ACADEMY OF NEUROLOGY
Customer Service
2221 University Avenue SE
Suite 335
Minneapolis, MN 55414
612-623-8115
Fax: 612-623-2491
http://www.aan.com

- *Choosing the Medical Specialty of Neurology.* 6 pages. Describes the field of neurology, the educational and training requirements, and board certification.

30
AMERICAN ACADEMY OF NURSE PRACTITIONERS
Capitol Station, LBJ Building
PO Box 12846
Austin, TX 78711
512-442-4262
Fax: 512-442-6469
admin@aanp.org
http://www.aanp.org

- *The Nurse Practitioner: A Primary Health Care Professional.* 8 pages. Provides an overview of the profession, its specialties, the duties involved, and the working environment.

- *Scope of Practice for Nurse Practitioners.* 1 page. Defines the professional role, educational requirements, and responsibilities of nurse practitioners.

- *Standards of Practice.* 4 pages. Lists the standards of practice for nurse practitioners.

31
AMERICAN ACADEMY OF OPHTHALMOLOGY
655 Beach Street
PO Box 7424
San Francisco, CA 94120-7424
415-561-8500
Fax: 908-935-2761
http://www.eyenet.org

- *Envision Ophthalmology: A Practical Guide to Ophthalmology as a Career Choice.* 16 pages. Defines the field and its subspecialties. Provides information on related topics, such as applying for a residency and residency program structure.

32
AMERICAN ACADEMY OF PEDIATRICS
141 NW Point Boulevard
PO Box 927
Elk Grove Village, IL 60009-0927

- *Pediatrics Career Fact Sheets.* 12 pages. Includes a profile of pediatrics, as well as information on pediatric residency training, career options and lifestyles, and minority health status indicators.

- *Your Career in Pediatrics.* 12 pages. Highlights the roles and duties of a pediatrician, the subspecialties in the field, the work environment, and residency training.

- *Selecting a Pediatric Residency: An Employment Guide.* ($5 prepaid, for medical students only) Highlights employment opportunities in pediatric residencies.

33
AMERICAN ACADEMY OF PHYSICAL MEDICINE AND REHABILITATION
1 IBM Plaza
Suite 2500
Chicago, IL 60611
312-464-9700
Fax: 312-464-0227
http://www.aapmr.org

- *What is a Physiatrist?* (#PE101) 6 pages. Discusses the types of conditions these specialists treat, their role in treatment, their diagnostic tools, and their work environment.

- *Physical Medicine & Rehabilitation: Diversity in a Profession.* (#PR101)

34
AMERICAN ACADEMY OF PHYSICIAN ASSISTANTS
950 North Washington Street
Alexandria, VA 22314-1552
703-836-2272
aapa@aapa.org
http://www.aapa.org/

- *Financial Aid Resources for PA Students.* 35 pages. Contains information on finding funds for a physician assistant education. Lists scholarships, traineeships, grants, constituent chapters of the AAPA, and physician assistant programs.

- *Information on the Physician Assistant Profession.* 8 pages. Includes information on the profession and a list of the accredited programs located throughout the United States.

35
AMERICAN ADVERTISING FEDERATION
1101 Vermont Avenue NW
Suite 500
Washington, DC 20005-3521
202-898-0089
Fax: 202-898-0159
http://www.aaf.org

- *Careers in Advertising.* 7 pages. Contains descriptions of the various careers in the advertising industry.

36
AMERICAN AGRICULTURAL ECONOMICS ASSOCIATION
1110 Buckeye Avenue
Ames, IA 50010-8063
515-233-3202
Fax: 515-233-3101
http://www.aaea.org

- *Careers for the Future...Agricultural Economics and Agricultural Business.* 8 pages. Describes specific career opportunities, the type of work involved, and typical employers in the field of agricultural economics.

37
AMERICAN ALLIANCE FOR HEALTH, PHYSICAL EDUCATION, AND DANCE
1900 Association Drive
Reston, VA 20191-1599
703-476-3400
http://www.aahperd.org

- *Career Opportunities for Safety Educators.* 8 pages. Lists the employment fields that provide career opportunities for safety educators.

- *Careers in Special Education and Related Services.* 4 pages. Discusses the nature of the work, education required, personal qualities, job outlook and advancement, and how to prepare for a career.

- *Dance Education: What Is It? Why Is It Important?* Communication tool for students, parents, administrators, and community leaders; explains the need for and benefits of dance education at all levels.

38
AMERICAN ALLIANCE FOR THEATRE AND EDUCATION
Theatre Department, Arizona State University
PO Box 872002
Tempe, AZ 85287-2002
602-965-6064
Fax: 602-965-5351
aateinfo@asuvm.inre.asu.edu

- *Teacher Preparation and Certification Standards.* 8 pages. This publication offers standards for preparation and certification of theatre specialists, speech/communication/theatre teachers, and speech-communication specialists.

39
AMERICAN ANTHROPOLOGICAL ASSOCIATION
4350 North Fairfax Drive
Suite 640
Arlington, VA 22203
703-528-1902
Fax: 703-528-3546
http://www.ameranthassn.org

Check AAA's web site for current career information.

- *Federal Employment Opportunities for Anthropologists.* 1 page.

40
AMERICAN APPAREL MANUFACTURERS ASSOCIATION
2500 Wilson Boulevard
Suite 301
Arlington, VA 22201
703-524-1864
Fax: 703-522-6741
grbates@americanapparel.org

- *Careers in the Apparel Manufacturing Industry/College Directory.* 32 pages. Provides brief descriptions and actual case studies of careers in the apparel industry. Also contains a list of colleges offering major programs in apparel manufacturing management and engineering technology, as well as information on curricula and degrees offered.

41
AMERICAN ARBITRATION ASSOCIATION
140 West 51st Street
New York, NY 10020-1203
212-484-4000
Fax: 212-765-4874
http://www.adr.org

- *You Want to Be a Labor Arbitrator?* 11 pages. Discusses qualifications, application procedures, and sources of information.

- *So You Want to Be a Mediator?* 6 pages. Discusses qualifications, application procedures, and sources of information.

42
AMERICAN ART THERAPY ASSOCIATION, INC.
1202 Allanson Road
Mundelein, IL 60060
847-949-6064
Fax: 847-566-4580
estygariii@aol.com
http://www.arttherapy.org

- *Art Therapy Model Job Description.* ($1)

- *General Information Packet.* ($4 to individuals; no charge to high school guidance counselors and college resource centers) Includes *Art Therapy: The Profession* ($1 without packet) 4 pp; *Art Therapy Educational Program List* ($2 without packet) 15 pages., listing AATA-approved graduate degree programs, clinical programs, and institute programs, as well as unapproved undergraduate and graduate programs; *Educational Standards for Programs Providing Art Therapy Education* ($1 without packet) 7 pages.; and *Resource Sheet,* listing publication materials available.

43
AMERICAN ARTIST MAGAZINE
Billboard Publications/Affiliated Publications
1515 Broadway
New York, NY 10036
800-745-8922
Fax: 212-536-5294

- *Directory of Art Schools.* ($4.50) Contains contact, financial, and enrollment information for art schools, summer schools, classes with private teachers, traveling workshops. Annual supplement appearing every March and available at local newsstands.

44
AMERICAN ASSEMBLY OF COLLEGIATE SCHOOLS OF BUSINESS
Subscription Office
600 Emerson Road
Suite 300
St. Louis, MO 63141-6762
314-872-8481
Fax: 314-872-8495
http://www.aacsb.edu

- *After the Boom: Management Majors in the 1990s.* 4 pages. Provides information on trends in undergraduate business degrees, freshman interest in business majors, academic background of male and female business majors, specialization preferences of male and female business majors, and activities in high school (by major).

- *Members of the Accreditation Council (Accredited Schools) of the AACSB.* 17 pages. Lists accredited business schools and accredited accounting programs, addresses, phone numbers, and degrees offered.

- *Accreditation: Achieving Quality and Continuous Improvement through Self-Evaluation and Peer Review.* 6 pages. Discusses the accreditation process and the benefits to schools and programs.

45
AMERICAN ASSOCIATION FOR CAREER EDUCATION
2900 Amby Place
Hermosa Beach, CA 90254
310-374-7378
Fax: 310-374-1360

- *Free Listing of Materials.* (self-addressed 55-cent stamped envelope) A pamphlet listing more than 100 books, workbooks, handbooks, guides, charts, videos, and software materials that connect careers, education, and work.

- *Career Education That Works.* ($4.50) 20 pages. Highlights 18 programs, practices, and publications that link career, education, and work. Includes descriptions and contact information.

46
AMERICAN ASSOCIATION FOR CLINICAL CHEMISTRY, INC.
2101 L Street NW
Suite 202
Washington, DC 200037-1526
800-892-1400 or 202-857-0717
Fax: 202-887-5093
http://www.aacc.org

- *Clinical Chemistry: Partnerships in Health Care.* 8 pages. Defines a clinical chemist and describes a typical day as part of a healthcare team.

- *Graduate and Postdoctoral Training Programs in Clinical Chemistry.* ($5) 48 pages. Lists only those programs approved by the Commission on Accreditation in Clinical Chemistry.

47
AMERICAN ASSOCIATION FOR HEALTH EDUCATION
1900 Association Drive
Reston, VA 20191-1599
703-476-3437
Fax: 703-476-6638
http://www.aahperd.org/aahe.html

- *AAHE Directory of Institutions Offering Specialization in Undergraduate and Graduate Professional Preparation Programs in School, Community and Public Health Education.* ($4.50) 18 pages.

48
AMERICAN ASSOCIATION FOR LABORATORY ANIMAL SCIENCE
70 Timber Creek Drive
Suite 5
Cordova, TN 38018
901-754-8620
Fax: 901-753-0046
http://www.aalas.org

- *Careers in Laboratory Animal Science.* 8 pages. Defines laboratory animal science, profiles the careers in the field, and lists sources of information.

- *Candidate Bulletin for Certification.* 28 pages. Discusses how to apply, the cost, and the qualifications for certification.

- *Use of Animals in Biomedical Research.* 4 pages. Explains why and how animals are used in biomedical research and the importance of such research.

49
AMERICAN ASSOCIATION FOR MARRIAGE AND FAMILY THERAPY
1133 15th Street NW
Suite 300
Washington, DC 20005
202-452-0109
Fax: 202-223-2329
http://www.aamft.org

- *Accredited and Candidacy Status Programs by State. 12 pages.* Includes listing of marriage and family therapy educational programs in Canada and the United States, as well as information on applying to a marriage and family therapy program.

50
AMERICAN ASSOCIATION FOR MEDICAL TRANSCRIPTION
PO Box 576187
Modesto, CA 95357-6187
209-551-0883
Fax: 209-551-9317
http://www.aamt.org/aamt

- *AAMT Model Job Description: Medical Transcriptionist.* 2 pages. SASE. Gives an overview of the position; details the necessary knowledge, skills, and abilities; and describes working conditions, physical demands, job responsibilities, and performance standards.

- *MTs Partners in Medical Communications.* 4 pages. SASE. Provides an overview of the medical transcriptionist profession.

- *Tip Sheet for Prospective Medical Transcription Students.* 1 page. SASE. Provides questions you should ask before enrolling in a medical transcription program.

- *You Called with Questions about Medical Transcription?* 2 pages.

51
AMERICAN ASSOCIATION FOR MUSIC THERAPY
PO Box 80012
Valley Forge, PA 19484
610-265-4006

- *Introducing the American Association for Music Therapy.* 8 pages. Includes educational requirements, approved schools, and certification information.

- *Music Therapy Makes a Difference.* Outlines the types of patients music therapists help, as well as qualifications, skills, possible work environments, duties, and responsibilities of music therapists.

52
AMERICAN ASSOCIATION FOR PARALEGAL EDUCATION
PO Box 40244
Overland Park, KS 66204
913-381-4458
Fax: 913-381-9308
http://www.chattanooga.net/cisce/aaspe

- *How to Choose a Paralegal Education Program.* 9 pages. Recommends factors to consider in choosing a paralegal education program.

53
AMERICAN ASSOCIATION FOR RESPIRATORY CARE
11030 Ables Lane
Dallas, TX 75229
214-243-2272
Fax: 972-484-2720
http://www.aarc.org

- *The AARC Career Guide: Climbing the Professional Ladder.* 9 pages. Discusses career planning and employment.

- *Respiratory Therapy Educational Programs.* 28 pages. Includes a historical summary of the respiratory therapy occupation, occupational and job descriptions, employment characteristics, information about educational programs, and a list of accredited educational programs by state.

- *Decisions.* 6 pages. Details careers in respiratory care. Designed for high school students.

- *Transitions.* 6 pages. Details careers in respiratory care. Designed for adults (college students and beyond).

- *Hello I'm Your Respiratory Care Practitioner.* 4 pages. Provides a basic overview of the respiratory care practitioner.

54
AMERICAN ASSOCIATION FOR STATE AND LOCAL HISTORY
530 Church Street
Suite 600
Nashville, TN 37219-2325
615-255-2971
Fax: 615-255-2979
http://www.nashville.net/~aaslh

AASLH Career Information Packet ($5) includes:

- *Careers for Graduates in History.* Guides history students through the process of considering advanced education or choosing a career in the private, public, or nonprofit sectors; cites numerous career opportunities.

- *A Guide to Resource Organizations.* 4 pages. Identifies a core group of national resources representing 13 areas regarding which inquiries are most often received.

- *Historians.* 4 pages.

- *History News Dispatch.* (sample issue free) Contains a list of job openings and defines the qualifications, education, and experience required for certain positions in the history field.

55
AMERICAN ASSOCIATION FOR THE ADVANCEMENT OF SCIENCE
Directorate for Science and Policy Programs
1200 New York Avenue NW
Washington, DC 20005
202-326-6600
Fax: 202-289-4950
science_policy@aaas.org
http://www.aaas.org

- *Guide to Education in Science, Engineering, and Public Policy.* (94-37S) ($10) 144 pages. For each institution lists contact information, background on the program, degrees offered, admission and degree requirements, student and faculty information, positions for graduates, and financial information.

- *Environmental Science and Engineering Fellows Program Reports.* Available from an AAAS Science, Engineering & Fellowship Program.

56
AMERICAN ASSOCIATION OF ADVERTISING AGENCIES
Publications Department
405 Lexington Avenue, 18th Floor
New York, NY 10174-1801
212-682-2500

- *Want a Job in Advertising?*

57
AMERICAN ASSOCIATION OF BLOOD BANKS
Coordinator, Professional Education Programs
8101 Glenbrook Road
Bethesda, MD 20814-2749
301-907-6977

- *Directory of SSB Education Programs.* 2 pages.

58
AMERICAN ASSOCIATION OF BOTANICAL GARDENS AND ARBORETA
786 Church Road
Wayne, PA 19087-4713
610-688-1120
Fax: 610-293-0149
http://www.aabga.mobot.org/

- *Careers in Public Gardens.* 2 pages. Describes the types of jobs available in public gardens, the training and education, and sources of information.

59
AMERICAN ASSOCIATION OF CEREAL CHEMISTS
3340 Pilot Knob Road
St. Paul, MN 55121-2097
612-454-7250
Fax: 612-454-0766
http://www.scisoc.org/aacc

- *Careers in Cereal Chemistry.* 17 pages. Details career opportunities and educational requirements in the field.

60
AMERICAN ASSOCIATION OF COLLEGES OF OSTEOPATHIC MEDICINE
5550 Friendship Boulevard
Suite 310
Chevy Chase, MD 20815
301-968-4100
http://www.aacom.org

- *Osteopathic Medical College Information.* ($2) 35 pages. Identifies 17 member schools and provides a brief description of the campus and the curriculum, admissions criteria, minimum entrance requirements, application material requirements, class size and enrollment, and application deadlines.

- *Osteopathic Medical Education.* 8 pages. Describes osteopathic medicine, education required, and postdoctoral programs and specialties. Provides a list of member colleges of osteopathic medicine.

- *Application packet.* Information and application materials for applying to the 17 member schools of osteopathic medicine.

61
AMERICAN ASSOCIATION OF COLLEGES OF PHARMACY
Publications Department
1426 Prince Street
Alexandria, VA 22314-2841
703-739-230
Fax: 703-836-8982

- *Academic Pharmacy's Vital Statistics.* 2 pages. Includes a list of institutions (names only; no contact information) offering degrees in pharmacy.

- *Pharmaceutical Education Today.* 6 pages. Lists the colleges and schools of pharmacy in the United States.

- *Shall I Study Pharmacy?* 31 pages. Describes the industry, subspecialties, work environments, personal qualifications, educational requirements, professional courses, and educational expenses. Also lists related publications, sources of financial aid, and U.S. colleges and schools of pharmacy.

62
AMERICAN ASSOCIATION OF COLLEGES OF PODIATRIC MEDICINE
1350 Piccard Drive
Suite 322
Rockville, MD 20850
800-922-9266.or 301-990-7400
Fax: 301-990-2807

- *Podiatric Medicine as a Career: What is a DPM?* 12 pages. Defines podiatric medicine; explains what doctors of podiatric medicine do and where they work; lists admission, licensing, and board certification requirements; discusses benefits and income potential; and lists the six colleges that participate in the centralized application service known as AACPMAS.

- *Fact Sheet-Podiatric Medicine.* 2 pages. Describes admission requirements, facts about podiatric medical students and graduates, residency training, licensing and credentialing, and benefits and income potential.

- *Podiatric Medicine's Advising Kit.* Provides help for those who want to present clear and accurate information about podiatric medicine when advising students interested in the health care profession. The kit includes *Podiatric Medicine as a Career, College Information Booklet* of AACPM's six member colleges, and other materials.

63
AMERICAN ASSOCIATION OF COMMUNITY COLLEGES
Publications
National Center for Higher Education
One Dupont Circle NW
Suite 410
Washington, DC 20036-1176
202-728-0200
http://www.aacc.nche.edu

Check out AACC's web site, where you can find the latest information on community colleges, government, education, and other helpful resources.

- *Community College Facts...at a Glance.* 2 pages. Provides information on the number of colleges, the background of students, tuition and fees, career programs, and other topics.

- *FACTS.* 4 pages. Contains factual information on AACC.

64
AMERICAN ASSOCIATION OF DENTAL SCHOOLS
1625 Massachusetts Avenue NW
Washington DC 20036-2212
202-667-9433

- *Careers in the Dental Profession: Dentistry.* 14 pages. Includes information on specialties in the field, advice on getting a dental education, and a message to parents.

- *Accredited Program Listing: Advanced Specialty and General Dentistry Education.* 17 pages. Lists schools providing accredited advanced education programs, including programs in dental specialties, general practice residencies, and advanced programs in general dentistry in Canada and the United States.

- *Accredited Program Listing: Dental Educational Programs.* 3 pages. Lists contact information for schools offering programs in Canada and the United States (as accredited by the Canadian Dental Association).

- *Accredited Program Listing: Dental Assisting, Dental Hygiene, and Dental Laboratory Technology Educational Programs.* 7 pages. Provides contact information for schools in Canada and the United States.

- *Fact Sheets.* Including such titles as *Dentistry as a Career, Dental Hygiene Today,* and *Dental Laboratory Technology.*

65
AMERICAN ASSOCIATION OF HOMES AND SERVICES FOR THE AGING
901 E Street NW
Suite 500
Washington, DC 20004-2011
202-783-2242
Fax: 202-783-2255
http://www.aahsa.org

- *Considering a Career in Long-Term Care and Senior Housing.* 12 pages. Describes careers in the field of aging services and lists additional resources.

66
AMERICAN ASSOCIATION OF MEDICAL ASSISTANTS
Publications Department
20 North Wacker Drive
Suite 1575
Chicago, IL 60606-2903
800-228-2262 or 312-899-1500
Fax: 312-899-1259
http://www.aama.ntl.org

- *Medical Assisting Career Pack.* Contains fact sheet on the profession, scholarship information, and a list of accredited programs.

67
AMERICAN ASSOCIATION OF NURSE ANESTHETISTS
Bookstore, 222 South Prospect Avenue
Park Ridge, IL 60068-4001
847-692-7050, ext. 3009
Fax: 847-692-6968
http://www.aana.com

- *Focus on Your Future.* 6 pages. Includes factors to consider in becoming a nurse, the duties of certified registered nurse anesthetists, how to become a CRNA, educational requirements, program requirements, and advantages of the profession.

- *Questions and Answers about a Career in Nurse Anesthesia.* 1 page. Includes the most frequently asked questions about the profession, the answers to those questions, and suggestions on where to get answers to other questions.

- *Council on Accreditation of Nurse Anesthesia Educational Programs: List of Recognized Educational Programs.* 10 pages. Lists the programs by state, along with pertinent program information.

- *Certified Registered Nurse Anesthetists and the American Association of Nurse Anesthetists.* 8 pages. Describes the impact of CRNAs on health care, their responsibilities, and their educational requirements.

68
AMERICAN ASSOCIATION OF ORIENTAL MEDICINE
433 Front Street
Catasauqua, PA 18032-2506
610-264-2768
Fax: 610-264-2768
aaom1@aol.com
http://www.aaom.org

- *Facts.* (donations appreciated) 2 pages. Describes the oriental medicine practice and the training and certification of acupuncturists.

- *Comprehensive Listing of Schools.* 1 page. Lists names, addresses, and telephone numbers of the American Association of Oriental Medicine schools and those offering accredited and candidate programs.

- *State Acupuncture Associations.* 1 page. Lists acupuncture associations by state.

- *Acupuncture: A Successful and Cost Effective Treatment.* 4 pages. Describes acupuncture and compares the costs and results of traditional medicine to acupuncture.

- *State Licensing.* 2 pages. Lists the licensing requirements for each state.

- *State Listing of Individuals Certified in Acupuncture.* Lists individuals by state.

69
AMERICAN ASSOCIATION OF ORTHODONTISTS
401 North Lindbergh Boulevard
St. Louis, MO 63141-7816
800-222-9969

- *Advanced Orthodontic Education Programs Approved by the Commission on Dental Accreditation of the American Dental Association.* 12 pages. Gives contact information, department head, program length, degree granted, number of students accepted, program starting date, and an application deadline for each school.

- *Career Planning-Consider ALL The Angles: Orthodontics.* Describes the profession, required skills, and career opportunities.

- *Orthodontist.* 2 pages.

70
AMERICAN ASSOCIATION OF PETROLEUM GEOLOGISTS
PO Box 979
Tulsa, OK 74101-0979
918-584-2555
Fax: 918-560-2636

- *Careers in Geoscience.*

71
AMERICAN ASSOCIATION OF PHYSICAL ANTHROPOLOGISTS
Career Development Committee
Department of Anthropology
College of Arts and Sciences
University of South Florida, SOC 107
Tampa, FL 33620-8100
813-974-6237
Fax: 813-974-2668

- *A Career in Biological Anthropology.* 6 pages. Defines anthropology and biological anthropology, details a biological anthropologist's duties, and describes the advantages of a career in the field and opportunities for study.

72
AMERICAN ASSOCIATION OF PHYSICISTS IN MEDICINE
One Physics Ellipse
College Park, MD 20740-3846
301-209-3350
Fax: 301-209-0862
aapm@aapm.org
http://www.aapm.org

- *The Medical Physicist.* 8 pages. Describes the field, the duties, professional position, work environment, training, demand, and occupational outlook of medical physicists.

73
AMERICAN ASSOCIATION OF RETIRED PERSONS
AARP Fulfillment Section
1909 K Street NW
Washington, DC 20049
202-434-2277
http://www.aarp.org

- *Directory of Centers for Older Learners.* (D13973) Lists educational opportunities for retired persons.

- *How to Plan Your Job Search, Your Work Life.* (D 12403) 28 pages. Provides a good listing of the main essentials.

- *How to Stay Employable: A Guide for the Midlife and Older Worker.* Has the best available summary of the changes that affect job search today. The best sections describe the employment changes that have appeared in the job market in the last few decades and then tell how they impact on older workers.

- *The Social Security Book: What Every Woman Absolutely Needs to Know.* (D14117)

74
AMERICAN ASSOCIATION OF SCHOOL ADMINISTRATORS
1801 North Moore Street
Arlington, VA 22209
888-782-2272
Fax: 703-841-1543
http://www.aasa.org

- *Guidelines for the Preparation of School Administrators.* (#21-00816) ($4.20) 12 pages. Describes initial preparation and training of a school administrator, as well as continued in-service education for better performance of all school administrators and university personnel. Includes chapters on The Guidelines in Context, Leadership Outcome Goals, Competencies and Skills, and Program Delivery Components.

75
AMERICAN ASSOCIATION OF TEACHERS OF SPANISH AND PORTUGUESE, INC.
Butler-Hancock Hall
Room 210
University of Northern Colorado
Greeley, CO 80639
970-351-1090
Fax: 970-351-1095
http://www.aatsp.org

- *Career Handbook.* 25 pages. Includes information on the growing presence of Hispanics in the United States, the importance of Spanish in work places, and special language training for careers and internships, career planning and development, job outlook, job search, job sources, and careers in the classroom. Also provides an annotated bibliography of additional career materials.

76
AMERICAN ASSOCIATION OF UNIVERSITY WOMEN EDUCATIONAL FOUNDATION
2201 North Dodge Street
Iowa City, IA 52243-4030
319-337-1716
Fax: 319-337-1204
http://www.aauw.org

- *Fellowships and Grants.* 15 pages. Describes AAUW Educational Foundation fellowships and grants for women. Encourages women of color to apply for these fellowships and grants.

77
AMERICAN ASTRONOMICAL SOCIETY
Education Office, Adler Planetarium
1300 South Lakeshore Drive
Chicago, IL 60605

312-294-0340
aased@aas.org
http://www.aas.org/education/career.html

- *A New Universe to Explore: Careers in Astronomy.* 19 pages. Describes the astronomy field and employment possibilities and outlines an academic plan for becoming an astronomer.

78
AMERICAN ATHLETIC TRAINERS ASSOCIATION AND CERTIFICATION BOARD, INC.
146 East Duarte Road, #200
Arcadia, CA 92662

- *Why Be an Athletic Trainer?* 6 pages.

79
AMERICAN AUTOMOBILE MANUFACTURERS ASSOCIATION
Statistics and Information Services
7430 Second Avenue
Suite 300
Detroit, MI 48202
313-872-4311
Fax: 313-871-2274
http://www.aama.com

- *Rewarding Careers in the Automotive Service Industry.* 12 pages. Discusses the industry, career opportunities in the field, training and education, and certification.

80
AMERICAN BANKERS ASSOCIATION
1120 Connecticut Avenue NW
Washington, DC 20036
800-338-0626 or 202-663-5000

- *Building Your Future? Banking is the Answer.* 8 pages. Describes banking career opportunities, necessary qualifications, training and advancement, and employment outlook.

- *Occupational Outlook Handbook.* 9 pages. Contains information on banking careers. Excerpted from the *Occupational Outlook Handbook*, published by the U.S. Bureau of Labor Statistics.

81
AMERICAN BAR ASSOCIATION
Order Fulfillment
750 North Lake Shore Drive
Chicago, IL 60611-4497
800-285-2221
Fax: 312-988-5568
http://www.abanet.org

- *Life in the Law.* (#235-0036) ($2.50) 16 pages. Discusses career opportunities in the legal field, skills needed, and pre-law studies; profiles lawyers; and suggests additional reading materials about careers in the law.

- *Law in the Workplace.* (#235-0036) ($2.50) Touches on all the major areas of employment law-recruiting and hiring, employees' rights and responsibilities, unemployment benefits, workers' compensation, and retirement planning.

- *Resource Careers.* (#535-0005) ($3) More than 20 articles discussing the practice of law, as well as career options regarding environmental law.

82
AMERICAN BEEKEEPING FEDERATION, INC.
PO Box 1038
Jessup, GA 31598-1038
912-427-4233
Fax: 912-427-8447
tfore@beta.jesupnet.com
http://www.absnet.org

- *Beekeeper: Career Summary.* 1 page. Describes beekeeping duties, working conditions, personal qualifications, education and training, earnings, hours, and occupational outlook.

83
AMERICAN BOARD OF FUNERAL SERVICES EDUCATION
PO Box 1305
Brunswick, ME 04011
207-798-5801
Fax: 207-798-5988
abfse@clinic.net

- *In Service of Others: The Professional Director.* 6 pages. Lists educational requirements, accredited schools of mortuary science, and responsibilities.

- *Have You Considered...Funeral Service?* 6 pages. Details the duties and responsibilities in the funeral service field, career opportunities, and educational requirements. Lists mortuary science programs.

84
AMERICAN CAMPING ASSOCIATION
Bradford Woods
5000 State Road 67 North
Martinsville, IN 46151-7902
765-342-8456
Fax: 765-342-2065
http://www.aca-camps.org

- *Careers in Camping.* 8 pages. Provides job descriptions, as well information on qualifications and salaries. Describes how to prepare for a career in camping and how to find employment opportunities.

- *Colleges and Universities Offering Study in Camping Administration and Related Courses.* 20 pages. Lists colleges and universities in Canada and the United States

- *Summer Camp Employment Opportunity Booklet.* 33 pages. Provides comprehensive nationwide job listings for day and resident camps. Lists positions for all majors. Includes detailed descriptions, salary ranges, and employment benefits for some camps.

- *The Outdoor Living Skills Training Program.* 4 pages. Describes the goals for participants, training fees, and other topics.

- *Camp Counselor.* 2 pages. Describes the duties, working conditions, personal qualifications, education and training, earnings, and hours. Lists additional sources of information for camp counselors.

85
AMERICAN CERAMIC SOCIETY
735 Ceramic Place
Westerville, OH 43081-8720
614-890-4700
Fax: 619-899-6109
http://www.acers.org

- *Ceramic Engineering: Career Opportunities for You.* 8 pages. Details how to prepare for a career in ceramic engineering. Lists career options and accredited institutions.

- *Ceramic Engineers.* 4 pages. Provides an overview of the ceramic engineering field, including work performed, education and training, personal qualifications, and employment outlook.

86
AMERICAN CHEMICAL SOCIETY
Education Division
1155 16th Street NW
Washington, DC 20036
800-227-5558 or 202-872-4600
Fax: 202-833-7732
http://www.acs.org/

Career Publications Set includes:

- *A Career as a Chemical Technician.* 5 pages. Describes the duties and responsibilities, necessary skills and preparation, salary range, employment outlook, and advancement potential.

- *Chemistry and Your Career: Questions and Answers.* 16 pages. Answers the questions asked most often by high school students.

- *Employment Outlook.* 23 pages. Discusses the demand for chemical engineers, their starting salaries, nontraditional careers for chemists, career planning resources, and the infiltration of Generation X into management. Reprinted from *Chemical Engineering News.*

• *Futures through Chemistry: Charting a Course.* 13 pages. Designed for undergraduates. Discusses academic preparation, career options, job hunting, how to prepare for and find a graduate school, and financial assistance.

• *I Know You're a Chemist, but What Do You Do?* 11 pages. Includes discussions by chemists in various types of work environments. Provides advice on job hunting.

• *List of Approved Schools.* 13 pages. Lists ACS approved schools by state. Also includes information on financial aid.

• *Chemical Careers in Brief.* 2 pages each. Discusses responsibilities, working conditions, places of employment, personal characteristics, required education and training, job outlook, and salary range. Briefs available on agriculture chemistry, biotechnology, chemical information, environmental chemistry, food and flavor chemistry, hazardous waste management, materials science, medicinal chemistry, polymer chemistry, and science writing.

87
AMERICAN CHIROPRACTIC ASSOCIATION
1701 Clarendon Boulevard
Arlington, VA 22209
703-276-8800
http://www.amerchiro.org/aca

Chiropractic Career Folder (for prospective chiropractic students) includes:

• *Planning a Career in Chiropractic.* 8 pages. Discusses the future of the profession, opportunities in chiropractic, advantages of practicing chiropractic, and education (includes a list of accredited institutions, licensure requirements, and curricula).

• *Chiropractic: State of the Art.* 25 pages. Provides information on the chiropractic profession, its policies, and its licensing.

• *Accredited Status Holding Institutions.* 6 pages. Lists institutions holding accredited status in the United States and abroad.

• *Doctor of Chiropractic: Occupational Description.* 2 pages. Provides an overview of the job of the doctor of chiropractic.

• *Preprofessional/Educational Requirements.* 2 pages.

88
AMERICAN COLLECTORS ASSOCIATION, INC.
PO Box 39106
Minneapolis, MN 55439-0106
612-926-6547
Fax: 612-926-1624
http://www.collector.com

• *Careers & Opportunities in Collections.* 12 pages. Describes a career in collection, duties and responsibilities, employment outlook, opportunities, and qualifications.

• *Starting & Managing a Collection Service.* 23 pages. Suggests procedures for establishing a collection service.

89
AMERICAN COLLEGE OF HEALTH CARE ADMINISTRATORS
325 South Patrick Street
Alexandria, VA 22314-3571
703-739-7900
Fax: 703-739-7901
http://www.achca.org

• *Starting Your Career in Long-Term Health Care Administration.* 8 pages. Describes the field, licensure requirements, and salary.

90

AMERICAN COLLEGE OF HEALTHCARE EXECUTIVES
1 North Franklin Street
Suite 1700
Chicago, IL 60606
312-424-2800
http://www.ache.org

- *Your Career as a Healthcare Executive: A Profile of the Profession Including a List of the Accredited Graduate Programs.* 24 pages. Describes career opportunities for health care executives, academic training, and necessary skills. Lists related health care organizations and accredited programs in Canada and the United States.

91

AMERICAN COLLEGE OF NURSE-MIDWIVES
818 Connecticut Avenue NW
Suite 900
Washington, DC 20006
202-728-9860
Fax: 202-728-9897
http://www.midwife.org

- *A Career in Nurse-Midwifery: Your Ticket to the World.* 9 pages. Includes a basic overview of the field, educational requirements, and sources of financial aid.

- *Education Programs Accredited by the ACNM Division of Accreditation.* 5 pages. Lists schools offering certificate and master's nurse-midwifery programs.

92

AMERICAN COLLEGE OF SPORTS MEDICINE
Public Information
PO Box 1440
Indianapolis, IN 46206-1440
317-637-9200
Fax: 317-634-7817
http://www.acsm.org/sportsmed

- *Viewpoint: The Sports Medicine Umbrella.* 2 pages. SASE. Describes career opportunities in the field of sports medicine.

- *What is an Exercise Physiologist?* 2 pages. SASE. Defines exercise physiology, the duties and responsibilities, work environments, and educational requirements.

- *ACMS Information and Publications Directory.* 27 pages. Contains an overview of the college and a mission statement; information on certification and education; and a publications list.

93

AMERICAN CONGRESS ON SURVEYING AND MAPPING
5410 Grosvenor Lane
Suite 100
Bethesda, MD 20814-2212
301-493-0200

- *Cartography and Geographic Information Systems: A Career Guide.* 20 pages. Lists career information (the nature of the work, types of jobs, etc.), educational programs with a cartography/GIS emphasis, readings, and federal government agencies related to the field.

94

AMERICAN COUNCIL FOR CONSTRUCTION EDUCATION
1300 Hudson Lane
Suite 3
Monroe, LA 71201
318-323-2816
Fax: 318-323-2413

- *ACCE Accredited Programs.* 3 pages. State by state listing of colleges and universities with accredited construction education programs.

95
AMERICAN COUNCIL OF NANNY SCHOOLS
Delta College
University Center, MI 48710
517-686-9417
Fax: 517-686-8736

- *ACNS Member Schools.* 1 page. Listing of ACNS schools.

96
AMERICAN COUNCIL ON PHARMACEUTICAL EDUCATION
311 West Superior Street
Suite 512
Chicago, IL 60610
312-664-3575
Fax: 312-664-4652

- *Accredited Professional Programs of Colleges and Schools of Pharmacy: Doctor of Pharmacy, Baccalaureate in Pharmacy.* 13 pages. Presents the accreditation status of each professional program, as well as a list of colleges or schools of pharmacy offering professional programs.

97
AMERICAN COUNCIL ON SCIENCE AND HEALTH
1995 Broadway, 2nd Floor
New York, NY 10023-5860
212-362-7044
Fax: 212-362-4919
http://www.acsh.org

- *Biotechnology and Food.* ($3.85) 22 pages. Describes biotechnology, the challenges for American agriculture with biotechnology solutions, and biotechnology foods.

98
AMERICAN COUNSELING ASSOCIATION
5999 Stevenson Avenue
Alexandria, VA 22304
703-823-9800, ext. 222
Fax: 703-823-0252
http://www.counseling.org

- *Choosing a Career in Counseling and Human Development.* 8 pages. Describes possible work environments, necessary training and education, licensing and certification information, and sources of additional information.

- *Great Minds in Counseling.* 8 pages. Discusses the work involved in helping children, adolescents, and adults, as well as education and training.

99
AMERICAN CULINARY FEDERATION EDUCATIONAL INSTITUTE
PO Box 3466
St. Augustine, FL 32085-3466
904-824-4468
Fax: 904-825-4758
http://www.acfchefs.org

- *ACFEI Apprenticeship Fundamentals/ Program Roster.* 7 pages. SASE. Lists apprenticeship programs available in the United States

- *ACFEI Accredited Programs.* 1 page. SASE. Lists accredited programs in the United States.

100
AMERICAN DANCE THERAPY ASSOCIATION
2000 Century Plaza
Suite 108
Columbia, MD 21044
410-997-4040
Fax: 410-997-4048

- *Educational Opportunities in Dance Movement Therapy.* ($2) 6 pages. Describes dance therapy and graduate and undergraduate degree programs. Lists approved schools.

101
AMERICAN DENTAL ASSISTANTS ASSOCIATION
203 North LaSalle Street
Suite 1320
Chicago, IL 60610-1225
312-541-1550
Fax: 312-541-1496
adaa1@aol.com
http://members.aol.com/adaa1/index.html

- *Careers in the Dental Profession/Dental Assisting.* 12 pages. Provides an overview of training and careers in the dental assisting field. Appropriate for high school students.

102
AMERICAN DENTAL ASSOCIATION
SELECT Program
211 East Chicago Avenue
Suite 1840
Chicago, IL 60611-2678
http://www.ada.org

- *Careers in the Dental Profession: Dental Assisting/Dental Hygiene/Dental Laboratory Technology/Dentistry.* Describes duties and responsibilities, advantages of a career in the field, work environments, education and training, accreditation, certification, earning potential, and sources of information.

- *Dental Assisting Today.* Includes information about the job, salary, educational requirements, and future trends in the field.

- *Dentistry Today.* Includes a professional profile, practice statistics, and information on salary and future trends in the field.

- *Listing of Accredited Dental Assisting, Dental Hygiene, and Dental Laboratory Technology Educational Programs.*

- *Listing of Accredited Predoctoral Dental Education Programs.*

103
AMERICAN DENTAL HYGIENISTS' ASSOCIATION
Division of Professional Development
444 North Michigan Avenue
Suite 3400
Chicago, IL 60611
800-243-2342 or 312-440-8900
Fax: 312-440-8929
adha@ix.netcom.com
http://www.adha.org

- *Dental Hygiene: A Profession of Opportunities.* 6 pages. Describes a career in dental hygiene and educational requirements.

- *Dental Hygiene Entry Level Education Programs.* 30 pages. Lists educational programs for individuals pursuing a career in dental hygiene.

- *Facts: Dental Hygiene Career Options in a Variety of Settings.* 1 page. Describes the work environments of dental hygienists and typical duties performed in each setting.

- *Facts: Dental Hygiene Education.* 1 page. Discusses admission requirements and prerequisites, degree programs, and curricula.

- *Facts: Dental Hygiene Licensure.* 1 page. Discusses dental hygiene licensur—who grants licenses and how they are obtained.

- *Salary Information for Dental Hygienists.* 1 page. Provides hourly and yearly national average salary ranges for dental hygienists.

104
AMERICAN DESIGN DRAFTING ASSOCIATION
PO Box 799
Rockville, MD 20848-0799
301-460-6875
Fax: 301-460-8591
national@adda.org
http://www.adda.org

- *Schools with Certified Curriculum.* 2 pages. Lists schools currently participating in the ADDA's certification program. The certificate, diploma, or degree level of the program is noted.

105
AMERICAN DIETETIC ASSOCIATION
Networks Team
216 West Jackson Boulevard
Chicago, IL 60606-6995
800-877-1600, ext. 4897 or 312-899-0040
Fax: 312-899-0008
http://www.eatright.org

- *Your Future with Food and Nutrition.* 6 pages. Defines dietetics, the dietitian, and dietetic technician for 4th to 6th grade students.

- *Check It Out...Careers in Dietetics.* Attempts to increase 6th to 8th grade students' awareness about careers in dietetics. Defines dietetics; describes where registered dieticians (RD) and dietetic technicians, registered (DTR), are employed and their job responsibilities; and lists resources for additional information.

- *Check It Out...Dietetics Educational Programs.* Describes the educational pathways required for students pursuing careers as registered dietitians or dietetic technicians, registered. Provides a list of the dietetic programs.

- *Check It Out...a Career as a Registered Dietitian.* 2 pages. Prepared for second career adults or college students who are interested in becoming a registered dietitian. Includes information on job outlook, requirements for registration, employment opportunities, and salary data for registered dietitians.

- *Check it Out...A Career as a Dietetic Technician, Registered.* 2 pages. Prepared for second career adults who are interested in becoming a dietetic technician, registered. Includes information on job outlook, requirements for registration, employment opportunities, and salary data for registered dietetic technicians, registered.

- *Check It Out...Careers in Dietetics Video.* 7 minutes. Illustrates career opportunities in dietetics by depicting RDs and a DTR in several food and nutrition practice settings. Designed to increase 6th to 8th grade students' awareness about careers in dietetics.

106
AMERICAN FARM BUREAU FEDERATION
225 Touhy Avenue
Park Ridge, IL 60068
847-685-8848
Fax: 847-685-8969
http://www.fb.com

- *Challenge in Agriculture.* 43 pages. Discusses employment opportunities; lists land grant colleges and universities by state; provides *Occupational Outlook Handbook* write-ups on agriculture, forestry, fishing, and related occupations; and lists scholarship information and computer sites.

107
AMERICAN FARRIER'S ASSOCIATION
Kentucky Horse Park
4059 Iron Works Pike
Lexington, KY 40511
606-233-7411
Fax: 606-231-7862

- *So You Want to be a Farrier.* 6 pages. Describes duties, working conditions, personal qualifications, training, earnings, and outlook.

- *Directory of North American Farrier Schools.* 6 pages.

- *AFA Certification Study Guide.* 10 pages. Lists the levels of the AFA examination, certification sites on record at the AFA office, and certification rules and study outlines.

- *AFA Certification: Questions and Answers.* 8 pages. Answers the most common questions about the AFA certification program.

- *Books of Interest to Farriers.* 1 page. Lists books relating to the farrier field.

108
AMERICAN FEDERATION OF LABOR AND CONGRESS OF INDUSTRIAL ORGANIZATIONS (AFL-CIO)
Department of Education
815 16th Street NW
Room 209
Washington, DC 20006
202-637-5000
Fax: 202-637-5058

- *AFL-CIO Guide to Union Sponsored Scholarships, Awards, and Student Financial Aid.* ($3) 130 pages.

- *Asian Americans in the Workforce.* ($.20) 8 pages.

- *Jobs for the Future: An AFL-CIO View.* ($.15) 10 pages.

109
AMERICAN FEDERATION OF TEACHERS
555 New Jersey Avenue NW
Washington, DC 20001-2079
202-879-4400

- *Teaching as a Career.* 8 pages. Intended as an introductory guide. Emphasizes the need for teachers and the rewards of the profession. Discusses how to prepare for the profession and find a job.

110
AMERICAN FISHERIES SOCIETY
5410 Grosvenor Lane
Suite 110
Bethesda, MD 20814-2199
301-897-8616
Fax: 301-897-8096

- *Careers in Fisheries.* ($.25) 12 pages. Discusses education, career choices, demand in the field, and employment opportunities.

- *Fisheries Programs and Related Courses at North American Colleges and Universities.* ($.25) 13 pages.

111
AMERICAN FOREST ASSOCIATION
PO Box 2000
Washington, DC 20013
202-667-3300
http://www.amfor.org

- *Growing Greener Cities & Environmental Education Guide.* ($9.50) Two volumes. Offers 13 adaptable lessons that help middle-school students interact with one another and with their environment. Helps students learn the value of trees and the correct way to plant them. Also helps sharpen their research, analysis, and communication skills.

112
AMERICAN FOUNDATION FOR THE BLIND
11 Pen Plaza
Suite 300
New York, NY 10001
800-232-3044 (orders only) or 212-502-7657
Fax: 212-502-7774

- *Braille Alphabet and Numbers.* (#28198-3) A learning tool for teachers and students. Shows the Braille alphabet and numbers.

113
AMERICAN FOUNDRYMEN'S SOCIETY, INC.
505 State Street
Des Plaines, IL 60016-8399
800-537-4237 or 847-824-0181
Fax: 847-824-7848
http://www.afsinc.org

- *Metalcasting: An Art...A Science...A Career!* (#CA-0001) 24 pages. Provides a brief background of the industry; an overview of the specialized careers in the field; scholarship information; a list of universities in the United

States offering cast metal studies; and a list of metalcasting organizations.

- *Casting Engineering Guidelines.* (#CA-0002) 27 pages. Provides an introduction to the foundry process. Directed toward the design engineer.

114
AMERICAN GEOLOGICAL INSTITUTE
National Center for Earth Science Education
4220 King Street
Alexandria, VA 22302-1507
703-379-2480
Fax: 703-379-7563
http://www.agiweb.org

- *Careers in the Geosciences.* 4 pages. Describes the field, career opportunities, work environment, and job and salary outlook.

115
AMERICAN GEOPHYSICAL UNION
Education and Research Department
2000 Florida Avenue NW
Washington, DC 20009-1231
202-462-6900
Fax: 202-328-0566

- *Careers in Geophysics.* Depicts careers in the geophysical field.

116
AMERICAN HEALTH INFORMATION MANAGEMENT ASSOCIATION
919 North Michigan Avenue
Suite 1400
Chicago, IL 60611-1683
312-787-2672
Fax: 312-787-9793
http://www.ahima.org

- *Accredited Educational Programs in Health Information (Medical Record) Administration and Health Information (Medical Record) Technology.* 9 pages. Lists colleges and universities offering programs in the field.

- *A Career in Health Information Management.* 8 pages. Describes career opportunities, employment outlook, salary information, work environment, and other topics.

- *You're in the Driver's Seat...with the Nation's Leader in Health Information Management!* 8 pages.

Contains information on the independent study programs in medical record technology and coding.

117
AMERICAN HEALTHCARE RADIOLOGY ADMINISTRATORS
PO Box 334
Sudbury, MA 01776
800-334-2472
Fax: 508-443-8046
http://www.ahra.com

- *Your Career Opportunities in Radiologic Technology.* 20 pages. ($1.25) This brochure details the eight specialty areas of radiologic technology: CT, MRI, radiography, special procedures, nuclear medicine, medical diagnostic sonography, radiation therapy, and management/education. Everyday duties, certification and educational requirements, and career opportunities for workers in all eight specialty areas are detailed in this full-color brochure.

118
AMERICAN HEALTHCARE RADIOLOGY ADMINISTRATORS
111 Boston Post Road
Suite 105
PO Box 334
Sudbury, MA 01776
508-443-7591
Fax: 508-443-8046
http://www.ahra.com

- *Your Career Opportunities in Radiologic Technology.* 17 pages. Describes the duties and responsibilities, certification requirements, educational programs, and career opportunities for a number of careers in the radiologic field.

119
AMERICAN HORSE COUNCIL
1700 K Street NW
Suite 300
Washington, DC 20006-3805
202-296-4031
Fax: 202-296-1970

- *Educational Opportunities in the Horse Industry.* 7 pages. Lists careers requiring daily contact with horses; support positions without daily contact; and careers in a number of disciplines. Also lists equine veterinary schools, equine organizations, intercollegiate information, and references.

120
AMERICAN HORTICULTURAL SOCIETY
Education Director
7931 East Boulevard Drive
Alexandria, VA 22308-1300
703-768-5700
Fax: 703-768-8700
gardenahs@aol.com
http://www.emall.com

- *Careers in Horticulture.* ($3) Includes articles on careers in the field, as well as a list of accredited schools in the United States and Canada offering degrees in horticulture and landscape architecture.

- *Horticulture Scholarships.* ($2.50) 5 pages. An AHS resource bulletin listing horticultural scholarship sources.

121
AMERICAN HOTEL & MOTEL ASSOCIATION
1407 South Harrison Road
PO Box 1240
East Lansing, MI 48826-1240
800-344-3320 or 517-353-5500

- *Lodging and Food Service Careers: A World of Opportunities.* 14 pages. Discusses career opportunities in the field and lists sources of additional information.

122
AMERICAN HUMANICS, INC.
4601 Madison Avenue
Kansas City, MO 64112
800-343-6466 or 816-561-6415
http://www.humanics.org

- *Make Your Mark on the World.* 6 pages. Describes AH as a national program devoted to preparing college students for careers in nonprofit youth and human service organizations; discusses requirements of the program, and financial assistance; and includes an insert on participating campuses and agencies.

123
AMERICAN INDIAN GRADUATE CENTER
4520 Montgomery Boulevard NE
Suite 1-B
Albuquerque, NM 87109-1291
505-881-4584
Fax: 505-884-0427

- *Fellowship Support for American Indian & Alaskan Native Graduate Students.* 6 pages. Discusses fellowship eligibility, review and award process, and application procedure and includes application packet order information.

124
AMERICAN INDIAN SCIENCE AND ENGINEERING SOCIETY
AISES Publishing, Inc.
5661 Airport Boulevard
Boulder, CO 80301-2339
303-939-0023
Fax: 303-939-8150
http://www.colorado.edu/AISES

- *Annual College Guide for American Indians.* ($7.50) 96 pages. Describes the top colleges as well as preparation and application information, emphasizing the schools with significant Indian communities and support programs; lists summer college-prep programs; and provides detailed financial information.

125
AMERICAN INDUSTRIAL HYGIENE ASSOCIATION
2700 Prosperity Avenue
Suite 250
Fairfax, VA 22031
703-849-8888
Fax: 703-207-3561
http://www.aiha.org

- *Careerworks.* (#170-PR-93) Targets students in grades 9 through 12; contains a description of the profession and its objectives; and promotes careers in the hygiene industry.

- *Careerworks for Kids.* (#185-PR94) 12 pages. For 3rd through 8th graders. Delivers a colorful presentation that both entertains and informs young students on hygiene careers.

- *Balancing Work, Health, Technology & Environment: Careers in Industrial Hygiene.* 19 pages. Provides an overview of the profession, a job description, typical employers, educational requirements, and salaries. Lists schools offering industrial programs.

- *Everything You Need to Know about Industrial Hygiene, Version 2.* 17 pages. Discusses the field, salary, educational requirements, work environment, levels of responsibility, and schools with accredited programs.

126
AMERICAN INSTITUTE FOR CONSERVATION OF HISTORIC AND ARTISTIC WORKS
1717 K Street NW
Suite 301
Washington, DC 20006
202-452-9545
Fax: 202-452-9328
infoaic@aol.com

- *Conservation Training in the United States.* 16 pages. Defines the field and describes the qualifications and responsibilities, work environment, rewards, training and apprenticeship, graduate programs, study abroad, financial aid, and conservation disciplines.

127
AMERICAN INSTITUTE OF ARCHITECTS
1735 New York Avenue NW
Washington, DC 20006-5292
800-365-ARCH or 202-626-7300
Fax: 802-864-7626

- *Career Profile: Architect.* ($10, pack of 25) 12 pages. Provides an overview of the profession, education and training requirements, and career options.

128
AMERICAN INSTITUTE OF BIOLOGICAL SCIENCES
1313 Dolley Madison Boulevard
Suite 402
McLean, VA 22101
800-992-2427
Fax: 703-790-2672
http://www.aibs.org

- *Careers in Biology.* Provides an overview of various life sciences careers, the required training, and the salary and employment outlook.

129
AMERICAN INSTITUTE OF CERTIFIED PUBLIC ACCOUNTANTS
Academic and Career Development Division
1211 Avenue of the Americas
New York, NY 10036-8775
212-596-6200
http://www.aicpa.org

- *Room Zoom: The CPA Sourcedisk.* ($5 plus shipping) Designed for high school and college students. Contains information on accounting education and CPA careers, technology tools used within the profession, scholarship and internship data, education required, and the CPA exam. Available online or by written request from the AICPA.

130
AMERICAN INSTITUTE OF CHEMICAL ENGINEERS
345 East 47 Street
New York, New York 10017-2395
800-242-4363
Fax: 212-705-8400
xpress@aiche.org
http://www.aiche.org//welcome/contacts.html

- *Career Services for Chemical Engineers.* Provides information on the Career Expo & Employment Clearinghouse, position wanted notices in *Chemical Engineering Progress*, a list of United States companies employing chemical engineers, help through its Resume Referral Service, a list of job-hunting books, and other career information.

- *From Microchips to Potato Chips: Chemical Engineers Make A Difference!* 8 pages. This color brochure gives a brief overview of the world of chemical engineers, including a description of their duties and responsibilities, prime employers, educational requirements, how to choose a college, and sources of additional information.

131
AMERICAN INSTITUTE OF PHYSICS
One Physics Ellipse
College Park, MD 20740-3843
301-209-3190
Fax: 301-209-0841
http://www.aip.org

- *Physics Is for You.* 12 pages. Provides an overview of the field and describes the required education, skills, and abilities, as well as career opportunities and sources of additional information.

132
AMERICAN INSTITUTE OF PROFESSIONAL GEOLOGISTS
7828 Vance Drive, #103
Arvada, Colorado 80003-2125
303-431-0831
Fax: 303-431-1332
aipg@aipg.com
http://www.nbmg.unr.edu/aipg/

- *Education for Professional Practice.* ($6) 16 pages. Provides information to students interested in becoming professional geologists and contains guidelines for curriculum development for university geology departments.

- *Guide to Federal and State Appointive Positions.* ($6) 10 pages. Contains information on how to get government geological positions at the state and federal levels.

133
AMERICAN INSTITUTE OF ULTRASOUND IN MEDICINE
14750 Sweitzer Lane
Suite 100
Laurel, MD 20707-5906
301-398-4100
Fax: 301-498-4450

- *Is Sonography for You?* 6 pages. Defines diagnostic and therapeutic ultrasound and discusses education and training, certification, and salary.

134
AMERICAN IRON AND STEEL INSTITUTE
Publication Orders
1101 17th Street NW
Suite 1300
Washington, DC 20036-4700
202-452-7100
Fax: 202-463-6573
http://www.steel.org

- *Iron and Steel Industry Workers.* 6 pages. Provides an overview of the work of iron and steel workers.

135
AMERICAN LEGION
PO Box 1055
Indianapolis, IN 46206-1055
317-630-1200

- *Need a Lift?* ($3) 134 pages. Discusses college financial aid (loans and scholarships), educational opportunities, and careers. Also includes a financial aid resource application.

136
AMERICAN LIBRARY ASSOCIATION
Office for Library Personnel Resources
Standing Committee on Library Education
50 East Huron Street
Chicago, IL 60611-2795
800-545-2433, ext. 4281 or 312-944-6780

- *Financial Assistance for Library and Information Studies.* ($1) Includes information on national awards, scholarships, fellowships, grants, and assistantships from state library agencies and associations, educational institutions, and local libraries. Most listings are for programs leading to the master's degree in library science.

The Future Is Information: Talented People Wanted. Folder includes:

- *Careers in Library and Information Science: Academic Librarianship.* 6 pages.

- *Careers in Library and Information Science: Technical Services.* 6 pages.

- *Library and Information Studies Directory of Institutions Offering Accredited Masters Programs.*

- *Graduate Library Education Programs: Master's Degree Program Academic Hour Requirements.* 1 page.

- *Graduate Library Education Programs: Distance Education.* 4 pages.

- *Graduate Library Education Programs: Joint Degree Programs Academic Hour Requirements.* 2 pages.

- *Guidelines for Choosing a Library and Information Studies Graduate Program.* 3 pages.

- *Librarians.* 2 pages. Reprinted from the *Occupational Outlook Handbook.*

- *Librarians: Information Sleuths.* 4 pages. Reprinted from *Career World.*

- *Library Education Scholarships for Which Foreign Students are Eligible to Apply.* 5 pages. Lists more than 30 programs by state.

- *Placements and Salaries.* 7 pages. Reprinted from the *Library Journal.*

137
AMERICAN MANAGEMENT ASSOCIATION
1601 Broadway
New York, NY 10019
800-262-9699 or 212-586-8100
Fax: 518-891-0368
http://www.amanet.org

Successful Office Skills Series. ($4 each) Available titles for these 64-page booklets include:

- *Becoming an Effective Leader.* (#07816)

- *Building Better Relationships on the Job.* (#07817)

- *Coaching and Counseling in the Workplace.* (#07818)

- *Conflict Resolution.* (#07820)

- *Creative Problem Solving.* (#07702)

- *Effective Teambuilding.* (#07819)

- *Get Organized!* (#07646)

- *How to Be a Successful Interviewer.* (#07697)

- *How to Be a Successful Manager.* (#07642)
- *How to Deal with Difficult People.* (#07674)
- *How to Delegate Effectively.* (#07700)
- *How to Make an Effective Speech or Presentation.* (#07672)
- *How to Negotiate a Raise or Promotion.* (#07643)
- *How to Read Financial Statements.* (#07644)
- *How to Run a Meeting.* (#07671)
- *How to Write an Effective Resume.* (#07669)
- *How to Write Easily and Effectively.* (#07641)
- *Improving your Reading Power.* (#07698-8)
- *Making Tough Decisions.* (#07821)
- *Managing Stress.* (#07673)
- *Polishing Your Professional Image.* (#07670-8)
- *Winning on the Telephone.* (#07699)

138
AMERICAN MASSAGE THERAPY ASSOCIATION
820 Davis Street
Suite 100
Evanston, IL 60201-4444
847-864-0123

- *List of Accredited Programs in Massage Therapy.*

139
AMERICAN MATHEMATICAL SOCIETY
PO Box 6248
Providence, RI 02940-6248
800-321-4AMS or 401-455-4000
Fax: 401-331-3842
http://www.ams.org/

- *Careers in Mathematics.* 6 pages. Contains helpful information for the college-bound high school student with an interest in mathematics. Discusses the difference between pure and applied mathematics, offers some important consideration when choosing a university, provides information on graduate mathematics programs and undergraduate scholarships and fellowships, and lists sources of additional information.

- *Seeking Employment in the Mathematical Sciences.* ($5) 21 pages. Assists mathematical science students at the bachelor's, master's, and doctoral levels who are or will be seeking professional employment. Discusses types of employment that are traditional for mathematicians, describes the relevance of certain courses to professional activities, contains some observations on strategies for finding employment opportunities, and suggests tactics for obtaining a position after a job opportunity has been identified.

140
AMERICAN MEAT SCIENCE ASSOCIATION
444 North Michigan Avenue
Chicago, IL 60611
312-670-9457
Fax: 312-670-9452

- *Careers in the Meat Industry.* An overview of careers, applicable to high school students.

141
AMERICAN MEDICAL ASSOCIATION
Division of Undergraduate Medical Education
515 North State Street
Chicago, IL 60610
800-621-8335 or 312-464-4662

- *Got That Healing Feeling? Study Medicine & Keep That Feeling Your Whole LIfe.* 12 pages. Discusses personal qualifications, career preparation, a list of U.S. medical schools offering combined college/MD programs, selecting the right school, applying for medical school, financial aid, income, alternative career choices.

- *Medical Education and Financial Assistance Programs Sponsored by U.S. Government Agencies.* 5 pages.

- *Medical Schools in the United States and Canada.* 9 pages. Contains tables listing—for each accredited U.S. and Canadian medical school—the ownership, year established, tuition and fees for residents and nonresidents, and dean's name; another table lists the number of in-state and out-of-state entering students, medical school enrollment data by gender, total enrollment, the number of graduate students of basic sciences, and the number of residents and fellows for each U.S. institution.

- *Medicine: A Chance to Make a Difference.* 12 pages. Explains how to prepare for medical school, acceptance guidelines, the application process, selecting the medical school for you, what to expect, expenses and financial aid information, sources of additional information.

- *Medicine as a Career.* Covers such topics as planning your medical education and what to expect in terms of practice, demand, salary, average work week, etc.

- *A Selected Bibliography of Financial Aid for Health Careers.* 4 pages.

- *State Educational Agencies (Sources of Information on Guaranteed Student Loans, PLUS Loans, SLS Loans, and State Aid).* 6 pages.

- *State Initiatives to Improve Rural Health Care: Education Assistance.* 7 pages.

- *You...the Doctor: Challenges and Opportunities in the Medical Profession.* (OP-416) ($2.50) Send check or money order to the AMA, Box 10946, Chicago, IL 60610.

142
AMERICAN MEDICAL STUDENT ASSOCIATION
Publications
1890 Preston White Drive
Reston, VA 22091-4325
703-620-6600

- *C.O.R.E.-Cancer Outreach and Relief Effort.* ($5) project guide. Describes project pairing medical students with siblings of pediatric cancer patients.

- *Community Connections: A Sourcebook for Local Community Health Projects.* ($5) A how-to for starting a community health project at your school, including identifying the need, planning, fundraising, and the logistics of setting up.

- *Financial Aid Resources for Minority Medical Students.* ($5)

- *Guide to Primary Care Residency Programs with an International Health Emphasis.* ($2) Describes 19 programs in family practice, internal medicine, pediatrics, and preventive medicine.

- *Hospice Directory.* ($4) A nationwide list of hospices that provide elective experiences for medical students.

- *Staying in Medical School: Understanding Your Student Rights.* ($5)

- *Visiting Clerkship Guide for Minority Students.* ($5) Lists programs offering formal and informal minority visiting clerkship opportunities.

For charges and purchase orders, send to the above address; for prepaid orders, send to AMSA Publications, PO Box 630818, Baltimore, MD 21263-0818.

143
AMERICAN MEDICAL TECHNOLOGISTS
710 Higgins Road
Park Ridge, IL 60068-5765
800-ASK-1AMT or 847-823-5169
Fax: 847-823-0458
amtmail@aol.com

- *Answers to Your Questions About an Exciting Career in Medical Technology.* ($.50) 6 pages. Describes the careers in the field and how to prepare for them.

- *RMA-Medical Assisting: A Career for Today and Tomorrow.* ($.50) 8 pages. Describes the medical assistant and registered medical assistant (RMA), as well as training programs, employment possibilities, and requirements for certification.

144
AMERICAN METEOROLOGICAL SOCIETY
45 Beacon Street
Boston, MA 02108-3693
617-227-2425
Fax: 617-742-8718
http://www.ametsoc.org/AMS

- *Challenges of our Changing Atmosphere: Careers in Atmospheric Research and Applied Meteorology.* 12 pages. Describes meteorology and the meteorologist, the duties and responsibilities, tools used, work environments, required education, employment outlook, and typical salaries.

- *Colleges and Universities with Degree Programs in the Atmospheric and Oceanic, Hydrologic, and Related Sciences.* 4 pages. Lists schools in the field.

- *Employment Outlook and Salaries in Meteorology.* 1 page. Includes employment outlook in meteorology and the average annual salaries for meteorologists with varying educational degrees.

145
AMERICAN MONTESSORI SOCIETY
281 Park Avenue South, 6th Floor
New York, NY 10010-6102
212-358-1250
Fax: 212-358-1256
http://www.seattleu.edu/ jcm/montessori/menu_link.html

- *Montessori Education Questions and Answers.* ($.25) 12 pages. Answers questions about the Montessori education philosophy.

- *Affiliated Teacher Education Programs.* ($.25)

- *1995 Salary Information.* ($5)

- *Some Comparisons of Montessori Education With Traditional Education.* ($.25) 1 page.

146
AMERICAN NUCLEAR SOCIETY
555 North Kensington Avenue
La Grange Park, IL 60525
708-579-8265

- *Careers for Women in Nuclear Science and Technology.* 28 pages. Discusses career opportunities in education, the government, industry, and national laboratories.

- *Nuclear Technology Creates Careers.* Lists typical duties and responsibilities, career opportunities in the field, income, employment outlook.

147
AMERICAN NURSES ASSOCIATION
600 Maryland Avenue SW
Suite 100 West
Washington, DC 20024-2571
800-637-4ANA

- *Career Letter.* 2 pages. Contains information on the nursing career.

148
AMERICAN OCCUPATIONAL THERAPY ASSOCIATION, INC.
4720 Montgomery Lane
PO Box 31220
Betheseda, MD 20824-1220
301-652-2682
Fax: 301-652-7711
http://www.aota.org

- *Occupational Therapy Educational Programs List.* ($5) 27 pages. Outlines the responsibilities of an occupational therapist, the job outlook, salaries, work environment, career choices, education and training, and financial assistance. Lists accredited occupational therapy educational programs at various levels, as well as occupational therapy assistant programs.

- *Occupational Therapy Careers.* 6 pages. Describes occupational therapy, the tasks of the field, and how to prepare for an occupational therapy career.

149
AMERICAN OPTOMETRIC ASSOCIATION EDUCATIONAL SERVICES
243 North Lindbergh Boulevard
St. Louis, MO 63141-7881
http://www.opted.org

- *Optometry: A Career with Vision.* Describes an optometric education, admission requirements, and financial aid and offers a statistical profile of students for each accredited school. Publication available at the web site.

150
AMERICAN ORNITHOLOGISTS' UNION
Division of Birds, MRC-116
National Museum of Natural History
Washington, DC 20560
202-357-2051

- *Career Opportunities in Ornithology.* ($1) 9 pages.

151
AMERICAN ORTHOPEDIC SOCIETY FOR SPORTS MEDICINE
6300 North River Road
Suite 200
Rosemont, IL 60018
847-292-4900
Fax: 847-292-4905
http://www.sportsmed.org

- *Pathways to Sports Medicine.* 7 pages. Details the various career opportunities in the field, the duties, and educational requirements.

- *Resource Directory for the Disabled Athlete.* ($2) Lists resources helpful to the disabled athlete.

152
AMERICAN OSTEOPATHIC ASSOCIATION
Public Relations
142 East Ontario Street
Chicago, IL 60611-2864
800-621-1773 or 312-280-7401
Fax: 312-280-5893
http://www.am-osteo-assn.org

- *Osteopathic Medical Education.* 6 pages. Describes admissions, the curriculum, training, and licensure. Lists accredited osteopathic medical colleges.

- *Osteopathic Medicine.* 6 pages. Provides an overview of the field and discusses education, training, and licensure requirements.

- *What Is a D.O. (Osteopathic Physician)?* 6 pages. Discusses the differences between the MD and DO, as well as basic principles behind osteopathic medicine.

153
AMERICAN OSTEOPATHIC HEALTHCARE ASSOCIATION
5301 Wisconsin Avenue NW
Suite 630
Washington, DC 20015
301-968-2642

- *Opportunities in Osteopathic Postdoctoral Education.* (free to students and libraries) Lists more than 100 programs approved by the AOHA and provides information on internships and residencies.

154
AMERICAN PHARMACEUTICAL ASSOCIATION
2215 Constitution Avenue NW
Washington, DC 20037-2985
202-429-7568

- *Pharmacy: A Caring Profession.* 6 pages. Discusses demand in the field, education and training, and work environments. Lists U.S. colleges and schools of pharmacy.

- *Interorganizational Financial & Experiential Information Document.* 20 pages. Lists pharmacy scholarships, loan sources, awards, grants, internships, residencies, research possibilities, and fellowships.

155
AMERICAN PHILOLOGICAL SOCIETY
Department of Classics
College of the Holy Cross
Worcester, MA 01610-2395
508-793-2203

- *Careers for Classicists.* ($1.50) 33 pages.

156
AMERICAN PHYSICAL SOCIETY
American Center for Physics
One Physics Ellipse
College Park, MD 20740-3844
301-209-3200
Fax: 301-209-0865

- *Physics Is for You.* 14 pages. Discusses the field, various work environments, education and training, career opportunities, and sources of additional information.

157
AMERICAN PHYSICAL THERAPY ASSOCIATION
1111 North Fairfax Street
Alexandria, VA 22314-1488
800-999-APTA or 703-684-2782
Fax: 703-706-3396
http://www.apta.org

- *A Future in Physical Therapy.* Outlines the field and provides information on education, training, certification, and employment outlook.

- *Accredited PT Education Programs.* Lists all accredited PT and PTA programs in the United States.

- *Patient Information Brochures.* Various brochures describing specific types of care.

158
AMERICAN PHYSIOLOGICAL SOCIETY
Education Office, 9650 Rockville Pike
Bethesda, MD 20814-3991
301-530-7164
educatio@aps.faaseb.org
http://www.faseb.org/aps

- *Careers in Physiology.* 8 pages. Discusses the field, education and training, career opportunities, salary levels, and other topics.

159
AMERICAN PHYTOPATHOLOGICAL SOCIETY 3340 PILOT KNOB ROAD
St. Paul, MN 55121-2097
612-454-7250
Fax: 612-454-0766
http://www.scisoc.org

- *Careers in Plant Pathology.* 7 pages. Defines the plant pathologist, typical duties and responsibilities, current technology, and education and training. Lists the departments of plant pathology by state. Also available in Spanish.

160
AMERICAN PLANNING ASSOCIATION
1776 Massachusetts Avenue NW
Suite 704
Washington, DC 20036
202-872-0611

Career Kit includes:

- *Accredited University Planning Programs.* 6 pages.

- *Urban and Regional Planners.* 21 pages. Describes the field, work environment, how to find a planning job, opportunities for women and minority groups, sources of information, and specialties in the field.

- *Urban Planners: Movers and Shakers.* 7 pages. Discusses the profession, salary range, qualifications, the career ladder, and other topics.

161
AMERICAN PODIATRIC MEDICAL ASSOCIATION, INC.
9312 Old Georgetown Road
Bethesda, MD 20814-1698
301-571-9200
Fax: 301-530-2752
http://www.apma.org

- *Podiatric Medicine: The Physician, The Profession, The Practice.* 6 pages. Includes background information on the profession, educational requirements, areas of practice, and other topics.

- *The Podiatric Medical Assistant.* 6 pages. Describes the profession, opportunity and employment outlook, scope of duties, education requirements, and certification.

162
AMERICAN POLITICAL SCIENCE ASSOCIATION
Publications
1527 New Hampshire Avenue NW
Washington, DC 20036
202-483-2512
http://www.apsanet.org

- *Careers and the Study of Political Science: A Guide for Undergraduates.* ($3.50 plus $1 shipping)

- *Storming Washington: An Intern's Guide to National Government.* ($6) Filled with practical advice on such subjects as how to line up an internship, how to get the most out of it, and finally, how to win it, including a list of options for internships, and even advice on how to locate bed and board.

- *Earning a Ph.D. in Political Science.*

163
AMERICAN POLYGRAPH ASSOCIATION
PO Box 8037
Chattanooga, TN 37414-0037
800-272-8037 or 423-892-3992
Fax: 423-894-5435
http://www.polygraph.org

- *Polygraph: Issues and Answers.* 12 pages. Presents a few essential facts about polygraph testing. Includes information on polygraph examinations, errors and accuracy of polygraph examinations, and polygraph screening in police agencies.

- *APA Accredited Polygraph Schools.* 1 page. Lists polygraph schools accredited by the APA.

164
AMERICAN PSYCHIATRIC ASSOCIATION
Public Affairs Division
1400 K Street NW
Suite 501
Washington, DC 20005
202-682-6220

- *What is a Psychiatrist?* 6 pages. Discusses the field, education and training, subspecialties, work environments, and salaries.

165
AMERICAN PSYCHOLOGICAL ASSOCIATION
Public Interest Directorate
750 First Street NE
Washington, DC 20002-4242

800-374-2721 or 202-336-5500
Fax: 202-336-5978
http://www.apa.org

- *Psychology: Scientific Problem Solvers-Careers for the 21st Century.* 20 pages. Provides an overview of psychology, job outlook for the next two decades, educational preparation for work in psychology, and several charts depicting various aspects of the field.

- *Is Psychology the Major for You?* ($9.95) 137 pages.

- *APA-Accredited Doctoral Programs in Professional Psychology.* 11 pages. (available through the Accreditation Department at 202-336-5979)

166
AMERICAN PUBLIC WORKS ASSOCIATION
2345 Grand Boulevard
Suite 500
Kansas City, MO 64108
816-472-6100
apwa@bbs.pubworks.org
http://www.FileShop.Com/apwa/main.html

- *Civil Engineering and Other Career Paths into Public Works.* Available online or by writing to the association.

167
AMERICAN SOCIETY FOR BIOCHEMISTRY AND MOLECULAR BIOLOGY
9650 Rockville Pike
Bethesda, MD 20814-3996
301-530-7145
Fax: 301-571-1824
http://www.faseb.org/asbmb

- *Unlocking Life's Secrets: Career Opportunities in Biochemistry and Molecular Biology.* 16 pages. Addresses career opportunities, duties and responsibilities, education and training, college admission requirements, and financial aid in the biochemistry and molecular biology field.

- *Institutions That Offer Bachelor's Degrees in Biochemistry/Molecular Biology.* 21 pages.

- *Biologists Discover Amazing Things.* Depicts various animals and describes how they aid us in biology. Suitable for middle school and high school students.

168
AMERICAN SOCIETY FOR CELL BIOLOGY
9650 Rockville Pike
Bethesda, MD 20814-3992
301-530-7153
Fax: 301-530-7139
http://www.acsb.org/acsb

- *Opportunity and Adventure in Cell Biology.* 17 pages. Discusses cell biology, employment opportunities and outlook, education and training, and other topics.

- *Opportunities in Cell Biology.* 13 pages. Contains information for minority students interested in pursuing a career in cell biology.

- *How to Get a Teaching Job at a Primarily Undergraduate Institution.* 8 pages. Written to assist those seeking alternative careers in the field. Provides suggestions for obtaining employment in cell biology at a primarily undergraduate institution.

- *How to Get a Research Job in Academia and Industry.* 15 pages. Intended for those at the postdoctoral level seeking a position with a large research component. Also helpful for students at an earlier stage in their career who are preparing for their first real job hunt.

169
AMERICAN SOCIETY FOR CLINICAL LABORATORY SCIENCE
7910 Woodmont Avenue
Suite 1301
Bethesda, MD 20814

- *Clinical Laboratory Science.* Tells why the field is important, cites activities performed by clinical laboratory professionals, summarizes methods of preparing for the field, and points out the diversity of employment options.

170
AMERICAN SOCIETY FOR CLINICAL LABORATORY SCIENCE
7910 Woodmont Avenue., Suite 1301
Bethesda, MD 20814
301-657-2768

- *Career Resources for Clinical Laboratory Professionals.* 4 pages. This flyer lists materials pertaining to careers in clinical laboratory science. It includes videos, brochures, directories, and books.

- *Opportunities in Medical Technology.* ($10) 160 pages. This book provides current information on training and education requirements, salary levels, and employment outlook for careers in medical technology.

171
AMERICAN SOCIETY FOR ENGINEERING EDUCATION
1818 N Street NW
Suite 600
Washington, DC 20036
202-331-3500
Fax: 202-265-8504
pubsinfo@asee.org
http://www.asee.org

- *An Academic Career: It Could Be for You.* ($2) 12 pages. Describes personal and professional rewards of an engineering faculty career.

- *Thinking of an Academic Career.* ($2) 4 pages. Includes employment trends—geographically and by discipline—salary levels, and job hunting suggestions.

172
AMERICAN SOCIETY FOR INDUSTRIAL SECURITY
1655 North Fort Myer Drive
Suite 1200
Arlington, VA 22209-3198
703-522-5800
Fax: 703-525-2694
http://www.asisonline.org

- *Careers in Security.* 8 pages. Describes employment opportunities, careers in the field, certification, education, and training.

173
AMERICAN SOCIETY FOR INFORMATION SCIENCE
8720 Georgia Avenue
Suite 501
Silver Spring, MD 20910-3602
301-495-0900
Fax: 301-495-0810
http://www.asis.org

- *Challenging Careers in Information: Join the Information Age.* 7 pages. Includes information on career and employment opportunities, salary, education and training, and further references.

174
AMERICAN SOCIETY FOR INTEGRATIVE AND COMPARATIVE BIOLOGY
401 North Michigan Avenue
Chicago, IL 60611-4267
312-527-6697
Fax: 312-245-1085
sicb@sba.com
http://www.sicb.org

- *Careers in Animal Biology.* 21 pages. Discusses opportunities in academic fields, fields of special interest, opportunities in health-related fields and other nonacademic fields, financing your education, and sources of information.

175

AMERICAN SOCIETY FOR INVESTIGATIVE PATHOLOGY, INC.
9650 Rockville Pike
Bethesda, MD 20814-3993
301-530-7130
Fax: 301-571-1879
http://www.asip.uthscsa.edu

- *Pathology as a Career in Medicine.* 12 pages. Describes the field, duties and responsibilities, employment opportunities, education, and training.

176

AMERICAN SOCIETY FOR MICROBIOLOGY
Office of Education and Training
1325 Massachusetts Avenue NW
Washington, DC 20005
202-942-9283
Fax: 202-942-9329
http://www.asmusa.org

- *Your Career in Microbiology: Unlocking the Secrets of Life.* 16 pages. Defines the microbiologist and the various career options. Discusses the career avenues for each degree level, possible work environments, salary levels, and high school and college preparation.

- *Colleges and Universities with Programs in the Microbiological Sciences.* 17 pages. Lists schools and contact information.

- *Microbiology-Challenges for the 21st Century.* A poster illustrating microbiology careers and depicting what a microbiologist does. Suitable for high school students.

- *Seeing the Unseen.* Poster depicting what a microbiologist is. Suitable for middle school students.

- *Heroes of Microbiology.* Poster including short biographies on minorities in microbiology and various experiments to try. Suitable for middle and high school students.

177

AMERICAN SOCIETY FOR PHARMACOLOGY AND EXPERIMENTAL THERAPEUTICS
9650 Rockville Pike
Bethesda, MD 20814-3995
301-530-7060
Fax: 301-530-7061
http://www.faseb.org.aspet

- *Explore Pharmacology: Graduate Studies in Pharmacology.* 16 pages. Details the number of subdivisions in the field, career opportunities, and required education and training.

- *Graduate Training in Pharmacy Programs in the United States and Canada.* 16 pages. Lists colleges and universities in the United States and Canada and specific fields of study.

178

AMERICAN SOCIETY FOR PHOTOGRAMMETRY AND REMOTE SENSING
5410 Grosvenor Lane
Suite 210
Bethesda, MD 20814-2160
301-493-0290
Fax: 301-493-0208
asprs@asprs.org
http://www.asprs.org/asprs

- *Careers: Mapping Your Future in Photogrammetry, Remote Sensing, and GIS.* 8 pages. Discusses the field, employment and educational opportunities, and sources of additional information.

179

AMERICAN SOCIETY OF AGRICULTURAL ENGINEERS
2950 Niles Road
St. Joseph, MI 49085-9659
616-429-0300
Fax: 616-429-3852
http://asae.org/

- *Career Options: Agricultural Engineering.* ($.20) 6 pages. Describes typical duties, opportunities, and educational requirements.

- *Career Options: Biological Engineering* ($.20) 6 pages. Describes typical duties, opportunities, and educational requirements.

- *Careers for Engineers in Bio-Resource Industries.* 6 pages. Describes typical duties, opportunities, and educational requirements.

180
AMERICAN SOCIETY OF AGRONOMY
677 South Segoe Road
Madison, WI 53711
608-273-8080
Fax: 608-273-2021
http://www.agronomy.org

- *Exploring Careers in Agronomy, Crops, Soils, and Environmental Sciences.* 27 pages. Describes the agronomic sciences, duties and responsibilities, education and training, and salary. Lists colleges and universities in the United States.

181
AMERICAN SOCIETY OF ANESTHESIOLOGISTS
520 North Northwest Highway
Park Ridge, IL 60068-2573
847-825-5586
Fax: 847-825-1692
http://www.asahq.org

- *Anesthesiology: Challenge, Diversity, Flexibility, Rewards.* 6 pages. Discusses education and training, residency, employment opportunities, hours, and outlook.

- *Accredited Programs in Anesthesiology.* 12 pages.

182
AMERICAN SOCIETY OF ANIMAL SCIENCE
1111 North Dunlap Avenue
Savoy, IL 61874
217-356-3182
Fax: 217-398-4119
http://www.asas.uiuc.edu

- *Animal Science Involves People Learning.* 4 pages. (available spring 1998) Describes undergraduate animal science programs and career opportunities.

183
AMERICAN SOCIETY OF CARDIOVASCULAR PROFESSIONALS/NATIONAL SOCIETY FOR PULMONARY TECHNICIANS
910 Charles Street
Fredericksburg, VA 22401
540-370-0102
Fax: 540-370-0015
http://www.augusta.net/atlantic/acsp/acspscm.html

- *Electrocardiograph Technicians: Health Technologist and Health Technicians.* 5 pages. Describes the nature of the work, working conditions, employment, training and advancement, job outlook, earnings, related occupations, and sources of additional information.

- *Cardiology Salary Survey.* 3 pages. National salary survey conducted by the American Academy of Medical Administrators.

- *Accredited Programs.* 4 pages. Lists the 16 programs of cardiovascular technology accredited by the American Medical Association.

184
AMERICAN SOCIETY OF CIVIL ENGINEERS
Student Services Department
1801 Alexander Bell Drive
Reston, VA 20191
800-548-ASCE or 703-295-6025
Fax: 703-295-6132
dconnor@asce.org

- *Our Past, the Present, Your Future...in Civil Engineering.* 30 pages. Includes testimonials from engineers and a description of the seven major branches of civil engineering, employment opportunities, education, training, and registration.

- *Our Past, the Present, Your Future...in Civil Engineering.* 8 pages. Describes the civil engineering career.

- *Jump with Civil Engineers.* A poster highlighting David Robinson, an NBA superstar and former Navy civil engineer. Suitable for middle and high school students.

185
AMERICAN SOCIETY OF CLINICAL PATHOLOGISTS
Board of Registry
PO Box 12277
Chicago, IL 60612-0277
312-738-1336
Fax: 312-738-5808
bor@ascp.org
http://www.ascp.org

- *Careers in Medical Laboratory Technology.* 16 pages. Explores four different career paths in medical laboratory technology.

- *Cytotechnologist: A Career for You!* 1 page. Describes career opportunities, educational requirements, necessary personal characteristics, career preparation, and certification.

- *Histologic Technician: A Career for You!* 1 page. Describes career opportunities, educational requirements, necessary personal characteristics, career preparation, and certification.

- *Medical Laboratory Technician: A Career for You!* 1 page. Describes career opportunities, educational requirements, necessary personal characteristics, career preparation, and certification.

- *Medical Technologist: A Career for You!* 1 page. Describes career opportunities, educational requirements, necessary personal characteristics, career preparation, and certification.

- *BOR Guide to Certification and Careers in the Medical Laboratory.* 12 pages. Provides an overview of all areas of certification.

186
AMERICAN SOCIETY OF CYTOPATHOLOGY (EVALUATION OF CELLS BY MICROSCOPE)
CPRC Secretary
400 West Ninth Street
Suite 201
Wilmington, DE 19801
302-429-8802
Fax: 302-429-8807
indictor@cytopathology.org
http://www.cytopathology.org

- *Consider a Career in Cytotechnology.* 6 pages. Describes the responsibilities, opportunities, education, certification, and employment.

- *Consider A Career in Cytotechnology.* ($2) This poster depicts career opportunities in cytotechnology.

- *Accredited Programs in Cytotechnology.* 8 pages. Lists accredited cytotechnology training programs in the United States and Puerto Rico. Updated monthly.

187
AMERICAN SOCIETY OF ELECTRONEURODIAGNOSTIC TECHNOLOGISTS
204 West 7th Street
Carroll, IA 51401-2317
712-792-2978
Fax: 712-792-6962
aset@netins.net
http://www.aset.org

- *A Career in Electroneurodiagnostic Technology: Brain Power in Action.* ($.50) 12 pages. Describes the field, duties and responsibilities, common procedures performed, career outlook, salary, qualifications, education and training, credentials, and sources of additional information.

- *Schools for Electroneurodiagnostic Technology.* 4 pages. Lists schools in the field that are and are not accredited.

188
AMERICAN SOCIETY OF EXTRA-CORPOREAL TECHNOLOGY
11480 Sunset Hills Road
Suite 210E
Reston, VA 20190
703-435-8556
Fax: 703-435-0056
http://www.amsect.org

- *AmSECT & Perfusion: The Guide.* Includes the following fact sheets: Perfusion Education and Training, Career Outlook, Directory of Accredited Educational Programs in Perfusion, and Employment Opportunities. Much of this information is also available at their web site.

189
AMERICAN SOCIETY OF HEATING, REFRIGERATING, AND AIR-CONDITIONING ENGINEERS, INC.
Education Department
1791 Tullie Circle NE
Atlanta, GA 30329-2305
404-636-8400
Fax: 401-321-5478
http://www.ashrae.org

- *Career Profiles In Heating, Ventilating, Air Conditioning and Refrigeration.* 20 pages. Describes such positions as consulting, teaching and research, utilities, manufacturing, and government agencies.

- *Your Future in the Air-Conditioning, Heating, and Refrigeration Industry.* 8 pages. Lists educational requirements, areas of employment, and job descriptions for a number of job titles.

190
AMERICAN SOCIETY OF HOSPITAL PHARMACISTS
Resident Matching Program
7272 Wisconsin Avenue
Bethesda, MD 20814-1439
301-657-3000

- *Opportunities: Pharmacy Residencies-Preparing for Your Future.* 26 pages. Provides detailed information on residencies in pharmacy, accredited programs, and specialties.

191
AMERICAN SOCIETY OF HUMAN GENETICS
9650 Rockville Pike
Bethesda, MD 20814-3998
http://www.faseb.org/genetics

Check ASHG's web site for current career information.

- *Solving the Puzzle: Careers in Genetics.* Describes career opportunities in genetics.

192
AMERICAN SOCIETY OF ICHTHYOLOGISTS AND HERPETOLOGISTS
Texas Natural History Collection
University of Texas, R 4000
Austin, TX 78712-1100
512-471-0998
Fax: 512-471-9775
http://www.utexas.edu/depts/asih/

- *Careers in Herpetology.* 3 pages. Profiles careers in the field, employment opportunities, and education and training.

- *Careers in Ichthyology.* 5 pages. Covers education and training, employment opportunities, and schools with graduate programs in ichthyology.

193
AMERICAN SOCIETY OF INTERIOR DESIGNERS
Student Affairs Coordinator
608 Massachusetts Avenue NE
Washington, DC 20002-6006
202-546-3480
Fax: 202-546-3240
http://www.asid.org

- *Interior Design Career Guide.* 12 pages. SASE (legal-size envelope). Describes the field, skills and education needed, career options, and future outlook. Includes a list of other resources, as well as a list of accredited interior design schools (with information on design programs and ASID student chapters).

194
AMERICAN SOCIETY OF LANDSCAPE ARCHITECTS
Education Department
636 I Street NW
Washington, DC 20001
202-898-2444

- *Career Packet.* Contains information about accredited programs and general information about the landscape architect profession.

- *Landscape Architecture: Shaping Our Land.* 12 pages. Discusses the profession and typical projects.

- *Accredited Programs in Landscape Architecture.* 12 pages. Lists schools offering accredited programs in landscape architecture.

195
AMERICAN SOCIETY OF LIMNOLOGY AND OCEANOGRAPHY
5400 Bosque Boulevard
Suite 680
Waco, Texas 76710-4446
800-929-2756
Fax: 817-776-3767
business@aslo.org
http://www.aslo.org/

- *Aquatic Science Career Information.* A free article available by mail or online at the web site. Defines the field of aquatic science and discusses job opportunities, employment outlook, earnings, working conditions, and educational preparation.

196
AMERICAN SOCIETY OF MAGAZINE EDITORS
919 Third Avenue
New York, NY 10022
212-872-3700
Fax: 212-906-0128

- *Guide to Careers in Magazine Publishing.* 14 pages. Discusses the industry, finding a job in magazine publishing, careers in the field (e.g., editorial, advertising, circulation, production and distribution, and finance and accounting), and other resources.

197
AMERICAN SOCIETY OF MAMMALOGISTS
269 MLBM, Brigham Young University
Provo, UT 84602
801-378-2492
duane@museum.byu.edu

- *The Science of Mammalogy.* 6 pages. Describes the field, necessary education and training, and employment opportunities.

198
AMERICAN SOCIETY OF MECHANICAL ENGINEERS
345 East 47th Street
New York, NY 10017-2392
212-705-7746

- *Mechanical Engineering.* 8 pages.

199

AMERICAN SOCIETY OF MEDIA PHOTOGRAPHERS, INC.
14 Washington Road
Suite 502
Princeton Junction, NJ 08550-1033
609-799-8300
Fax: 609-799-2233
http://www.asmp.org

- *Career and School Information.* 1 page. Lists photographic schools and institutions in the United States.

200

AMERICAN SOCIETY OF MICROBIOLOGY
Office of Education
1325 Massachusetts Avenue, NW
Washington, DC 20005

- *Your Career in Microbiology: Unlocking the Secrets of Life.*

- *Seeing the Unseen* (poster).

- *Microbiology: Challenges for the 21st Century* (poster).

- *Undergraduate Funding in the Life Sciences.*

201

AMERICAN SOCIETY OF PLUMBING ENGINEERS
3617 East Thousand Oaks Boulevard
Suite 210
Westlake Village, CA 91362-3649
805-495-7120
Fax: 805-495-4861
aspehq@aol.com

- *A Career in Plumbing Engineering.* 6 pages. Describes plumbing engineers and what they do.

202

AMERICAN SOCIETY OF RADIOLOGIC TECHNOLOGISTS
15000 Central Avenue SE
Albuquerque, NM 87123-3917
505-298-4500
Fax: 505-298-5063
http://www.asrt.org

- *Discover the Possibilities...the Radiologic Sciences.* 6 pages. Discusses various educational programs, curricula, duties and responsibilities, and specialties for a number of fields in the radiologic sciences.

203

AMERICAN SOCIETY OF SAFETY ENGINEERS
1800 East Oakton Street
Des Plaines, IL 60018

- *Careers in Safety.*

- *Directory of College and University Safety and Related Career Programs.*

204

AMERICAN SOCIETY OF TRAVEL AGENTS
1101 King Street
Suite 200
Alexandria, VA 22314
703-739-2782

- *ASTA Travel School Members.* 17 pages.

- *Choosing a Travel School.* 1 page.

- *Off to the Right Start with ASTA.* 12 pages. Describes the field, training, agencies, etc.

- *What is a Travel Agent?*

205

AMERICAN SOCIOLOGICAL ASSOCIATION
1722 N Street NW
Washington, DC 20036
202-833-3410

Fax: 202-785-0146
apap@asanet.org
http://www.asanet.org

- *Careers in Sociology.* 25 pages. Discusses the specialties; teaching, research, and practice; employment outlook; and career prep.

- *How to Approach Term Papers with Professionalism: A Style Guide for Students.* 2 pages. Details ASA's guidelines for authors who submit scholarly articles to journals. Provides helpful hints for the student writer, including sections on the craft of writing, organization of a term paper, and mechanics of writing.

- *Majoring in Sociology: A Guide for Students.* 6 pages. Contains information for high school students on pursuing a bachelor's degree in sociology, the types of jobs available, and searching for a job.

- *The Sociology Major as Preparation for Careers in Business and Organizations.* 6 pages. Discusses coursework, tips for the job search, prospects for the MA/PhD, and sociological and academic roles.

- *Embarking upon a Career with an Undergraduate Degree in Sociology.* ($6) 65 pages.

- *Sociologists in the Corporate World: Academic Research and Practice Roles in Business and Industry.* ($6) 42 pages.

- *Mastering the Job Market with a Graduate Degree in Sociology.* ($6) 92 pages.

206
AMERICAN SPEECH-LANGUAGE-HEARING ASSOCIATION
Fulfillment Operations
10801 Rockville Pike
Rockville, MD 20852
301-897-5700
Fax: 301-897-7358

Careers in Speech-Language Pathology and Audiology Kit. (# 0111530) ($3.50) The kit includes:

- *Careers in Speech-Language Pathology and Audiology.* 6 pages.

- *Close-up on Your Future.* 8 pages. Describes the field and its specialties.

- *Exciting Opportunities Ahead for Speech, Language and Hearing Scientists.* 8 pages.

- *For Your Life after Graduate School.* (# 011205) ($5) 16 pages. Discusses the job market, job search resources, resume-writing tips, and interviewing techniques.

207
AMERICAN SPORTS MEDICINE ASSOCIATION BOARD OF CERTIFICATION
660 West Duarte Road
Arcadia, CA 91007
818-445-1978
Fax: 818-574-1999

- *Why Be a Sports Medicine or Athletic Trainer?* 6 pages. Details how to become a board certified sports medicine or athletic trainer.

208
AMERICAN SPORTSCASTERS ASSOCIATION, INC.
5 Beekman Street
Suite 814
New York, NY 10038
212-227-8080

Career packet includes:

- *Interview Guidelines.* 1 page.

- *Radio: career profiles for broadcaster, broadcaster producer, engineer, promotions, and sales.* 6 pages.

- *Sportscaster: Career Profile.* 2 pages.

209
AMERICAN STATISTICAL ASSOCIATION
1429 Duke Street
Alexandria, VA 22314-3402

703-684-1221
Fax: 703-684-2037
http://www.amstat.org

- *Careers in Statistics.* 6 pages. Describes a career as a statistician.

- *Minorities in Statistics/Minorities: Looking for a Challenging Career?* 6 pages. Contains information on the field of statistics, job opportunities, programs of study, salaries, and additional topics useful to minority students.

- *Meeting Today's Challenges: Women in Statistics.* 12 pages. This booklet profiles various women that have made valuable contributions in statistics; describes how to become a statistician, job duties, employment outlook and earnings.

210
AMERICAN SYMPHONY ORCHESTRA LEAGUE
777 14th Street NW
Suite 500
Washington, DC 20005-3201
202-628-0099

- Orchestra Librarian/Music Preparation Packet ($4)

- *The Orchestra Librarian: A Career Introduction.*

- *The Major Orchestra Librarians' Association (MOLA) Music Preparation Guidelines for Orchestral Music.*

- *Senior Citizens as Volunteers.* ($5)

211
AMERICAN TEXTILE MANUFACTURERS INSTITUTE
1130 Connecticut Avenue
Suite 1200
Washington, DC 20036
202-862-0500
http://www.atmi.org

- *A High-Tech World of Textiles.* Provides a general overview of careers in the textile industry.

212
AMERICAN TRANSLATORS ASSOCIATION
1800 Diagonal Road
Suite 220
Alexandria, VA 22314
703-683-6100
http://www.atanet.org

- *A Guide to ATA Accreditation.* 6 pages.

- *Profile of a Competent Translator.* 2 pages.

- *Setting Up an Independent Translation Business.* 5 pages.

- *Steps Toward a Full-Time Career in Translation.* 2 pages.

213
AMERICAN TRUCKING ASSOCIATION, INC.
Office of Public Affairs
2200 Mill Road
Alexandria, VA 22314
703-838-1873

- *Careers in Truck Driving.* 8 pages. Outlines the necessary qualifications for trucking, how to choose a truck driver training school, and how to get hired and promoted in the trucking field.

214
AMERICAN VETERINARY MEDICAL ASSOCIATION
1931 North Meacham Road
Suite 100
Schaumburg, IL 60173-4360
847-925-8070

- *Your Career in Veterinary Technology.* 8 pages. SASE. Discusses the required education, curriculum, personal attributes, admission requirements, registration and certification, and salaries.

- *Programs in Veterinary Technology.* SASE. Lists veterinary technology schools. Updated annually.

- *Today's Veterinarian.* 20 pages. SASE. Describes the veterinarian career and lists U.S. schools and colleges of veterinary medicine.

215
AMERICAN VOCATIONAL ASSOCIATION
1410 King Street
Alexandria, VA 22314
703-683-3111
Fax: 703-683-7424
http://www.avaonline.org

- *Get Your Career in Gear!* 6 pages. Explains to students the school-to-career concept.

- *Career Options Planner.* ($7) Helps students answer tough career questions and assess their academic performance, personal interests, and work preferences.

- *Making the Connection from School to Careers.* 4 pages. Contains information on the new trends toward school-to-career systems and the integration of vocational-technical and academic education; provides a concise summary of what state-of-the-art career preparation programs are all about; and includes statistics on locating jobs.

- *You Can Be What You Want to Be: Careers in Vocational Education.* 7 pages. Contains career quizzes for middle school and high school students as they think about their future career goals.

- *Eight Facts Every Parent Should Know.* 6 pages. Offers eight reasons why parents should encourage their teenagers to include vocational education courses in their high school curriculum.

- *Tech Prep: The Success Option.* 8 pages. Shows students that tech prep means focus, applied learning, skills, college, and success.

- *Tech Prep: A Way to the Future.* 6 pages. Written for parents. Provides reasons why tech prep is a good option for students.

216
AMERICAN WATCHMAKERS-CLOCKMAKERS INSTITUTE, INC.
701 Interprise Drive
Harrison, OH 45030
513-367-9800
Fax: 513-367-1414
http://www.awi-net.org

- *Careers in Watch/Clock Repairing.* 8 pages. Includes information on career opportunities, salary, employment outlook, scope of work, education and training, working conditions, and the proficiency exam.

217
AMERICAN WATER WORKS ASSOCIATION
6666 West Quincy Avenue
Denver, CO 80235-3098
303-794-7711

- *Employment Opportunities in the Water Industry.* 23 pages. Provides a general job description and discusses required skills, education, employment opportunities, and the average entry-level salary for 20 positions in the field.

218
AMERICAN WELDING SOCIETY
550 Northwest LeJeune Road
Miami, FL 33126
800-443-9353 or 305-443-9353
Fax: 305-443-7559

- *Welding and Joining...the Future is Bright.* 6 pages. Aimed at the high school student. Includes information on the field of welding and joining.

- *Student Scholarship Handbook.* Offers a question and answer format about scholarships available through AWS National Scholarship Committee. Includes application.

- *Future Watch: Young Welders Paid Well to Hold the World Together.* 1 page. Describes what welders do, type of education required, and salary range.

- *Welding: Land of Opportunities.* 9 pages. Contains information on the opportunities and challenges for the welding profession.

219
AMERICAN ZOO AND AQUARIUM ASSOCIATION
7970-D Old Georgetown Road
Bethesda, MD 20814-2493
http://www.aza.org

- *Zoo and Aquarium Careers.* 8 pages. SASE. Describes career opportunities, educational and training requirements, salaries, and positions.

- *A Listing of Universities and Schools Having Courses and Classes Professionally Relevant to Zoo Keeping.* 15 pages. SASE. Lists U.S. and international universities and schools.

220
AMIDEAST
Advising Quarterly
1100 17th Street NW
Washington, DC 20036-4601
202-785-0022
Fax: 202-822-6563

The following career publications generally include a description of the field, accredited institutions, program requirements, and additional sources of information. Prices vary according to publication length: ($.70) 1 or 2 pages.; ($.90) 3 pages.; ($1.15) 4 pages.; ($1.40) 5 pages.; ($1.70) 6 pages.; ($1.95) 7 pages.; ($2.25) 8 pages.; ($2.80) 10 pages.; ($3.85) 12 pages.; ($4.05) 13 pages.

- *Accounting.* 3 pages.

- *Aerospace/Aeronautical Engineering.* 2 pages.

- *Agricultural Engineering.* 2 pages.

- *Agriculture.* 6 pages.

- *American Studies.* 2 pages.

- *Applied Arts and Design.* 7 pages.

- *Architecture First Professional Degree.* 3 pages.

- *Asian Studies.* 2 pages.

- *Basic Medical Sciences.* 4 pages.

- *Botany.* 3 pages.

- *Business Administration.* 8 pages.

- *Certified Copies (notary public)* 7 pages.

- *City, Community, and Regional Planning.* 2 pages.

- *Computer Science and Related Fields.* 4 pages.

- *Computer Engineering.* 2 pages.

- *Dentistry in the United States.* 4 pages.

- *Environmental Sciences.* 3 pages.

- *Finance and Banking.* 6 pages.

- *Fish, Game, and Wildlife Management.* 2 pages.

- *Food Sciences and Technology, and Nutrition.* 2 pages.

- *Forestry.* 2 pages.

- *Geography-Graduate.* 3 pages.

- *Geosciences.* 7 pages.

- *Graduate Engineering Studies.* 10 pages.

- *International Relations/International Studies.* 4 pages.

- *Journalism, Mass Communications, and Related Fields.* 6 pages.

- *Landscape Architecture.* 2 pages.

- *Library and Information Sciences.* 2 pages.

- *Linguistics.* 3 pages.

- *Marketing.* 2 pages.

- *Metallurgy, Metallurgical Engineering, Materials Science, Material Science Engineering, Polymer Science, and Ceramic Engineering.* 6 pages.

- *Microbiology.* 4 pages.

- *Music.* 8 pages.

- *Nutrition/Dietetics/Food Science.* 4 pages.

- *Optometry.* 3 pages.

- *Petroleum Engineering.* 2 pages.

- *Pharmacy.* 3 pages.

- *Physical Therapy.* 3 pages.

- *Political Science.* 4 pages.

- *Psychology.* 7 pages.

- *Public Policy and Administration.* 2 pages.

- *Real Estate.* 3 pages.

- *Social Work.* 5 pages.

- *Sociology.* 5 pages.

- *Sports Administration.* 1 pages.

- *Undergraduate Engineering Studies.* 12 pages.

- *U.S. Graduate Programs in Business and Management.* 13 pages.

- *Veterinary Medicine.* 2 pages.

Also offered:

- *College Application Essays.* 1 page. Discusses the purpose of admission essays and some suggestions for topics and what to include.

- *Public Junior/Community Colleges.* 3 pages. Lists public two-year colleges that offer residential halls or other student housing, with indication of whether certain majors are offered.

- *Summer Programs Proposed by American Universities of Interest to Foreign Lawyers and Advanced Law Students.* ($3.50) 15 pages.

221
APPRAISAL INSTITUTE
875 North Michigan Avenue
Suite 2400
Chicago, IL 60611-1980
312-335-4473
Fax: 312-335-4200
http://www.appraisalinstitute.org

- *Career Opportunities.* 5 pages. Describes duties and responsibilities, qualifications, and employment outlook in the appraisal field.

222
THE ARC: A NATIONAL ORGANIZATION ON MENTAL RETARDATION
500 East Border Street
Suite 300
Arlington, TX 76010
817-261-6003 or 817-277-0553 (TDD)
Fax: 817-277-3491
http://www.thearc.org/welcome.html

- *Make a Difference! Exploring Careers in Disability-Related Fields.* (#30-21) 8 pages. SASE. Focuses on the varied career opportunities in the disability-related field.

223
ARCHAEOLOGICAL INSTITUTE OF AMERICA
656 Beacon Street, 4th Floor
Boston, MA 02215-2010
617-353-6550
http://csaws.brynmawr.edu:443/aia.html

- *Archaeologist Fact Sheet.* 1 page. Covers duties, working conditions, personal qualifications, education, earnings and hours, outlook, and related careers.

- *Frequently Asked Questions about a Career in Archaeology in the United States.* 4 pages.

- *Participate in Archaeology.* 16 pages.

224
ARIZONA DEPARTMENT OF ECONOMIC SECURITY
Research Administration
Labor Market Information Publications
Site Code 733A
PO Box 6123
Phoenix, AZ 85005-6123
800-827-4966 or 602-542-3871
Fax: 602-542-6474

- *Arizona Occupational Employment Forecasts, 1994-2005.* Information for the state and by particular county.

- *Job Bank Wage Data.* Information available for the state (#PAL 379A) and for Maricopa County-Phoenix Metropolitan area (#PAL 379), Pima County (#PAL 379C), and nonmetropolitan counties (#PAL 544).

- *Arizona's Workforce.* Monthly release.

- *Arizona Economic Trends.* Quarterly review.

- *Employment, Firms, and Wages by Industry.*

- *Job Seekers Kit.*

225
ARIZONA OCCUPATIONAL INFORMATION COORDINATING COMMITTEE
Research Administration
Labor Market Information Publications
Site Code 733A
PO Box 6123
Phoenix, AZ 85005-6123
602-542-3871

- *Arizona Apprenticeship Data by Training Program.*

226
ARKANSAS EMPLOYMENT SECURITY DEPARTMENT
Labor Market Information Section
PO Box 2981
Little Rock, AR 72203-2981
501-682-3198
Fax: 501-682-2942

- *Arkansas Labor Market Trends.* 8 pages. Monthly publication concerning nonfarm payroll jobs in manufacturing industries and metropolitan areas. Details employment by industry, hours, and earnings.

- *Directory of Licensed Occupations.*

- *Occupational Trends.* Available for the state of Arkansas, the city of Little Rock, and the following regions: Central, Eastern, North Central, Northeast, Southeast, Southwest, West Central, and Western.

227
ARMSTRONG WORLD INDUSTRIES, INC.
Corporate Relations Department
313 West Liberty Street
PO Box 3001
Lancaster, PA 17604-3001
717-396-2436
Fax: 717-396-2555
http://www.armstrong.com

- *A Career as a Lab Technician.* 6 pages. Discusses how to get started in a flooring career, necessary education and knowledge, traits of a good technician, and more.

- *A Career as a Professional Flooring Installer.* 4 pages. Defines a flooring installer, describes the type of work, and suggests ways to learn the flooring trade.

228
ARMY MEDICAL SPECIALIST CORPS
AMSC Personnel Counselor
8610 North New Braunfels
Suite 419
San Antonio, TX 78217-6358

- Army Medical Specialist Corps. 14 pages.

229
ARMY RECRUITING STATION

Contact your local Army recruiter. Distributed publications include:

- *Army Opportunities for Women, Benefits, College and the Working Musician, Medical Specialist, Today's Warrant Officer, Training, Warrant Officer Flight Training, We Speak Your Language (linguist),* and *You and the Army.*

230
ARMY ROTC
U.S. Army Cadet Command Headquarters
Attn: ATCC-MM
Fort Monroe, VA 23651
757-727-4616
Fax: 757-727-3860
http://www.tradoc.army.mail/rotc/index.html

- *ROTC-The Facts.* 24 pages. Describes the four-year and two-year programs, ROTC course guide, and scholarship information.

- *ROTC Science and Engineering.* 7 pages. Includes information on scholarships, Army opportunities after graduation, and today's high-tech Army.

- *ROTC Nursing.* 12 pages. Describes the ROTC nursing program and the Army nursing career.

231
ASPIRA
1444 I Street NW
Suite 800
Washington, DC 20005
202-835-3600
http://www.incacorp.com/aspira

- *Preparing for College.* ($5) 41 pages. Written for parents. Discusses the importance of college and the parent's role in preparing a child for college.

- *Planning for College.* ($5) 47 pages. Also written for parents. Contains suggestions on when to begin planning for college and the steps to take in the 9th through 12th grades.

- *Paying for College.* ($5) 34 pages. Offers parents suggestions on saving for college, facts about financial aid and how to apply, and the steps to take if the aid received is not enough.

232
ASSOCIATED COLLEGES OF THE MIDWEST
205 West Wacker Drive, Suite 1300
Chicago, IL 60606
312-263-5000

- The Pre-College Planner. 13 pages. Offers information on campus visits, college evaluation, financial assistance, applications, and other tools students can use to pick the college that matches their personalities and interests.

233
ASSOCIATED GENERAL CONTRACTORS OF AMERICA
1957 E Street NW
Washington, DC 20006
202-393-2040
Fax: 202-737-5011
http://www.agc.org

- *Construction: A Brochure Describing Career Opportunities for Men and Women in the Construction Industry.* ($2.25) 8 pages. Describes the industry, career opportunities, and education and training.

- *Construction: Apprenticeship Opportunities Unlimited for Young Men and Women.* ($2.25) 16 pages. Acquaints high school students and their counselors with the opportunities available in construction through the various craft apprenticeship programs.

234
ASSOCIATED LANDSCAPE CONTRACTORS OF AMERICA
150 Elden Street
Suite 270
Herndon, VA 20170
800-395-2522 or 703-736-9666
Fax: 703-736-9668
http://www.alca.org

- *The Landscape Industry: Growing Careers for You!* 8 pages. Discusses the required education and training, co-op education, the industry outlook, and careers in the industry.

235
ASSOCIATION FOR AMERICAN MEDICAL COLLEGES
Office of Communications
2450 N Street NW
Washington, DC 20037
202-828-0542

- *Careers in Medicine: A Guide for High School Students.* 14 pages. This brochure uses a question and answer format to explore education, training, and career information pertaining to the medical field.

236
ASSOCIATION FOR APPLIED PSYCHOPHYSIOLOGY AND BIOFEEDBACK
10200 West 44th Avenue
Suite 304
Wheat Ridge, CO 80033-2837
303-422-8436
Fax: 303-422-8894
http://www.aapb.org

- *The Psychology Major as Biofeedback Therapist.* 4 pages. Describes biofeedback, necessary training involved, certification requirements, and employment.

237
ASSOCIATION FOR CHILDHOOD EDUCATION INTERNATIONAL
11501 Georgia Avenue
Suite 315
Wheaton, MD 20902-1924
800-423-3563 or 301-942-2443
Fax: 301-942-3012
http://www.udel.edu/bateman/acei

- *Careers in Education.* 6 pages. SASE. Describes ways to prepare for careers in education, career possibilities in teaching and related fields, and other sources of information.

238
ASSOCIATION FOR EDUCATION AND REHABILITATION OF THE BLIND AND VISUALLY IMPAIRED
4600 Duke St.
Suite 430
PO Box 22397
Alexandria, VA 22304
703-823-9690

- *Don't Settle for Just a Job—Choose a Career.* This brochure lists career information for jobs dealing with teaching and aiding the blind or visually impaired. Includes job outlook, salary information, and education and training information.

239
ASSOCIATION FOR EDUCATION IN JOURNALISM AND MASS COMMUNICATION
121 LeConte College
Room 121
University of South Carolina
Columbia, SC 29208-0251
803-777-2005
Fax: 803-777-4728
aejmc@sc.edu
http://www.aejmc.sc.edu/online/home.html

- *A Look at Careers in Journalism and Mass Communications.* 12 pages.

240
ASSOCIATION FOR GERONTOLOGY IN HIGHER EDUCATION
1001 Connecticut Avenue NW
Suite 410
Washington, DC 20036-5504
202-429-9277
Fax: 202-429-6097
http://www.aghe.org

- *Careers in Aging: Consider the Possibilities.* ($.50) 12 pages. An introductory booklet on careers in aging appropriate for high school and college students. Discusses the field of gerontology, jobs and careers available, how to select a program, and how to find jobs in aging.

- *Careers in Aging: Opportunities and Options.* ($2) 28 pages. Defines gerontology, discusses education and training, and provides sources of additional information, and suggestions for finding employment in the field.

- *Sources of Information about Fellowships in Gerontology and Geriatrics.* ($4) 9 pages. Descriptions of national fellowship programs at the pre- and postdoctoral level for gerontological education and training. Also includes a list of newsletters and directories that publish fellowship opportunities in aging.

- *Search the National Database on Gerontology in Higher Education.* 6 pages. Information about the National Database on Gerontology in Higher Education, including general directions and how to request a search.

241
ASSOCIATION FOR INTERNATIONAL PRACTICAL TRAINING
10400 Little Patuxent Parkway
Suite 250
Columbia, MD 21044-3510
410-997-2200
Fax: 410-992-3924
http://www.aipt.org

- *Training for a Global Economy.* 6 pages. Describes the international training opportunities available through three key programs: the Student Exchanges Program for university students, providing on-the-job work experience overseas in a number of technical fields; Career Development Exchanges for trainees with a background in their fields; and Hospitality/Tourism Exchanges, allowing students and graduates of the field to train overseas in the hotel, food service, or travel/tourism fields.

242
ASSOCIATION FOR THE ADVANCEMENT OF MEDICAL INSTRUMENTATION
Certification Program Administrator
3330 Washington Boulevard
Suite 400
Arlington, VA 22201-4598
703-525-4890

- *Certification of Biomedical Equipment Technicians, Radiology Equipment Specialists, and Clinical Laboratory Equipment Specialists.* 19 pages. Covers eligibility requirements, the application process, preparing for the examination, sample questions, available readings, the exam, and certification renewal.

243
ASSOCIATION FOR WOMEN IN MATHEMATICS
Career Booklets Order
4114 Computer and Space Sciences Building
University of Maryland
College Park, MD 20742-2461
301-405-7892
awm@math.umd.edu

- *Careers That Count: Opportunities in the Mathematical Sciences.* ($1.50) 18 pages. Describes mathematics careers and profiles women working in various mathematical fields.

244
ASSOCIATION MONTESSORI INTERNATIONAL -USAA
410 Alexander Street
Rochester, NY 14607
716-461-5920
Fax: 716-461-0075

- *AMI Invites You...Become a Montessori Teacher.* 6 pages. Contains a brief history of AMI, descriptions of training for prospective teachers and of educational requirements, and a list of AMI training courses in the United States.

245
ASSOCIATION OF ACCREDITED COSMETOLOGY SCHOOLS
901 North Washington Street
Suite 206
Alexandria, VA 22314
703-683-1700
Fax: 703-683-2376
ronsmith@ix.netcom.com
http://www.beautyschools.org

- *Choosing a Career in Cosmetology.* 3 pages. Describes cosmetology, different types of salons, and what they have to offer.

- *Occupational Outlook Handbook.* 4 pages. A reprint from the U.S. Department of Labor. Covers barbers and cosmetologists, the nature of the work, working conditions, employment, training, job outlook, earnings, and related occupations.

- *AACS Schools List.* 114 pages. Lists schools of cosmetology in the United States.

247
ASSOCIATION OF AMERICAN GEOGRAPHERS
1710 16th Street NW
Washington, DC 20009-3198
202-234-1450
Fax: 202-234-2744
gaia@aag.org
http://www.aag.org

- *Careers in Geography.* ($1.50) 16 pages. Discusses career opportunities, education, and graduate school. Lists institutions that offer a geography major and related professional associations.

- *Geography: Today's Career for Tomorrow.* 6 pages. Describes the fields in geography and geographers at work.

- *Why Geography?* 6 pages. Discusses the need for geography and how it affects natural and human environments.

- *Geography as a Discipline.* 6 pages. Describes what geographers do and the training required for a career in the geography field.

248
ASSOCIATION OF AMERICAN MEDICAL COLLEGES
2450 N Street NW
Washington, DC 20032-1129
202-828-0400

- *List of Combined-Degree Programs.*

- *Medicine: A Chance to Make a Difference.* 14 pages. Brief summary of medical schools, their academics, and how some students pay for the process.

249
ASSOCIATION OF AMERICAN PUBLISHERS
220 East 23rd Street
New York, NY 10010
212-689-8920

- *Getting into Book Publishing.* 19 pages.

250
ASSOCIATION OF BOARDING SCHOOLS
1620 L Street NW
Suite 1100
Washington, DC 20036-5605
202-973-9753
Fax: 202-973-9790
http://www.schools.com

- *Boarding School Directory.* Published annually to assist families, counselors, and consultants in matching a student with a boarding school. Contains profiles of 291 elementary and secondary boarding schools.

251
ASSOCIATION OF COLLEGIATE SCHOOLS OF ARCHITECTURE
1735 New York Avenue NW
Washington, DC 20006
800-232-2724 or 202-785-2324
Fax: 202-628-0448

- *Accredited Programs in Architecture.* 18 pages. Lists accredited architecture programs and indicates program types (by identifying the professional degree received upon the completion of the program).

- *The Education of an Architect.* 24 pages. Contains a brief history of architectural education, as well as information on high school preparation, architectural programs and degrees, selecting a school, internships, and employment opportunities.

252
ASSOCIATION OF ENERGY SERVICE COMPANIES
6060 North Central Expressway
Suite 428
Dallas, TX 75206
214-692-0771
Fax: 214-692-0162
http://www.alphatx.com/aesc

- *Consider a Career in Well Servicing.* 6 pages. Describes well servicing crews, their jobs, training programs, and necessary personal traits of a well servicing employee.

253
ASSOCIATION OF FLIGHT ATTENDANTS
1625 Massachusetts Avenue NW
Washington, DC 20036
202-328-5400

- *Selected United States Airlines.* 4 pages. Lists U.S. airlines (including contact information) that may be accepting flight attendant applications.

254
ASSOCIATION OF INFORMATION TECHNOLOGY PROFESSIONALS
505 Busse Highway
Park Ridge, IL 60068-3191
800-224-9371
Fax: 847-825-1693
http://www.aitp.org

- *Computer Careers.* 4 pages. Describes education and training available for information technologists; profiles computer careers by listing job titles and descriptions; and describes types of career opportunities available.

255
ASSOCIATION OF MEDICAL ILLUSTRATORS
1819 Peachtree Street NE
Suite 620
Atlanta, GA 30309
404-350-7900
Fax: 404-351-3348
http://www.medical-illustrations.org

- *Medical Illustration as a Career.* 8 pages. Describes the nature of the work, required skills and education, employment, advancement, and salary.

- *Accredited Graduate Programs of Medical Illustration.* 2 pages.

256
ASSOCIATION OF OFFICIAL SEED ANALYSTS
268 Plant Science, IANR
University of Nebraska-Lincoln
Lincoln, NE 68583-0911
402-492-7211

- *Career Opportunities in Seed Analysis.* Discusses responsibilities, education, and training.

257
ASSOCIATION OF OPERATING ROOM NURSES, INC.
2170 South Parker Road
Suite 300
Denver, CO 80231-5711
303-755-6300
dsmith@aorn.org/
http://www.aorn.org

- *Career Packet on Operating Room Nursing.* 55 pages. Discusses the everyday duties and responsibilities, education and training, salaries, and other topics.

258
ASSOCIATION OF SCHOOLS AND COLLEGES OF OPTOMETRY
6110 Executive Boulevard
Suite 510
Rockville, MD 20852
301-231-5944
http://www.opted.org

- *Optometry: A Career with Vision.* 12 pages. Designed for students contemplating a career in optometry. Provides general information about the profession, offers guidelines concerning the recommended course of graduate study, and includes a list of accredited schools and colleges of optometry.

- *Is Your Future in Sight? Consider Optometry.* 8 pages. Details the career opportunities in optometry available to minorities.

- *List of Accredited Schools and Colleges of Optometry.* 1 page.

259
ASSOCIATION OF SURGICAL TECHNOLOGISTS
7108-C South Alton Way
Suite 100
Englewood, CO 80112-2106
303-694-9130
http://www.ast.org

- *Surgical Technology: A Growing Career.* 36 pages. Discusses duties and responsibilities, personal characteristics, working conditions, employment, education, and curriculum. Lists accredited surgical technology programs and career opportunities.

260
ASSOCIATION OF SYSTEMATICS COLLECTIONS
730 11th Street NW, Second Floor
Washington, DC 20001-4521
202-347-2850

- *Careers in Biological Systematics.* 12 pages.

261
ASSOCIATION OF THEOLOGICAL SCHOOLS
10 Summit Park Drive
Pittsburgh, PA 15275-1103
412-788-6505
Fax: 412-788-6510
ats@ats.lm.com
http://www.ATS.edu

- *Directory and Membership List.* ($8 plus shipping) 148 pages. Provides brief descriptions of the major institutional and organizational resources for graduate theological education in North America.

262
ASSOCIATION OF UNIVERSITY PROGRAMS IN HEALTH ADMINISTRATION
1911 North Fort Myer Drive
Suite 503
Arlington, VA 22209
703-524-550
Fax: 703-525-4791
http://www.aupha.com

- *Health Administration Employment: A Survey of Early Career Opportunities.* 26 pages. Contains observations on career opportunities in health care, various tables regarding employment status, and information about job searching and education.

- *The Official List of Accredited Programs in Health Services Administration in Canada and the United States.* 8 pages.

263
ASSOCIATION OF WOMEN SURGEONS
414 Plaza Drive
Suite 209
Westmont, IL 60559
630-655-0392

- *A Manual for Surgical Interns and Residents.* A guide for women in the surgical specialties.

264
ASSOCIATION ON HIGHER EDUCATION AND DISABILITY (AHEAD)
PO Box 21192
Columbus, OH 43221-0192
614-488-4972
Fax: 614-488-1174
http://www.ahead.org

- *College Students with Learning Disabilities.* ($.35) 8 pages. Offers suggestions for college students with learning disabilities, and for faculty dealing with students with learning disabilities.

- *Ready, Set, Go: Helping Students with Learning Disabilities Prepare for College.* ($.35) 6 pages. Lists activities that high school students with learning disabilities can do as they prepare for college.

265
AUTOMOTIVE SERVICE ASSOCIATION
PO Box 929
Bedford, TX 76095-0929
800-ASA-SHOP or 817-283-6205
Fax: 817-685-0225
http://www.asashop.org

- *Automotive Technician: A Challenging and Changing Career.* 10 pages. Contains job description and discusses areas of specialty, employers of technicians, employment outlook, career advancement, training, earnings, and opportunities for women and minorities.

- *Career Opportunities...in the Automotive Collision Repair and Refinishing Industry.* 10 pages. Includes job description and discusses earn while you learn programs, advancement opportunities, opportunities for women, areas of specialty, and outlook and earnings.

266
BIOLOGICAL PHOTOGRAPHIC ASSOCIATION, INC.
115 Stoneridge Drive,
Chapel Hill, NC 27514-9737

- *Biophotography.* 4 pages. Details a typical week in the life of a biophotographer working in a medical center; discusses certification, training, and education.

267
BIOMEDICAL ENGINEERING SOCIETY
PO Box 2399
Culver City, CA 90231
310-618-9322
http://www.mecca.mecca.org/BME/BMES/society/bmeshm.html

- *Planning a Career in Biomedical Engineering.* 8 pages. Outlines typical duties, the specialty areas, employment opportunities, and career preparation.

268
BIOPHYSICAL SOCIETY OFFICE
9650 Rockville Pike
Bethesda, MD 20814-3998
301-530-7114
Fax: 301-530-7133
http://www.biosci.cbs.umn.edu/biophys/biophys.html

- *Career in Biophysics.* 20 pages. Provides an introduction to careers in biophysics for high school and college students, as well as information on the nature of the work, employment opportunities, and education.

269
BIOTECHNOLOGY INDUSTRY ORGANIZATION
1625 K Street NW
Suite 1100
Washington, DC 20006-1604
202-857-0244
Fax: 202-857-0237
http://www.bio.org

- *Biotechnology: The Choice for Your Future.* 24 pages. A general resource on careers in biotechnology.

- *Careers in Biotechnology.* 90 pages. Describes the responsibilities and training required for various careers in the field. Lists schools offering biotechnology programs and Dedicated Biotechnology Companies by state.

- *Do You Know What to Do with Your Future?* 6 pages.

- *What is Biotechnology?* ($3) 27 pages. Explains methodologies and applications of biotechnology in easily understood language.

- *Biotechnology at Work Series.* Describes biotechnology's applications and role in the study of various fields. Titles include *Agriculture and the New Biology; Animals, People and Biotechnology; Food for the Future; Diagnostics; Medicine and the New Biology;* and *Protecting our Environment.*

270
BOTANICAL SOCIETY OF AMERICA
Business Office
1735 Neil Avenue
Columbus, OH 43210-1293
614-292-3519
http://www.botany.org

- *Careers in Botany: A Guide to Working with Plants.* 13 pages. Discusses specialties in the field, employment opportunities, salary, job availability, educational requirements and preparation, and additional sources of information.

271
BOY SCOUTS OF AMERICA
Professional Selection Service
1325 West Walnut Hill Lane
PO Box 152079
Irving, TX 75015-2079
972-580-2000

- *Have You Thought about Being an Executive with the Boy Scouts of America?...A Career of Character.* 4 pages. Explains professional BSA work, philosophy, and compensation.

- *Why Not Consider Something Different?...A Career in the Boy Scouts of America.* 6 pages. Explains the work, qualifications, and advantages of the BSA for those considering a career change.

- *Why Not Make the Boy Scouts of America Your Life's Work?...A Career of Character.* 6 pages. Describes a career in the Boy Scouts. Suitable for those still in high school.

272
BRICK INSTITUTE OF AMERICA
11490 Commerce Park Drive
Reston, VA 20191-1525
703-620-0010

- *Playing in the Big Leagues as a Brick Mason.* Outlines the benefits and advantages of a mason and how to get started in the field.

- *Brick by Brick, Block by Block.* A poster depicting a brick layer. Suitable for a school counselor or career adviser.

- *Brick Laying.* A poster showing brick laying tools and providing brief statements about the brick laying craftsman. Suitable for school counselors and career centers.

273
BUILDING OFFICIALS AND CODE ADMINISTRATORS (BOCA) INTERNATIONAL
4051 West Flossmoor Road
Country Club Hills, IL 60478-5795

- *Careers in Code Enforcement.* 12 pages. Describes the code enforcement process, duties of code officials, types of inspectors, working conditions, compensation, education and certification, and employment outlook.

274
BUREAU FOR AT-RISK YOUTH
645 New York Avenue
Huntington, NY 11743
516-673-4584

- *Becoming a Civilian Family: Successfully Getting Through the Transition.* ($3) 14 pages. Discusses the obstacles facing a military family returning to civilian life and how to avoid them.

- *How to Be a Successful Young Military Family.* ($3) 14 pages. Discusses the military lifestyle and how to prepare for and deal with its unique set of challenges.

- *Set of six leaflets for teens.* ($4) Titles include: *Choosing a Career Path, Finding a Part-Time or Summer Job, How to Keep Your Job Once You're Hired, Interviewing Techniques that Get the Job, Matching Your Talents to Employers' Needs, Where and How to Find Job Opportunities.*

275
BUREAU OF APPRENTICESHIP AND TRAINING
U.S. Department of Labor
200 Constitution Avenue NW
TWA (Room N-4649)
Washington, DC 20210
202-219-5921

- *National Apprenticeship Program.* 15 pages. Describes the National Apprenticeship Program and apprenticeable occupations. Lists state apprenticeship councils and agencies.

276
BUREAU OF INDIAN AFFAIRS
Office of Indian Education Programs
U.S. Department of the Interior
18th and C Streets NW
Washington, DC 20240
202-208-4871

Call or write for a list of current publications.

277
BUREAU OF LABOR STATISTICS
U.S. Department of Labor
Washington, DC 20212

202-606-5700
http://stats.bls.gov/ocohome.htm

- *The College Labor Market: Outlook, Current Situation, and Earnings.*

- *Twenty Occupations Most Often Hired by the Federal Government.*

278
BUREAU OF LABOR STATISTICS
Publication Sales Center, PO Box 2145
Chicago, IL 60690
312-353-1880
http://stats.bls.gov

Prepayment required on all orders.

- *Employment Outlook: 1994-2005.* (#2472) ($5.50) 76 pages. Aids planners and policy makers in creating training and educational programs attuned to labor market demands. Contains career information and detailed statistics.

- *Occupational Projections and Training Data.* (#2471) ($6) 76 pages. Assists in planning education and training programs. Includes comparisons between 500 occupations on factors such as job openings expected, percent self-employed, and significant sources of training.

- *Occupational Outlook Quarterly.* ($3 per issue) Contains pertinent and timely occupational and educational information. Helps students and jobseekers explore career interests, discover new and emerging occupations, tailor education to career goals, and learn about the best job prospects in a competitive labor market. For subscription information contact Superintendent of Documents, PO Box 371954, Pittsburgh, PA 15250-7954 (202-512-1800).

- *Occupational Outlook Handbook Reprints.* Provides information on working conditions, employment, training, qualifications, advancement, job outlook, earnings, and related fields.

- *Business and Managerial Occupations.* (2450-2) ($3.50) 53 pages.

- *Clerical and Other Administrative Support Occupations.* (2450-13) ($3) 40 pages.

- *Communications, Design, Performing Arts, and Related Occupations.* (2450-10) ($2) 23 pages.

- *Computer and Mathematics-Related Occupations.* (2450-4) ($1.75) 20 pages.

- *Construction Trades and Extractive Occupations.* (2450-17) ($2.25) 28 pages.

- *Dietetics, Nursing, Pharmacy, and Therapy Occupations.* (2450-8) ($1.50) 16 pages.

- *Education and Social Service Occupations and Clergy.* (2450-6) ($2.75) 28 pages.

- *Engineering, Scientific, and Related Occupations.* (2450-3) ($2.50) 31 pages.

- *Health Diagnosing Occupations and Assistants.* (2450-7) ($1.50) 15 pages.

- *Health Technologists and Technicians.* (2450-9) ($1.50) 18 pages.

- *Mechanics, Equipment Installers, and Repairers.* (2450-16) ($2.50) 32 pages.

- *Metalworking, Plastic-working, and Woodworking Occupations.* (2450-18) ($1.50) 18 pages.

- *Production Occupations.* (2450-19) ($2.50) 30 pages.

- *Protective Service Occupations and Compliance Inspectors.* (2450-14) ($1.50) 16 pages.

- *Sales Occupations.* (2450-12) ($1.75) 18 pages.

- *Service Occupations: Cleaning, Food, Health, and Personal.* (2450-15) ($2) 22 pages.

- *Social Scientists and Legal Occupations.* (2450-5) ($1.50) 19 pages.

- *Technologists and Technicians, Except Health.* (2450-11) ($1.50) 19 pages.

- *Tomorrow's Jobs: An Overview.* (2450-1) ($1.75) 15 pages.

- *Transportation, Forestry, Fishing, and Related Occupations.* (2450-20) ($1.75) 21 pages.

279
BUREAU OF LABOR STATISTICS
Office of Compensation and Working Conditions U.S. Department of Labor
Postal Square Building, Room 4175
2 Massachusetts Avenue NE
Washington, DC 20212
202-606-6220
Fax: 202-606-6647
http://stats.bls.gov/ocshome.htm

- *Occupational Compensation Surveys.* Cites salary wages and hourly wages for a number of occupations in various U.S. cities.

280
BUREAU OF LABOR STATISTICS
Office of Publications and Special Studies
Special Publications Branch, Room 2850
2 Massachusetts Avenue NE
Washington, DC 20212-0001

- *Issues in Labor Statistics.* This Bureau of Labor Statistics publication deals with a wide variety of labor topics. Recent *Issues in Labor Statistics* titles include the following: *Growth of Jobs With Abovoe Average Earnings Projected at All Educational Levels, Part-time Work: A Choice or a Response,* and *Warm Areas Continue Hottest Job Growth.* Write to to be added to the mailing list.

281
CALIFORNIA EMPLOYMENT DEVELOPMENT DEPARTMENT
Labor Market Information Division
Occupational Information Unit
7000 Franklin Street
Suite 1100
Sacramento, CA 95823

- *California Occupational Guide Series.* Will send set to career counselors; individual titles available upon request. These 2-page fact sheets describe typical duties; working conditions; employment outlook; wages, hours, and fringe benefits; entrance requirements and training; advancement; finding the job; and related occupational guides for a number of occupations, including bell person, copywriter, numerical-control machine operator, and tool designer.

282
CALIFORNIA LIBRARY ASSOCIATION
717 K Street
Suite 300
Sacramento, CA 95814-3477
916-447-8541
Fax: 916-447-8394

- *From Books to Bytes: Careers for Librarians and Information Professionals.* Covers careers in public libraries and children's librarianship, as well as opportunities for minorities.

283
CALIFORNIA SEA GRANT COLLEGE
University of California
9500 Gilman Drive, Department 0232
La Jolla, CA 92093-0232
619-534-4444
Fax: 619-453-2948
http://www-cgsc.uscd.edu

- *Marine Science Careers.* ($5) 40 pages. Comprehensive guide to marine career areas. Contains question and answer profiles, as well as photos of 38 marine scientists and other professionals in the field. Contact Sea Grant Communications, Kingman Farm, University of New Hampshire, Durham, NH 03824, for information on this publication.

- *Directory of Academic Marine Programs in California.* 82 pages. Lists and describes for students, teachers, and counselors the marine programs at 48 two- and four-year schools of higher learning in California.

284
CALIFORNIA STATE UNIVERSITY AT LONG BEACH
College of Business Administration
Admissions and Advisement Center
1250 North Bellflower Boulevard
Long Beach, CA 90840-6006
562-985-4514
http://www.csulb.edu/~dchand/student.htm

- *Student Guide to Accounting.* Provides information on accounting careers, including income tax planning and preparation, small vs. large CPA firms, government and not-for-profit accounting, and other career options. Also available online.

285
CALIFORNIA STUDENT AID COMMISSION
PO Box 510845
Sacramento, CA 94245-0845
916-322-3189 or 916-327-4609 (voice mail)
Fax: 916-323-1748
http://www.csac.ca.gov

- *Financial Aid for Students: Workbook.* 20 pages. For high school students and parents. Describes many financial aid opportunities available, including state-funded programs administered by the commission and low-interest federally supported student loans.

- *Financial Aid for Students.* 8 pages. Describes financial aid options, and how to apply.

286
CAMPUS COMPACT
Brown University
PO Box 1975
Providence, RI 02912
401-863-1119
Fax: 401-863-3779

- *Campus Compact: The Project for Public and Community Service.* Publishes a list of fellowships for those involved in volunteer service projects.

287
CANADIAN ASSOCIATION OF PHYSICISTS
150 Louis Pasteur
Suite 112
McDonald Building
Ottawa, Ontario
K1N 6N5 Canada
613-562-5614
Fax: 613-562-5615

- *Careers in Physics.* 9 pages. Describes the main fields of physics and lists Canadian universities offering physics programs.

- *Physicist.* 3 pages. Discusses the nature of the work, working conditions, qualifications and preparation, employment outlook, and salary.

288
CANADIAN VETERINARY MEDICAL ASSOCIATION
Communications Officer
339 Booth Street
Ottawa, Ontario
K1R 7K1 Canada
613-236-1162
Fax: 613-236-9681
http://www.upei.ca/~cvma/

- *Veterinary Medicine in Canada: Your Career Choice.* ($.75) 4 pages. Describes the various fields and types of practice, educational requirements, necessary personal attributes, and salary range. Lists the four veterinary colleges in Canada. In English or French.

- *Veterinarians Caring for Animals.* ($1.25) For children to age 11. Includes a basic introduction to veterinarians and animal care. In English or French.

- *Jr. Veterinarian Club Kit.* ($.50) Contains activity book suitable for elementary and middle school students, with basic facts about veterinarians. Includes ruler and pin. In English or French.

289
CAREER CHOICES CENTER
PO Box 43257
Cincinnati, OH 45253

- *General Career Guide.* 14 pages. Contains basic information about resume writing, job searching, networking, interviewing, salary negotiating, and writing cover letters.

- *Marketing.* 14 pages. Contains information on careers in marketing, including salary data, types of jobs and descriptions of jobs; interviews with people in the industry; and professional associations.

- *Money and Finance.* 14 pages. Contains information on types of jobs in money and finance, including accountants, consultants, investment bankers, and insurance professionals.

- *Off the Beaten Path.* 14 pages. Contains information on a variety of careers, including travel, education, entrepreneuring, non-profit humanitarian work, and volunteer work.

- *Communications and Entertainment.* 14 pages. Includes information on careers in such fields as broadcasting, publishing, film and television, music, and theater.

290
CAREER DEVELOPMENT SERVICES
Library
14 Franklin Street
Suite 1200
Rochester, NY 14604
716-325-2275

- Barriers and Breakthroughs: Executive Development Topics for Women. *Annotated ($3) 6 pages.*

- *Career Options for Teachers.* Annotated ($1.50) 3 pages.

- *Finding the Job You Want Through Your Ears: An Annotated Bibliography of Job Search Audiocassettes.* ($2.50)

- *How to Change Careers.* Annotated ($1) 2 pages.

- *Making the Connection: Networking for Success.* Annotated ($1.50) 3 pages.

- *New Directions: Job Search Guides for Women Re-Entering the Work Force.* Annotated. ($1.50) 3 pages.

- *Overseas Odysseys: International Jobs.* Annotated. *($1.50) 3 pages.*

- *Professional Job Search.* ($2.50) 5 pages.

- *Real World 101: A Bibliography of Resources for New College Graduates.* Annotated ($1.50) 3 pages.

- *Recareering: Job Search Guides for Retirees.* Annotated ($1.50) 3 pages.

- *Starting Your Own Business: Books, Periodicals, Organizations, Agencies and Courses to Help You Get Started.* Annotated. ($5) 12 pages.

- *Successful Reemployment: A Selection of Books to Help You Survive Layoff and Return to the Work Force.* Annotated. ($2) 4 pages.

291
CAREER PUBLISHING, INC.
910 North Main Street
PO Box 5486
Orange, CA 92863-5486
800-854-4014
Fax: 714-532-0180

- *20/20 Career Planning: How to Get a Job & Keep It!* ($2.95) 32 pages. Gives guidelines for analyzing job potential and provides specific instructions to help the job seeker get the right job. Lists 20 steps toward getting a job and 20 tips on keeping a job.

- *15 Tips on Handling Job Interviews.* ($2.50) 24 pages. Provides information on how to succeed at a job interview. Includes advice on how to handle every part of the interview from preparation to follow-up.

- *15 Tips on Writing Resumes.* ($2.50) 24 pages. Offers an easy-to-follow method to help plan, write, and prepare a resume that will get noticed. Includes sample resumes.

292
CAREER TRANSITION FOR DANCERS
1727 Broadway, Second Floor
New York, NY 10019-5284
212-581-7043
Fax: 212-262-9088

- *Careers in Transition: Building on Experience.* 4 pages. Details the job opportunities for dancers leaving the stage.

- *Dancers Managing Change.* 2 pages.

- *Puzzled about Your Future?* 6 pages. Reviews the steps for identifying and pursuing a rewarding new career. Explains the group's free consulting services.

- *CareerLine.* A national career consultation line (800-581-2833) for dancers seeking information about a career transition. Schedules career counseling sessions with a member of the counseling staff.

293
CAREERS & COLLEGES MAGAZINE
Career Watch
989 Avenue of the Americas
Sixth Floor
New York, NY 10018

- *Career Watch Profiles.* ($1 each) Choose from more than 150 occupations, including animation designer, bankruptcy lawyer, corporate librarian, engraver, executive chef, fish farmer, glassblower, jingle writer, literary agent, municipal financier, museum curator, public relations person, special education teacher, storm tracker, TV commercial producer, umpire, wilderness instructor.

294
CAREERS, INC.
PO Box 135
Largo, FL 33779-0135
813-584-7333

- *Career Briefs.* ($2.50 each) 4 pages each. Provides comprehensive information on general occupational fields and on careers requiring extensive descriptions. Briefs on hundreds of occupations.

- *Career Summaries.* ($2 each) 2 pages each. Provide concise information on specific careers.

- *Career Job Guides.* ($2 each) 2 pages each. Describes careers requiring a short period of time of on-the-job training.

295
CASUALTY ACTUARIAL SOCIETY
1100 North Glebe Road
Suite 600
Arlington, VA 22201
703-276-3100
Fax: 703-276-3108
office@casactsoc.com
http://www.casact.org

- *Actuaries Make a Difference.* 22 pages. Profiles actuaries in various actuarial careers. Discusses an actuary's duties, work environment, employment outlook, and qualifications, as well as how to prepare for a career, achieve professional status, the exams, and related organizations.

- *Actuarial Training Programs.* 30 pages. Provides information on some of the actuarial training programs in Canada and the United States available for actuaries. Suitable for those entering the actuarial profession.

- *Canadian and United States Schools Offering Actuarial Science Courses Including Actuarial*

Mathematics. 4 pages. Identifies schools in Canada and the United States offering actuarial courses.

296
CATALYST
250 Park Avenue South
New York, NY 10003-1459
212-777-8900

- *Info Briefs.* ($4 each) 2 pages each. Presents current facts and figures on issues affecting women in the work force. Topics include child care, flexible work arrangements, parental leave, women in corporate management, women in engineering, family and medical leave act, sexual harassment, and mentoring.

297
CENTER FOR WOMEN POLICY STUDIES
2000 P Street NW
Suite 508
Washington, DC 20036
202-872-1770 or 888-SAT-BIAS
Fax: 202-296-8962

- *The SAT Action Kit.* Reports on gender bias in the SAT and actions that can be taken.

- *Looking for More Than a Few Good Women in Traditionally Male Fields.* ($5)

- *Women Faculty at Work in the Classroom, or, Why It Still Hurts to Be a Woman in Labor.* ($5)

298
CHANNING L. BETE COMPANY, INC.
200 State Road
South Deerfield, MA 01373
800-628-7733 or 413-665-7611
Fax: 800-499-6464
http://www.channing-bete.com

The following booklets are each 16 pages; add $5.75 for shipping.

- *About Career Planning.* (B18630) ($1.25)

- *About Job Interview Skills.* (B18648) ($1.25)

- *About Job Services.* (B14340) ($1.25)

- *About RNs.* (B37101) ($1.25)

- *About Setting Goals to Reach Your Potential.* (B48363) ($1.25)

- *About Writing Your Resume.* (B16139) ($1.25)

- *Adult Learners.* (B48843) ($1.25)

- *Be a Volunteer.* (B18382) ($1.25)

- *Career Opportunities for Women.* (B55111) ($1.60)

- *Financing the Cost of College Education.* (B55137) ($1.60)

- *Getting a Job.* (B55046) ($1.60)

- *How to Balance Work and Family.* (B48835) ($1.25)

- *How to Choose a College.* (B55087) ($1.60)

- *How to Develop Your Leadership Skills.* (B18465) ($1.25)

- *How to Have Successful Meetings.* (B18507) ($1.25)

- *What Everyone Should Know about Career Planning.* (B18630) ($1.25)

- *What You Should Know about Getting a Job.* (B55046) ($1.60)

- *What You Should Know about Job Interviewing Skills.* (B18648) ($1.25)

299
CHEFS DE CUISINE ASSOCIATION OF AMERICA
155 East 55th Street
Suite 302B
New York, NY 10022
212-832-4939

- *List of Culinary Schools.* 1 page. Lists schools in the United States and abroad.

300
CHILD CARE ACTION CAMPAIGN
330 Seventh Avenue, 17th Floor
New York, NY 10001-5010
212-239-0138
Fax: 212-268-6515

CCAC Information Guides (up to 3 guides free). SASE business-size. Titles include:

- *Careers in Child Care.* (#23)

- *Child Care Liability Insurance.* (#25)

- *Current State Day Care Licensing Offices.* (#28)

- *Employer Supported Child Care: Current Options and Trends.* (#10)

- *How to Start a Child Care Center.* (#24)

- *How to Start a Family Day Care Home.* (#26)

- *Speaking with Your Employer about Child Care Assistance.* (#9)

- *Wages and Benefits in Child Care.* (#27)

301
CHRONICLE GUIDANCE PUBLICATIONS, INC.
66 Aurora Street
PO Box 1190
Moravia, NY 13118-1190
800-622-7284
Fax: 315-497-3359
http://www.chronicleguidance.com

- Chronicle Occupational Briefs and Reprints. (minimum order $5: $2 each plus $1 shipping and handling up to $10) Present career information on hundreds of occupations from academic dean to marble setter to zoologist. Each brief offers a job description and presents educational requirements, salaries, employment outlook, and other topics.

302
CITY UNIVERSITY OF NEW YORK
University Office of Affirmative Action
Office of Faculty and Staff Relations
535 East 80th Street
Room 604
New York, NY 10021
212-794-5374
Fax: 212-794-5667

- *Have You Considered Becoming a College Professor?* 16 pages. Describes the typical duties and responsibilities, educational preparation, admissions factors considered by graduate schools, financial aid, and advancement.

303
CLEARINGHOUSE ON DISABILITY INFORMATION
Office of Special Education and Rehabilitative Services, U.S. Department of Education
330 C Street SW
Switzer Building
Room 3132
Washington, DC 20202-2425
202-205-8241
Fax: 202-410-2680
http://www.ed.gov/offices/osers

- *Federally Supported Clearinghouses on Disability.* 1 page. Lists clearinghouses offering information on disability.

- *Pocket Guide to Federal Help for Individuals with Disabilities.* 24 pages. Summarizes benefits and services available to individuals with disabilities.

- *A Summary of Existing Legislation Affecting People with Disabilities.* 235 pages. A history and description of all relevant federal laws enacted through 1991.

- *OSERS Magazine.* A collection of various articles on disability. No longer published, although individual copies of some back issues are still available.

304
COLLEGE BOARD
45 Columbus Avenue
New York, NY 10023-6992
212-713-8000
http://www.collegeboard.org

- *Bibliography of Financial Aid Information Sources.* 6 pages. Lists over 40 publications with information on thousands of scholarships, grants, loans, and fellowships from private, state, and federal sources. Contains a short description of each publication.

- *Basic Facts about Paying for College.* 11 pages. Intended to help parents and students better understand the financial aid process and to address some of their concerns, this brochure has been developed to answer a few of the most frequently asked questions.

- *College Credit: Education Loans from an Organization Dedicated to Education.* 10 pages. Discusses student and parent loan programs from the College Board.

305
COLLEGE BOARD PUBLICATIONS
PO Box 886
New York, NY 10101-0886
800-323-7155 or 212-713-8165
Fax: 212-713-8143

- *Student Survival Guide: How to Work Smarter, Not Harder.* ($4.95-minimum order of 2 required) 44 pages.

306
COMMERCE CLEARING HOUSE, INC.
Cash Item Dept. 3376
4025 West Peterson Avenue
Chicago, IL 60646
800-248-3248

- *Social Security Benefits-Including Medicare.* (5335) ($5) 48 pages.

307
COMMISSION ON GRADUATES OF FOREIGN NURSING SCHOOLS
3600 Market Street
Suite 400
Philadelphia, PA 19104-2651
215-349-8767
Fax: 215-662-0425

- *An Overview of the Commission on Graduates of Foreign Nursing Schools.* 4 pages. Provides an overview of the history and mission of the CGFNS.

- *CGFNS International Evaluator.* Quarterly reports on nursing education and licensure.

308
COMMISSION ON OPTICIANRY ACCREDITATION
10111 Martin Luther King, Jr. Highway
Suite 100
Bowie, MD 20720-4299
301-459-8075

- *Description of the Profession.* Discusses careers in ophthalmic dispensing and ophthalmic laboratory technology. Lists accredited schools.

309
COMMISSION ON WOMEN IN THE PROFESSIONS
750 North Lake Shore Drive
Chicago, IL 60611
800-285-2221
Fax: 312-988-5528
http://www.abanet.org/women

- *Options and Obstacles: A Survey of the Studies of the Careers of Women Lawyers.* ($10) 60 pages. Identifies issues that continue to create barriers in women's careers and points out where gathering more information would assist the profession in understanding and eliminating those barriers.

- *Pathways to Leadership: An ABA Roadmap.* ($5) 24 pages. Provides information on the various paths to leadership positions within the American Bar Association.

- *The Basic Facts from Women in Law: A Look at the Numbers.* ($6) 6 pages. A quick summary of the most asked questions regarding statistics on women in the legal profession.

- *Goal IX Report Card.* Issued by the commission. Provides statistics on women's involvement in the ABA and measures women's progress in attaining leadership positions in ABA sections and divisions and in ABA governance.

310
COMMUNITY JOBS
1001 Connecticut Avenue NW
Suite 838
Washington, DC 20036-5504
202-785-4233
Fax: 202-785-4212
http://www.essential.org/access/

- *Community Jobs: The National Employment Newspaper for the Non-Profit Sector.* ($10 for a current sample copy and one back issue)

311
COMMUNITY SERVICE SOCIETY
Office of Information
105 East 22nd Street
New York, NY 10010
212-614-5322
Fax: 212-614-5390

- *Youth Enterprises: A How-to Manual for Starting a Youth Business in Your Community.* ($5) 41 pages. Helpful to the staff in youth programs and organizations serving youth. Provides a general approach for community-based enterprise development.

- *Critical Choices: Education and Employment among New York City Youth.* ($10) 115 pages. A study on New Yorkers between the ages of 16 and 24. Provides a detailed analysis of their connection to education and employment and evaluates school enrollment, labor force participation, educational attainment, work history, fertility, and poverty status by race, ethnicity, age, and sex.

312
COMPLETE COLLEGIATE/TRAVELER
Department GA, PO Box 11145
Fairfield, NJ 07004
201-808-9249

- *Complete Collegiate Catalog and Dorm Essential Checklist.* 16 pages. SASE business-size.

- *Financing Your Child's Education.* ($2) Helps predict your child's future college costs.

313
COMPUTING RESEARCH ASSOCIATION
1875 Connecticut Avenue NW, Suite 718
Washington, DC 20009
202-234-2111
http://cra.org

- *Women in Computer Science.* 20 pages. Profiles eighteen women involved in computer careers. Some of the careers profiled include computer engineer, software engineer, astronaut, electrical engineer, research scientist, university professor, research assistant, and Director of Defense Research and Engineering/Department of Defense.

314
CONFERENCE BOARD OF THE MATHEMATICAL SCIENCES
1529 18th Street NW
Washington, DC 20036
202-293-1170

- *Career Information in the Mathematical Sciences.* 25 pages. Lists and describes career-related materials pertaining to the mathematical sciences, The list includes videos, pamphlets, posters, and brochures. Entries are organized by education level of intended readers.

315
CONGRESSIONAL RESEARCH SERVICE
United States Capitol
Washington, DC 20510
202-224-3121.

- *Internships and Fellowships Info Pack.* (IP0631) Request from your congressman by writing to his or her attention at the above address.

316
CONSUMER INFORMATION CENTER
U.S. General Services Administration
PO Box 100
Pueblo, CO 81002
719-948-4000
Fax: 719-948-9724
http://www.pueblo.gsa.gov

A variety of federal publications of consumer interest are also available online.

- *Planning for College.* (507D) 10 pages. Includes strategies to help plan for tuition and fees along with helpful charts for estimating future costs.

- *Preparing Your Child for College: A Resource Book for Parents.* (508D) 57 pages. Contains worksheets and checklists to help plan for college academically and financially.

- *Resumes, Application Forms, Cover Letters, and Interviews.* (102D) ($1) 8 pages. Includes tips on tailoring a resume to specific jobs and sample interview questions.

- *Tomorrow's Jobs.* (103D) ($1.75) 14 pages. Discusses the changes in the economy, labor force, future demand for occupations, and more.

- *Tips for Finding the Right Job.* (131D) ($1.75) 28 pages. Discusses how to develop skills and interests, prepare a resume, write cover letters, and interview for a job.

- *Occupational Outlook Quarterly.* (250D) ($9.50 for one-year subscription, 4 issues) Reviews new occupations, salaries, job trends, and more.

- *Consumer Information Catalog.* Published quarterly. Lists free and low-cost federal publications of consumer interest.

317
COOPERS & LYBRAND
1800 M Street NW
Washington, DC 20036
202-822-4000

- *United States Nationals Working Abroad: Tax and Other Matters.* ($2) 48 pages. Answers questions regarding the income tax implications of working abroad.

318
CORNELL UNIVERSITY
Undergraduate Programs
Department of Agricultural and Biological Engineering
425 Riley-Robb Hall
Ithaca, NY 14853
http://www.cals.cornell.edu/dept/aben/homepage.html

- *Agricultural Currents.* Publishes articles on recent developments in agricultural engineering. Check out Cornell University's web site for general information about agricultural and biological engineering, undergraduate and graduate programs, course listings, and more.

319
CORNELL UNIVERSITY
Publications Resource Center
7-8 Business and Technology Park
Ithaca, NY 14850
607-255-2080
Fax: 607-255-9946
http://www.cce.cornell.edu/publications/catalog.html

- *Your Teen's Career: A Guide for Parents.* ($2) 6 pages.

320
CORPORATION FOR PUBLIC BROADCASTING
Publications
901 E Street NW
Washington, DC 20004-2037
202-879-9600

- *Careers in Public Broadcasting.* 12 pages. Describes careers in the field and cites minority job banks and minority media professional organizations.

- *Guide to Volunteer and Internship Programs in Public Broadcasting.*

321
COSMETOLOGY ADVANCEMENT FOUNDATION
208 East 51st Street
Suite 143
New York, NY 10022
212-753-4806

- *Where Do I Go from Here?* 12 pages.

322
COUNCIL FOR ACCREDITATION OF COUNSELING AND RELATED EDUCATIONAL PROGRAMS
5999 Stevenson Avenue
Alexandria, VA 22304
703-823-9800, ext. 301
http://www.counseling.org/CACREP/main.html

- *Directory of Accredited Programs.* 8 pages. Lists accredited master's and doctoral degree programs in counseling (community, marriage and family counseling/therapy, mental health, and school), student personnel service in higher education, and student affairs practice in higher education.

323
COUNCIL FOR EARLY CHILDHOOD PROFESSIONAL RECOGNITION
1341 G Street NW
Suite 400
Washington, DC 20005-3105
800-424-4310 or 202-265-9090
Fax: 202-265-9161

- *Improving Child Care through the Child Development Associate Program.* 6 pages. Describes the role of a child development associate and credentialing information.

- *CDA Information Brochure.* Contains information about the assessment processes for center-based, family child care and home visitor personnel. Provides information on the CDA Professional Preparation Program and state regulations related to CDAs.

- *Council News & Views Newsletter.* Published three times a year. Provides program updates, profiles of CDAs, and news affecting the early care and education professional.

324
COUNCIL OF AMERICAN SURVEY RESEARCH ORGANIZATIONS
3 Upper Devon
Belle Terre
Port Jefferson, NY 11777
516-928-6954
Fax: 516-928-6041
http://www.casro.org

- *Careers in Survey Research.* 6 pages. Defines survey research, marketing research, and public opinion research and explains what is involved in conducting research, employment opportunities, and educational requirements.

- *Surveys and You.* ($.25) 7 pages. Answers questions about survey research: what it is, who does it, how it involves people, and how it helps people.

325
COUNCIL OF GRADUATE SCHOOLS
One Dupont Circle NW
Suite 430
Washington, DC 20036-1173
202-223-3791
Fax: 202-331-7157
http://www.cgsnet.org

- *Graduate School and You: A Guide for Prospective Graduate Students.* ($5 plus shipping) 36 pages. Designed for people of all ages considering graduate study. Discusses the purpose of graduate education and contains information on career options, choosing a school, timetables for applying, and guidelines for financing graduate education.

- *Graduate Studies in the United States: A Guide for Prospective International Graduate Students.* ($5) 19 pages. Written expressly for students from other countries interested in American graduate education. Provides information on appropriate backgrounds for graduate education, how to apply, points about living in the United States, and other topics related to graduate study.

326
COUNCIL OF LOGISTICS MANAGEMENT
2803 Butterfield Road
Suite 380
Oak Brook, IL 60521-1156
630-574-0985
Fax: 630-574-0989
http://www.clm1.org

- *Careers in Logistics.* 20 pages. Describes the field, required education and training, career profiles, and where the jobs are.

- *Executive Placement Guide.* 7 pages.

- *Career Patterns in Logistics.* 20 pages. Also available online.

- *Transportation & Distribution College/University Directory.* 13 pages. Also available online.

327
COUNCIL ON CHIROPRACTIC EDUCATION
7975 North Hayden Road
Suite A-210
Scottsdale, AZ 85258
602-443-8877
Fax: 602-483-7333
cceoffice@aol.com

General Information Packet includes:

- *Chiropractic Programs & Institutions Holding Accredited Status.* 2 pages.

- *General Information Letter.* 3 pages. Includes information on preprofessional requirements, transfer students, transfer of credit from foreign health profession institutions, and licensure.

- *CCE-The Council on Chiropractic Education.* 6 pages. Includes information on CCE and a list of CCE accredited institutions.

328
COUNCIL ON EDUCATION FOR PUBLIC HEALTH
1015 15th Street NW
Suite 402
Washington, DC 20005
202-789-1050

- *United States Schools of Public Health and Graduate Public Health Programs Accredited by the Council on Education for Public Health.* 2 pages. Lists schools.

329
COUNCIL ON HOTEL, RESTAURANT AND INSTITUTIONAL EDUCATION
1200 17th Street NW
Washington, DC 20036-3097

- *United States and International Directory of Schools.*

330
COUNCIL ON INTERNATIONAL EDUCATIONAL EXCHANGE
205 East 42nd Street
New York, NY 10017-5706
212-822-2600
http://www.ciee.org

- *Student Travels Magazine.* 48 pages. Includes information on studying, working, and traveling abroad for students.

- *Students Work Abroad.* 27 pages. Describes working abroad opportunities for college students.

331
COUNCIL ON REHABILITATION EDUCATION, INC.
1835 Rohlwing Road
Suite E
Rolling Meadows, IL 60008
847-394-1785
Fax: 847-394-2108

- *CORE Recognized Master's Degree Programs in Rehabilitation Counselor Education.* 9 pages.

332
CUNA & AFFILIATES
Credit Union and Consumer Publications
5710 Mineral Point Road
PO Box 431
Madison, WI 53701-0431
800-356-8010
Fax: 608-231-1869
ccsd@meteor.org

- *Your Guide to Careers in Credit Unions.* Describes credit unions and careers in credit unions.

333
CURRICULUM PUBLICATIONS CLEARINGHOUSE
Curriculum Publications Clearinghouse
Western Illinois University
Horrabin Hall 46
Macomb, IL 61455
800-322-3905
Fax: 309-298-1917

- *A Guide to free Career guidance Materials.* ($3.25) Lists free career-related materials produced and made available by corporations, government agencies, and national associations.

334
DADANT & SONS, INC.
51 South Second Street
Hamilton, IL 62341-1399
217-847-3324
Fax: 217-847-3660

- *Beginning with Bees.* ($2.00 plus shipping) A set of five pamphlets on beekeeping.

- *First Lessons in Beekeeping.* ($2.80 plus shipping) A beginner's manual to beekeeping.

- *Me? Beekeeping?* Details how to get started in beekeeping.

335
DANCE MAGAZINE
33 West 60th Street, 10th Floor
New York, NY 10023
800-221-3148 or 212-245-9050
http://www.dancemagazine.com

- *Summer Study Issue.* ($3.95, January issue) Lists summer dance programs at colleges, universities, and dance schools in the United States and abroad. Available at your local newsstand.

336
DEVRY, INC.
Publications Office
One Tower Lane
Oakbrook Terrace, IL 60181-4624
800-73-DEVRY or 708-571-7700
Fax: 630-571-0317
http://www.devry.edu

- *Career Update Workshop and Student Guide.* 12 pages. Contains exercises to help students investigate different career fields.

- *Career Navigator: Guiding Today's Students in Their Search for 21st Century Careers.* 24 pages. Includes tools for helping students match their skills and preferences with careers; a career chart, providing information about educational plans; and projections for growth for each career listed. Works in conjunction with the information students gain from the *Career Update Workshop and Student Guide* listed above.

- *Undergraduate Degree Programs in Electronics and Technology-Based Business (Academic Catalog).* 128 pages. Outlines the undergraduate programs in accounting, business operations, computer information systems, electronics engineering technology, electronics, and telecommunications management.

- *Evening and Part-Time Degree Opportunities for Working Adults.* 10 pages. Answers the most frequently asked questions and contains a list of programs.

337
THE DIETARY MANAGERS ASSOCIATION
One Pierce Place
Suite 1220W
Itasca, IL 60143-3111

- *What It Means to be a Certified Dietary Manager.*

- *Answers to Your Questions about Dietary Managers.*

338
DIRECT MARKETING EDUCATIONAL FOUNDATION, INC.
1120 Avenue of the Americas
New York, NY 10036
212-768-7277
http://www.the-dma.org

Assorted brochures on various direct marketing career opportunities. Write, call, or check the web site for the most up-to-date brochures.

339
DIRECT SELLING ASSOCIATION
1666 K Street NW
Suite 1010
Washington, DC 20006-2808
202-293-5760

- *Who's Who in Direct Selling.* 15 pages. SASE business size. Explains how to become a distributor for DSA-member companies.

340
DISTANCE EDUCATION AND TRAINING COUNSEL
1601 18th Street NW
Washington, DC 20009-2529
202-234-5100

- *Directory of Accredited Institutions.* 16 pages. Lists the 59 accredited home-study institutions, as well as the subjects taught by them.

341
DISTRICT OF COLUMBIA DEPARTMENT OF EMPLOYMENT SERVICES
Labor Market Information Research Staff
500 C Street NW
Suite 201
Washington, DC 20001
202-724-7213

- *Occupational Employment Projections-Year 2005.* 4 pages. Contains occupational employment projections for the District of Columbia to the year 2005.

342
DOW JONES & COMPANY, INC.
Special Publications Department
PO Box 435
Chicopee, MA 01021-0435
609-520-4306

Reprint booklets on important job search topics. ($5 each) 24 pages. Write or call for a list of the topics covered.

- *Managing Your Career.* ($5) 36 pages. Advice for graduating college students.

- *National Business Employment Weekly.* ($3.95 per issue) 60 pages.

343
DOW JONES NEWSPAPER FUND, INC.
PO Box 300
Princeton, NJ 08543-0300
800-DOW-FUND or 609-452-2820
Fax: 609-520-5804
newsfund@wsj.dowjones.com
http://www.dowjones.com/newsfund

- *Journalist's Road to Success: A Career and Scholarship Guide.* ($3) 150 pages. Answers questions about newspaper jobs, describes how to prepare for a journalism career, and provides the latest statistics on beginning salaries. Lists more than 400 colleges and universities that offer majors in print journalism, financial aid available to news-editorial students at those schools, and grants available from newspapers and media organizations.

- *Newspapers, Diversity & You.* 48 pages. Includes an overview of the journalism field, a career and salary report, and material about academic preparation, job hunting, and financial aid programs designated specifically for minority students.

344
ECOLOGICAL SOCIETY OF AMERICA
Business Manager
Center for Environmental Studies
Arizona State University
Tempe, AZ 85287-3211
602-965-3000

- *Careers in Ecology.* 8 pages.

345
EDITOR & PUBLISHER
Editorial Department
11 West 19th Street
New York, NY 10011
212-675-4380
http://www.mediainfo.com

- *Editor & Publisher.* ($4) The December issue lists hundreds of scholarships, fellowships, and other award programs in journalism.

346
EDUCATION COUNCIL OF THE GRAPHIC ARTS INDUSTRY, INC.
1899 Preston White Drive
Reston, VA 20191-4367
703-648-1768
Fax: 703-620-0994

- *A Counselor's Guide: Careers in Graphic Communications.* 13 pages.

- *Directory of Technical Schools, Colleges & Universities Offering Courses in Graphic Communications.* 90 pages. Spans all degree levels for technology, management, and education.

- *I Want a Great Future. Tell Me about Career Opportunities in One of America's Largest Industries.* 10 pages.

- *Scholarships.* 7 pages.

- *Guide to Audio/Visual Materials.* 21 pages.

- *National Association of Printers & Lithographers Industry Fact Sheet.* 1 page.

- *Printing Industries of America Fact Sheet.* 1 page.

347
EDUCATIONAL FOUNDATION OF THE NATIONAL RESTAURANT ASSOCIATION
250 South Wacker Drive
Suite 1400
Chicago, IL 60606-5834

800-765-2122 or 312-715-1010
Fax: 312-715-0807

- *Choose Foodservice: A Guide to Careers with a Future.* 12 pages. This booklet discusses career options in the foodservice industry, salaries and wage rates, education and training, and financial aid.

- *Choose Foodservice: A Guide to Two-Year and Four-Year Colleges and Universities with Food- service/Hospitality Programs.* 46 pages. Contains a list of schools with foodservice and hospitality programs.

348
EDUCATIONAL TESTING SERVICE
Publications Order Services
PO Box 6736
Princeton, NJ 08541-6736
609-771-7243
Fax: 609-406-5090
http://www.ets.org

Among the many free publications offered by ETS on test-taking preparation, as well as on specific testing programs (such as the GMAT, GRE, DANTES, SLEP, TOEFL, and Praxis), are:

- *Common Sense on Preparing for an Admission Test.*

- *GMAT Bulletin of Information.* Provides information on the Graduate Management Admission Test, sample questions, and a registration form.

- *GRE Descriptions of the Subject Tests.* Summarizes the purpose and scope of each Graduate Record Examination subject test and offers sample questions. Includes volumes on biochemistry, biology, cell and molecular biology, chemistry, computer science, economics, education, engineering, geology, history, literature in English, mathematics, music, physics, political science, psychology, and sociology.

- *GRE Services for Students and Institutions.*

- *HBCU-ETS Test-Taking Tip Sheets-General, Reading, Analytical, Writing.* Provides test-taking hints and strategies to maximize performance. Order from HBCU-ETS Collaboration, PO Box 6790, Princeton, NJ 08541-6790.

- *MBA: A Guide for International Students.* 8 pages. Contains information for international students interested in graduate management study in the United States.

349
EDUCATIONAL THEATRE ASSOCIATION
3368 Central Parkway
Cincinnati, OH 45225
513-559-1996
Fax: 513-559-0012
pubs@one.net

- *Dramatics Magazine College Theatre Directory.* ($3) 56 pages.

- *Dramatics Magazine Summer Theatre Directory.* ($3.50) 60 pages.

350
ELECTROCHEMICAL SOCIETY, INC.
10 South Main Street
Pennington, NJ 08534-2896
609-737-1902
Fax: 609-737-2743
ecs@electrochem.org
http://www.electrochem

- *What is Electrochemistry? Electrochemistry and Solid State Science in the Electrochemical Society.* 46 pages. Contains a series of essays on the work involved in such fields as corrosion, electrodeposition, energy technology, industrial electrolysis, electrochemical engineering, organic and biological electrochemistry, and physical electrochemistry.

351

ELECTRONIC INDUSTRIES ASSOCIATION
2500 Wilson Boulevard
Suite 210
Arlington, VA 22201-3834
703-907-7400
Fax: 703-907-7401

- *How to Choose and Use Home Office Products.*

352

ELECTRONICS TECHNICIANS ASSOCIATION, INTERNATIONAL
602 North Jackson Street
Greencastle, IN 46135
800-288-ETAI
Fax: 765-653-8262
http://www.eta-sda.com/etasda/index.html

For a complete listing of all ETA monographs, contact ETA or check the website. *ETA Employment Assistance Monographs* ($1.50 each). Titles include:

- *Learn New Skills for Employment.* (EA15)
- *Starting Your Own Business.* (EA13)
- *Fine Tuning Your Resume.* (EA8)
- *Employment Preparation.* (EA7)
- *Improve Your Value to Your Employer.* (EA3)
- *Job Hunting Techniques That Work.* (EA2)
- *Tech Training-Job Security.* (EA5)
- *Your Own Business (Antennas).* (EA10)

353

EMPLOYMENT SITUATION INFORMATION LINE
U.S. Department of Labor
202-606-7828

- *Employment Situation Information Line.* A recorded message offering current information on the unemployment rate in a number of fields.

354

ENERGIA PUBLISHING, INC.
PO Box 985
Salem, OR 97308-0985
800-639-6048 or 503-362-1480
Fax: 503-362-2123
energ123@aol.com

Several career and education booklets available. Contact Energia Publishing for a catalog. Titles include:

- *Career Development for the College Student.* (P0307) ($2.50) 8 pages. Contains a step-by-step system for career planning.

- *Choosing a Human Service Provider: Tips for Adult Students.* (P0313) ($2.50)

- *Conquering Test Anxiety.* (SPS0301) ($2.50)

- *Considering Your Significant Others: Techniques for Adult Students.* (P0312) ($2.50)

- *Finding Your Own Answers: The Four Year College & You.* (P0308) ($3)

- *Finding Your Own Answers: Voc Ed & You.* (SPS0311) ($3)

- *Getting, Keeping, and Growing in Your Job.* ($9.95) 128 pages. Contains information on a variety of job-related topics, including resumes, cover letters, office politics, interviews, and starting a new job.

- *Goal Tending: A Guide to Setting and Maintaining Goals.* (SPS0305) ($2.50)

- *How to Find a Job.* ($2.50) 16 pages. Provides a step-by-step system for finding jobs.

- *Orientation Tips for Returning Students.* (P0314) ($2.50)

- *Simple Research Techniques for the High School Student.* (SPS0303) ($2.50)

- *Successful Test Taking Techniques.* (SPS0333) ($3.50)

- *Time Management for High School Students.* (A0402) ($2.50)

- *Top Careers for the Next 30 Years.* (SPS0309) ($2.50) 8 pages. Outlines and lists major career opportunities for the next century.

- *Vocational Careers in the 21st Century.* (SPS0302) ($3) 16 pages. Contains information on vocational careers, past, present, and in the future.

- *What a Business College Can Do for You.* (SPS0306) ($2.50)

- *Your Educational Plan: A Simple Guide to Planning Your College Career.* (P0318) ($3)

- *Your Opportunities Series.* ($2.50 each) 8 pages. each. Describes the training required and employment opportunities for each career and includes salary and industry growth information. Careers include accounting, agriculture, bookkeeping, child care, computer programming, computers, dental assisting, drafting, electronics, emergency medical work, environment, fashion, food services, gas or diesel mechanics, law enforcement, legal support, medical support, massage therapy, nursing, physical therapy, printing industry, professional driving, real estate, recreation, travel and tourism, retail sales, secretarial work (executive and legal), and trades. Shipping and handling add $1 for 1 booklet, $2 for 2 to 5 booklets, and $3 for 6 to 10 booklets.

356
ENERGY EFFICIENCY AND RENEWABLE ENERGY CLEARINGHOUSE
PO Box 3048
Merrifield, VA 22116
800-363-3732
Fax: 703-893-0400
http://www.erecbbs.nciinc.com

- *Careers in Renewable Energy and Conservation Professions and Trades.*

- *Energy Education Resources.*

357
ENTOMOLOGICAL SOCIETY OF AMERICA
Public Relations Department
9301 Annapolis Road
Lanham, MD 20706-3115
301-731-4535
Fax: 301-731-4538
http://www.entsoc.org

- *Discover Entomology.* 12 pages. Describes entomology (the study of insects and related animals), provides reasons for insect research, and contains advice on how to prepare for the field.

358
ENTREPRENEUR MAGAZINE
2392 Morse Avenue
Irvine, CA 92713
800-421-2300

- *Business Development Catalog.* 64 pages. Lists more than 150 guides to starting your own business.

359
EQUAL OPPORTUNITY PUBLICATIONS
1160 East Jericho Turnpike
Suite 200
Huntington, NY 11743
516-421-9421
EOPub@aol.com
http://www.eop.com

The following magazines are published three times a year.

- *Minority Engineer.* (free to minority engineering professionals and minority college students within two years of graduation)

- *Woman Engineer.* (free to women engineers and female college students within two years of graduation)

- *Equal Opportunity.* (free to minority college students)

360

ERIC CLEARINGHOUSE ON ADULT, CAREER, AND VOCATIONAL EDUCATION
Ohio State University
Center on Education and Training for Employment
1900 Kenny Road
Columbus, OH 43210-1090
614-292-4353
Fax: 614-292-1260
http://coe.ohio-state.edu/cete/ericacve/

Visit the ERIC/ACVE web site for full text of many of the ERIC Digests, Trends and Issues Alerts, and other publications or for links to a variety of web sites related to adult, career, and vocational education and training. Write for a complete list of ERIC/ACVE publications, updated regularly.

361

ERIC CLEARINGHOUSE ON INFORMATION AND TECHNOLOGY
Syracuse University
4-194 Center for Science and Technology
Syracuse, NY 13244-4100
800-464-9107 or 315-443-3640
Fax: 315-443-5448
eric@ericir.syr.edu
http://ericir.syr.edu

- ERIC Digests are short reports giving an overview of topics of current interest and suggesting literature for other reading. The ERIC Networker is a help sheet providing instructions for using ERIC-related resources on the Internet. Contact ERIC via the web, e-mail, phone, or mail for a catalog listing other Digests, Networkers, and publications. Digest titles include:

- *The Bread and Butter of the Internet: A Primer Presentation Packet for Educators.*

- *Trends in Educational Technology.*

- *Computer Skills for Information Problem-Solving: Learning and Teaching Technology in Context.*

- *Internet Resources for K-12 Educators Part I: Information Resources.*

- *Internet Resources for K-12 Educators Part II: Question Answering, Listservs, Discussion Groups.*

- *Internet Basics.*

- *Local Area Networks for K-12 Schools.*

- *Strategies for Teaching at a Distance.*

ERIC Networkers titles include:
- *Internet Access Points to ERIC.*

- *LM_NET: A Worldwide Discussion Group for School Library Media.*

- *The AskERIC Service for Educators.*

- *The Field of Educational Technology: A Dozen Frequently Asked Questions.* ($1 for shipping and handling)

- *ERIC Digest,* 4 pages.

362

ERIC CLEARINGHOUSE ON TEACHING AND TEACHER EDUCATION
American Association of Colleges for Teacher Education
One Dupont Circle NW
Suite 610
Washington, DC 20036-1186
800-822-9229 or 202-293-2450
Fax: 202-457-8095
ericsp@inet.ed.gov
http://www.ericsp.org

- *ERIC Digests, Internet Bookmarks, InfoCards,* and other materials are available. Contact ERIC via e-mail, phone, or mail for a complete listing of their publications and materials. *ERIC Digests* are two-page overviews with bibliographies of topics of current interest in education. SASE business size. Titles include:

- *Alternative Career Paths in Physical Education: Fitness and Exercise.* (92-1)

- *Alternative Career Paths in Physical Education: Sport Management.* (93-1)

- *Coaching Certification.* (88-10)

- *Comprehensive School Health Education.* (92-2)

- *Demand and Supply of Minority Teachers.* (88-12)

- *Prekindergarten Teacher Licensure.* (90-6)

- *Preparation of Middle School Teachers.* (90-1)

- *Senior Citizens as School Volunteers: New Resources for the Future.* (93-4)

- *Status of Dance in Education.* (91-5)

- *Teacher-as-Researcher.* (92-7)

Internet Bookmarks are laminated, colorful bookmarks for students or adults and are helpful when searching the Internet. Topics include:

- *General Education.*

- *Student-Oriented.*

- *Physical Education, Sports, Kinesiology.*

- *Health Education.*

Info Cards give concise information on specific topics for those considering a career in elementary or secondary education. Titles include:

- *International Teaching Opportunities.* (#1)

- *Alternative Routes to Teacher Certification.* (#2)

- *Financial Aid for Teacher Education Students.* (#3)

- *Specialized Interests in Teaching.* (#4)

- *Choosing a Teacher Education College/University.* (#5)

- *Finding a Teaching Position.* (#6)

- *What is the ERIC Clearinghouse on Teaching and Teacher Education.* (#7)

- *What You Should Know about HIV/AIDS Education.* (#8)

- *Teaching in Elementary/Secondary Schools.* (#9)

363
EXECUTIVE ADVANCEMENT RESOURCE NETWORK (EARN)
777 Danforth Avenue
Toronto, Ontario
M4J 1L2 Canada
416-466-6039

- *E.A.R.N. Meetings and Seminars.*

364
FAIRTEST
342 Broadway
Cambridge, MA 02139
617-864-4810
http://fairtest.org

- *Tests Optional.* (SASE). A directory of nearly 300 colleges and universities that do not require SAT or ACT results for admission to bachelor's degree programs; published by the National Center for Fair and Open Testing.

365
FEDERAL ACQUISITION INSTITUTE (VF)
General Services Administration
18th and F Streets NW
Room 4019
Washington, DC 20405
202-501-0964

366–370 Free and Inexpensive Career Materials

- *Federal Contracting Careers.* 9 pages.

366
FEDERAL AVIATION ADMINISTRATION
Mike Monroney, Aviation Careers Division
Aeronautical Center, PO Box 26650
Oklahoma City, OK 73126
405-954-4657 or 405-954-4508
Fax: 405-954-0250
http://www.jobs.faa.gov

- *Remote Electronic Vacancy Announcements Merit Promotion (REVAMP).* Lists FAA vacancies nationwide. Available by mail, by phone, or at web site.

367
FEDERAL AVIATION ADMINISTRATION
Superintendent of Documents
Retail Distribution Division
Consigned Branch
8610 Cherry Lane
Laurel, Maryland 20707
http://www.tc.faa.gov/2DV/careers.html

The following brochures from the *FAA Aviation Career Series* may be obtained by writing to the FAA.

- *Pilots and Flight Engineers.*
- *Flight Attendants.*
- *Airline Non-Flying Careers.*
- *Aircraft Manufacturing.*
- *Aviation Maintenance and Avionics.*
- *Airport Careers.*
- *Government Careers.*
- *Aviation Education Offices.*
- *Aviation Education Resource Center.*
- *Women in Aviation and Space.* ($2.50) 21 pages. Profiles 46 women involved in various aviation and space careers including, general flight, federal government, space, education/training, engineering, airport management, aircraft maintenance/air traffic control, business/manufacturing, and the arts in aviation.

368
FEDERAL RESERVE SYSTEM
Publications Services, MS-127
Board of Governors
Washington, DC 20551
202-452-3245
Fax: 202-728-5886
http://www.bog.frb.fed.us

- *A Guide to Business Credit for Women, Minorities, and Small Business.* 12 pages. Describes funding sources for small business entrepreneurs.

369
FEDERAL STUDENT AID INFORMATION CENTER
U.S. Department of Education
PO Box 84
Washington, DC 20044
800-4-FED-AID

- *1997-1998 Student Guide: Financial Aid from the United States Department of Education.* 34 pages. Contains information on financial aid from the U.S. Department of Education. Financial aid programs include Pell Grants, Supplemental Educational Opportunity Grants (SEOG), College Work-Study (CWS), Perkins Loans, Stafford Loans, and PLUS Loans/Supplemental Loans for Students (SLS).

- *Directory of Ed Publications.* 131 pages. Lists Department of Education publications and information on how to obtain them.

370
FEDERAL TRADE COMMISSION
Public Reference
Room 130
Washington, DC 20580

202-326-2222
http://www.ftc.gov

- *Choosing a Career or Vocational School.* 6 pages. Describes some deceptive practices found by the FTC; recommends some precautions to take before enrolling in a career or vocational school; and suggests questions to ask school representatives in an early interview.

- *Help Wanted...Finding a Job.* 10 pages. Contains facts for consumers on types of employment service firms, and other information.

- *Modeling Agency Scams.* 8 pages. Provides tips on how to detect and avoid fraudulent modeling schemes and where to go for help if you become the victim of a scam.

- *Consumer & Business Publications.* 10 pages. Lists numerous FTC publications and order information.

371
FEDERAL TRADE COMMISSION
Enforcement Division
6th and Pennsylvania Avenue NW
Washington, DC 20580
202-326-3768

- *A Business Guide to the Federal Trade Commission's Mail or Telephone Order Merchandise Rule.* 16 pages. A helpful guide to planning and operating a business. Explains the merchandise rule's requirements and includes a question and answer section about the rule and full text of the rule.

372
FINANCIAL PUBLISHING COMPANY
PO Box 15698
Boston, MA 02215
617-262-4040
Fax: 617-247-0136

- *College 'Scope National College Directory.* 52 pages. Updated annually. Lists more than 1,500 accredited colleges and universities, as well as scholarships, fields of study, entrance tests required, tuition costs, student body size, room and board costs, deadlines, and more.

373
FIVE COLLEGE PROGRAM IN PEACE AND WORLD SECURITY STUDIES
Hampshire College
Amherst, MA 01002
413-549-4600
Fax: 413-582-5620

- *Guide to Careers, Internships, and Graduate Education in Peace Studies.* ($6) Describes career options in the field, lists related organizations and agencies, and examines internships, fellowships, and graduate programs worldwide.

374
FLIGHT TRAINING MAGAZINE
201 Main Street
Parkville, MO 64152-3733
816-741-5151
Fax: 816-741-6458
FlightTrng@aol.com

- *Choosing a Flight School: A Checklist for Finding Quality Training.* 12 pages. Contains general guidance information. Intended as an aid for anyone interested in learning to fly and for selecting the training organization that will meet specific needs.

- *Why College? Because Pilots Do More Than Just Fly.* 7 pages. Describes the aviation professional and the necessary education.

- *Learn to Fly...Stop Dreaming and Start Flying.* 30 pages. An excerpt from *Flight Training Magazine.* Includes a flight school directory.

- *How to Select an Aviation College.* 4 pages. A checklist for choosing an aviation college that meets specific needs.

- *Internships and Co-Ops.* 16 pages. An excerpt from *Flight Training Magazine*; contains information on internships and co-ops in aviation; includes college directory.

- *Collegiate Aviation: Programs and Options.* 8 pages. This is an excerpt from *Flight Training Magazine*. Discusses associate's and bachelor's degree programs, tuition, and finding work.

- *Flight Training Magazine.* ($3.95) Available at local newsstands. Published monthly.

375
FLOOR COVERING INSTALLATION BOARD
310 Holiday Avenue
Dalton, GA 30720
706-226-5488

- *Contractors Certification Program.* 6 pages.

376
FLORIDA DEPARTMENT OF LABOR AND EMPLOYMENT SECURITY
Division of Jobs and Benefits
Bureau of Labor Market Information
Hartman Building
Suite 200
2012 Capital Circle SE
Tallahassee, FL 32399-2151
904-488-1048
Fax: 904-414-6210
http://199.44.49.226

Contact for a *Labor Market Information Directory*, which includes the following materials and more:

- *Florida's WEB.* A newsletter published semiannually and featuring occupational, educational, and career information of statewide and national importance. Request from the Florida Occupational Information System Unit.

- *Florida LMI NET.* 6 pages. Contains information on how to access LMI NET, a computer-based bulletin board system that links data users with Florida's Bureau of Labor Market Information data and resources.

- *Florida Industry and Occupational Employment Projections, 1994-2005.* Published annually. Includes a ranking of the growing and declining occupations. Available from the Occupational Employment Statistics Unit.

- *Florida Labor Market Trends.* Published monthly. Contains nonagricultural employment by industry and unemployment rates. Available from the Economic Analysis Unit.

377
FOOD AND AGRICULTURAL CAREERS FOR TOMORROW
1140 Agricultural Administration Building
Purdue University
West Lafayette, IN 47907-1140
317-494-8473
Fax: 317-494-8977
adg@admin.agad.purdue.edu

- *Employment Opportunities for College Graduates in the Food and Agricultural Sciences: Agriculture, Natural Resources, and Veterinary Medicine.* 20 pages. Identifies major trends in professional employment opportunities for recent college graduates.

- *Living Science Poster Sets.* ($4 per set) Each set contains 40 (11 X 17) posters, which depict various food, agricultural, and natural resources careers.

378
FOOD MARKETING INSTITUTE
Information Service
800 Connecticut Avenue NW
Washington, DC 20006-2701
202-452-8444

- *New Opportunities-The Supermarket Industry and YOU!*

- *Super Careers in Supermarketing.* ($3.30) 24 pages. Includes detailed job descriptions and career options, as well as a comprehensive list of schools offering programs related to supermarketing.

379
FOREIGN PHARMACY GRADUATE EXAMINATION COMMITTEE
National Association of Boards of Pharmacy
700 Busse Highway
Park Ridge, IL 60068
847-698-6227

- *FPGEC Certification Program Information Booklet.* 30 pages. Includes certification information and application form.

380
FORENSIC SCIENCES FOUNDATION, INC.
PO Box 669
Colorado Springs, CO 80901-0669
719-636-1100
Fax: 719-636-1993
http://www.aafs.org

- *Career Brochure.* 32 pages. Describes various employment opportunities in the forensics field.

- *List of Schools.* 11 pages. Lists graduate and undergraduate schools that offer forensic science programs.

381
FOUNDATION FOR INTERIOR DESIGN EDUCATION RESEARCH
60 Monroe Center NW
Suite 300
Grand Rapids, MI 49503-2920
616-458-0400
Fax: 616-458-0460
http://www.fider.org

- *Directory of Interior Design Programs Accredited by FIDER.* Contains a list of FIDER accredited programs. Also available on FIDER's web site.

382
FRANCHISE RULE INFORMATION HOTLINE
Federal Trade Commission
6th and Pennsylvania Avenue NW
Washington, DC 20580
202-326-2222
http://www.ftc.gov

Franchise Information Package includes:

- *Franchise and Business Opportunities.* 8 pages. Contains consumer facts about the FTC Rule, information about buying a business, and other material.

- *The Franchise Rule; Questions and Answers.* 1 page. Describes the Trade Regulation Rule, what the rule does, and who is covered by the rule.

- *Franchise Rule Summary.* 7 pages. Contains information on businesses covered by the rule, disclosure documents, earnings claims, acts of practice that violate the rule, state franchise laws, and relevant legal citations.

- *A Consumer Guide to Buying a Franchise.* 21 pages. Discusses the benefits and responsibilities of owning a franchise, selecting a franchise, investigating franchise offerings, and additional sources of information.

- *State Agencies Administrating Franchise Disclosure Laws.* 1 page. Lists agencies administering franchise disclosure laws.

- *Federal Trade Commission Federal Register.* 14 pages. Describes disclosure requirements and prohibitions concerning franchising and business opportunity ventures.

383
GENERAL AVIATION MANUFACTURERS ASSOCIATION
1400 K Street NW
Suite 801
Washington, DC 20005

202-393-1500
http://www.generalaviation.org

- *General Aviation...A National Resource Video.* Available free for a 30-day period. Portrays the important role general aviation plays in the national transportation system and economy.

384
GENERAL MOTORS AUTOMOTIVE SERVICE EDUCATIONAL PROGRAM
National College Coordinator
General Motors Service Technology Group
30501 Van Dyke Avenue
Box 9008
Warren, MI 48090-9008
313-947-9857

- *Colleges and Universities Participating in the GM Automotive Service Education Program.* 18 pages. A listing of colleges and universities participating in the GM Automotive Service Educational Program in the U.S. and Canada.

- *Rewarding Careers in the Automotive Industry.* 12 pages.

385
GENETICS SOCIETY OF AMERICA
9650 Rockville Pike
Bethesda, MD 20814-3998
http://www.faseb.org/genetics

- *Solving the Puzzle: Careers in Genetics.* Available only on the Internet. Discusses various genetics careers and the training required.

386
GEOGRAPHICAL STUDIES AND RESEARCH CENTER
Roark 201, Eastern Kentucky University
Richmond, KY 40475-3129
606-622-1418

- *Schwendeman's Directory of College Geography of the United States.* ($8) 138 pages. Lists 605 colleges and universities with geography departments and includes information on enrollment, faculty, and degrees awarded.

387
GEOLOGICAL INQUIRIES GROUP
U.S. Department of the Interior Geological Survey
907 National Center
Reston, VA 20192
703-648-4383
http://www.geology.er.usgs.gov/eastern/careers.html

- *Selected References on Careers in Earth Science.* 4 pages. Lists pamphlets, leaflets, booklets, books, audiovisual aids, and related organizations.

388
GEOLOGICAL SOCIETY OF AMERICA
3300 Penrose Place
PO Box 9140
Boulder, CO 80301
303-447-2020
http://www.geosociety.org

- *Careers in the Geosciences.* 12 pages. Describes the work of the geoscientist, job and salary outlook, and other topics.

- *Future Employment Opportunities in the Geological Sciences.* 26 pages. Contains articles on Future Jobs in Geology, Academic Employment Opportunities, Minerals Industry, Oil and Gas Industry, Resumes and Interviews, and Networking.

- *Geological Science Reprints.* 15 pages. Discusses academic employment; the consulting industry; the impact of federal legislation; work in the federal government, state government, minerals industry, and petroleum industry; and resumes and interviews.

389
GEORGETOWN UNIVERSITY
Division of Interpretation and Translation
School of Languages and Linguistics
Washington, DC 20057-0993

- *Preparing for Studies in Interpretation and Translation.* 22 pages.

390
GERMAN STUDIES INFORMATION, LTD.
DAAD/Monatshefte Directory
818 Van Hise Hall
1220 Linden Drive
Madison, WI 53706
608-262-3008
Fax: 608-262-7949
http://polyglot.lss.wisc.edu/german/mona

- *DAAD/Monatshefte Directory of German Studies.* ($5) Contains a list of German departments, programs, and faculties at four-year colleges and universities in the United States and Canada.

391
GLASS CEILING COMMISSION
Office of the Secretary
U.S. Department of Labor
Women's Bureau
200 Constitution Avenue NW
Room S2233
Washington, DC 20210
202-619-6652
http://www.dol.gov/dol/wb/welcome.html

- *Don't Work in the Dark-Know Your Rights Series.* Each of the free, nine-page pamphlets focus on a discrimination issue that affects women in the workplace. Pamphlet titles include *Disability Discrimination*, *Wage Discrimination, Age Discrimination, Sexual Harassment, Pregnancy Discrimination,* and *Family and Medical Leave.* The following fact sheets are also available:

- *Women and Downsizing.* 4 pages. (96-1)

- *20 Facts on Women Workers.* 4 pages. (96-2)

- *Domestic Violence: A Workplace Issue.* 6 pages. (96-3)

- *Women of Hispanic Origin in the Labor Force.* 8 pages. (94-2)

- *Earnings Differences Between Women and Men.* 11 pages. (93-5)

392
GLENDON COLLEGE
Counseling and Career Center
2275 Bayview Avenue
Toronto, Ontario M4N 3M6
Canada

- *A Training and Reference Manual for Part-Time Staff and Volunteers.* ($20) 58 pages Outlines how staff members should handle such things as incoming job postings, address issues such as confidentiality of information, and discusses how to write a letter of application and resume.

393
GOODWILL INDUSTRIES, INC.
9200 Wisconsin Avenue
Bethesda, MD 20814-3896
301-530-6500

- *People with Disabilities Terminology Guide.* 6 pages.

394
GRADUATE MANAGEMENT ADMISSION COUNCIL
8300 Greenboro Drive
Suite 750
McLean, VA 22102
703-749-0131
Fax: 703-749-0169

- *Bulletin of Information and Registration Form.* 48 pages. Gives an explanation of the GMAT, provides sample questions and suggestions, and lists test dates and test centers locations.

- *MBA: A Guide for International Students.* 8 pages. Discusses the application process, admission, costs and finances, and visas.

395
GRAPHIC ARTS TECHNICAL FOUNDATION
4615 Forbes Avenue
Pittsburgh, PA 15213-3796
412-621-6941

- *Directory: Technical Schools, Colleges, & Universities Offering Courses in Graphic Communications.* 64 pages. Covers all degree levels for technology, management, and educational graphic arts programs.

396
GREATER WASHINGTON SOCIETY OF ASSOCIATION EXECUTIVES
Association Career Services Center
1426 21st Street NW
Suite 200
Washington, DC 20036-5901
202-429-9370
Fax: 202-833-1129
http://www.gwsae.org

- *A Guide to Association Careers.* 24 pages. Discusses the opportunities available, the various careers, salaries, and where to look for an association job.

397
HARNESS HORSE YOUTH FOUNDATION
14950 Greyhound Court
Suite 210
Carmel, IN 46032
317-848-5132
http://www.hhyf.org

- *Equine School and College Directory.* ($8) 101 pages. Lists equine degree programs, farrier schools, veterinary schools, veterinary technical programs, and related scholarships.

- *Careers in Harness Racing.* 28 pages. A brief description of various horse-related career opportunities.

398
HEALTH PROFESSIONS CAREER OPPORTUNITY PROGRAM
1600 Ninth Street
Room 441
Sacramento, CA 95814
916-654-1730
Fax: 916-654-3138

- *Health Pathways.* A quarterly newsletter containing timely information on health professional schools, admissions, postbaccalaureate and summer enrichment programs, financial aid, health careers, student health organizations, and health issues.

- *Financial Advice for Minority Students Seeking an Education in the Health Professions.* Discusses financial aid basics-costs, eligibility, availability, and resources.

- *The Physician Assistant: A Guide for Minority Students.* Covers career preparation, entry requirements, admissions procedures, financial aid, curriculum, training, and certification. Describes the physician assistant role, available opportunities, and employment outlook.

- *Minorities and Public Health Careers.* Highlights public health careers, how to apply to graduate school, and specific public health curricula.

- *The Many Roles of Nursing.* Includes information on career preparation, entry requirements, admission procedures, financial aid, and training.

- *Minorities in Medicine: A Guide for Premedical Students.* Contains descriptions of medical careers, information on how to prepare for them, and a list of sources.

- *Educational Survival Skills Study Guide.* Offers techniques for developing study skills and improving chances of academic success.

- *Time Management for Students.* Geared toward medical and other graduate students. Includes techniques for improving time usage.

- *Minority Public Health Student Contact List.* A list of individuals to contact for support, information, and networking. Designed for new or prospective public health students.

- *Minority Medical Student Contact List.* Lists persons to contact for support, information, and networking. Designed for new or prospective medical students.

- *Third World Student Organizations and Health Groups Directory.* A list of undergraduate minority student health science clubs and associations in California.

399
HEALTH RESOURCE CENTER
American Council on Education
One Dupont Circle NW
Suite 800
Washington, DC 20036-1193
202-939-9320
Fax: 202-833-4760
health@ace.nche.edu
http://www.acenet.edu

Prior to ordering, contact the HRC about the availability of publications.

- *Career Planning and Employment Strategies for Postsecondary Students with Disabilities.* ($2) 8 pages.

- *Distance Learning and Adults with Disabilities.* ($2) 6 pages. Describes the learning opportunities available via computer conferencing, cable television, and videocassette.

- *Financial Aid for Students with Disabilities.* ($2) 12 pages.

- *How to Choose a College: Guide for the Student with a Disability.* ($1) 17 pages.

- *National Clearinghouse on Postsecondary Education for Individuals with Disabilities Resource Directory.* ($5) 39 pages.

- *Vocational Rehabilitation Services: A Postsecondary Student Consumer's Guide.* ($2) 4 pages.

400
HEALTHCARE FINANCIAL MANAGEMENT ASSOCIATION
Career Development
Two Westbrook Corporate Center
Suite 700
Westchester, IL 60154-5700
800-252-HFMA or 708-531-9600
http://www.hfma.org

- *Careers in Healthcare Financial Management.* 4 pages. Provides an overview of the field and describes career opportunities and educational preparation.

401
HOBART INSTITUTE OF WELDING TECHNOLOGY
400 Trade Square East
Troy, OH 45373
800-332-9448
http://www.welding.org

- *Course Catalog.* 35 pages. Provides a description of skill and tech classes, lists costs, and includes an application form. Portions of the catalog are available at the web site.

- *Training Materials Catalog.* 23 pages. Provides a description of materials and publications available for purchase.

402
HOME ECONOMISTS IN BUSINESS
5008-16 Pine Creek Drive
Westerville, OH 43081-4899
614-890-4342

- *Business Career Opportunities for Home Economists.* ($3) 36 pages.

403
HOWARD HUGHES MEDICAL INSTITUTE
4000 Jones Bridge Road
Chevy Chase, MD 20815

- *Beyond Bio 101.* 88 pages. Describes opportunities in biology, reports on changes in teaching methods, points out the kinds of research being done by innovative students, and tells how institutions are attempting to recruit more minorities and women into the field.

404
HUMAN FACTORS AND ERGONOMICS SOCIETY
PO Box 1369
Santa Monica, CA 90406-1369
310-394-1811
http://www.hfes.org

- *Career Opportunities in Human Factors/Ergonomics.* 8 pages. Discusses career options in the field, educational requirements, employment areas, salaries, and related professions.

- *Human Factors & Ergonomics...Designing for Human Use.* 6 pages. Describes the history of ergonomics, areas of work, and more.

405
HUMAN RESOURCES DEVELOPMENT INSTITUTE
1101 14th Street NW
Suite 320
Washington, DC 20005
202-638-3912

- *It's Your Job...These Are Your Rights.* 13 pages. A guide to young workers' rights under federal laws. Includes information on wages, health and safety, and family and medical leave.

406
IDAHO DEPARTMENT OF EMPLOYMENT
Research and Analysis Publications
317 Main Street
Boise, ID 83735-0670
208-334-6168
http://www.doe.state.id.us

- *Basic Economic Data.* Lists information on nonagricultural wage and salary workers by industry, for each county.

- *Distribution of Wages Paid to Covered Workers in Idaho, by Industry.*

- *Economic Profiles.* Economic overviews in various areas, including income, housing, employment, health care, education, and tax rates. Specify county.

- *Idaho Employment Newsletter.* Contains data on employment, unemployment, and economic trends and indicators.

- *Idaho Occupational Wage Survey.* Covers over 750 occupations in more than 8,500 businesses around the state.

- *Occupational Employment Statistics.* Includes information on occupations and employment within specific industries in the state and for the state as a whole.

407
ILLINOIS ASSOCIATION OF CHAMBER OF COMMERCE EXECUTIVES
215 East Adams Street
Springfield, IL 62701
217-522-5512
Fax: 217-522-5518

- *Is a Career in Chamber of Commerce Management Right for You?* 6 pages. Defines the role of the chamber of commerce and its staff and discusses compensation and other topics.

408
IMMIGRATION AND NATURALIZATION SERVICE
U.S. Department of Justice
425 Eye Street NW
Washington, DC 20536

- *Administrative Careers with America.* 6 pages.

409
INDEPENDENT ELECTRICAL CONTRACTORS, INC.
507 Wythe Street
Alexandria, VA 22314
703-549-7351
Fax: 703-549-7448
http://www.ieci.org

- *We Build the Country.* ($.50) 9 pages. Highlights the code of ethics and training requirements of independent electrical contractors.

410
INDEPENDENT INSURANCE AGENTS OF AMERICA, INC.
127 South Peyton Street
Alexandria, VA 22314
800-221-7917 or 703-683-4422
Fax: 703-683-7556
http://www.iiaa.org

- *Take This I Test First.* 6 pages. Contains questions for career-bound students and a discussion about the answers.

- *What Do You Want to Be When You Grow Up?* 4 pages. Describes the insurance field and available opportunities.

411
INDUSTRIAL DESIGNERS SOCIETY OF AMERICA
1142-E Walker Road
Great Falls, VA 22066
703-759-0100
Fax: 703-759-7679
idsa@erols.com
http://www.idsa.org

- *Career Packet.* ($10) Includes comprehensive description of interior design, listing of industrial design school programs, code of ethics and articles of ethical practice, *Business Week* article reprint, annual design awards winners booklet, *Industrial Designers* (Chronicle Guidance Publication), copy of *Innovation* magazine, and more.

412
INDUSTRIAL RELATIONS RESEARCH ASSOCIATION
4233 Social Science Building
University of Wisconsin
1180 Observatory Drive
Madison, WI 53706-1393
608-262-2762
Fax: 608-265-4591
http://www.ilr.cornell.edu/irra/

- *Industrial Relations Degree Programs in the United States, Canada, and Australia.* 4 pages. Contains descriptions of degree programs in industrial/labor relations and human resources.

413
INDUSTRIAL TRUCK ASSOCIATION
1750 K Street NW
Suite 460
Washington, DC 20006
202-296-9880

- *Truck Operator, Industrial.* Summarizes career opportunities in the trucking industry.

414
INSTITUTE FOR OPERATIONS RESEARCH AND THE MANAGEMENT SCIENCES (INFORMS)
Customer Service
901 Elkridge Landing Road
Suite 400
Lithicum, MD 21090-2909
800-446-3676

Fax: 410-684-2963
http://www.informs.org

- *Is a Career in Operations Research/ Management Science Right for You?* 21 pages. Contains 12 questions to help people decide if the career is for them.

- *Career Information in the Mathematical Sciences: A Resource Guide.* 29 pages. Lists mathematical career materials and sources for a variety of audiences.

- *Educational Programs in Operations Research and the Management Sciences.* 85 pages. Contains descriptions of 123 degree programs supporting operations research and the management sciences at institutions in the United States and abroad.

415
INSTITUTE OF ELECTRICAL AND ELECTRONICS ENGINEERS, INC.
1828 L Street NW
Suite 1202
Washington, DC 20036
202-785-0017
Fax: 202-785-0835
http://www.ieee.org

- *Careers in Electrical, Electronics, and Computer Engineering.* 8 pages. Describes the field of engineering and the opportunities available.

- *Your Career in the Electrical, Electronics, and Computer Engineering Fields.* 12 pages. Contains information on specific careers in the field. Includes a sample high school and college curriculum.

416
INSTITUTE OF FOOD TECHNOLOGISTS
Scholarship Department
221 North LaSalle Street
Chicago, IL 60601
312-782-8424
Fax: 312-782-8348

- *Food Scientists.* 4 pages. Discusses food scientists and the work they perform, education and training required, employment outlook, and more.

- *Food Technology Career Booklet.* 16 pages. Sections include Your Future, Your Mission, Your Job, Your Boss, Your Reward, and Your First Step.

- *IFT Administered Fellowship/Scholarship Program.* 17 pages. Contains program descriptions and application procedures. In the 1997-98 year, the IFT administered 39 graduate fellowships and more than 95 undergraduate scholarships.

417
INSTITUTE OF INDUSTRIAL ENGINEERS
Customer Service Center
25 Technology Park/Atlanta
Norcross, GA 30092
770-449-0460
Fax: 770-449-0460
http://www.iienet.org

- *Industrial Engineering Updates.* 1 to 6 pages. each. Titles include *ABET Accredited IE & IET Programs, IE Jobs Today and in the Future, IE Ranks 18th Out of 250 Jobs, Understanding the IE Profession,* and *Salary Survey Results.*

- *Planning Your Career as an IE: The People-Orientated Engineering Profession.* 10 pages. Covers job demand, work environments, and education and training.

418
INSTITUTE OF INTERNAL AUDITORS
249 Maitland Avenue
Altamonte Springs, FL 32701-9983
407-830-7600
Fax: 407-831-5171
custserv@theiia.org
http://www.theiia.org

- *What is a Certified Internal Auditor?* 8 pages. Describes a certified internal auditor and the job duties.

- *What's Next? Could Internal Auditing Be the Answer?* 6 pages. Defines internal auditing, the scope of the work, qualifications and certification, and internships.

419
INSTITUTE OF INTERNATIONAL EDUCATION
PO Box 371
Annapolis Junction, MD 20701-0371
800-445-0443
Fax: 301-953-2838

Study Abroad-you can get there from here: A Guide for Women (* and men). 32 pages. Addresses the variety of issues involved in studying abroad. The guide, while geared specifically toward women who face many cultural and social barriers in their attempts to study abroad, also offers guidance to men seeking study overseas.

420
INSTITUTE OF MANAGEMENT ACCOUNTANTS
10 Paragon Drive
Montvale, NJ 07645-1760
800-638-4427 or 201-573-9000
Fax: 201-573-8601
http://www.imanet.org

- *Accounting as a Career.* 8 pages. Describes accounting education, preparation for an accounting career, and professional certification.

421
INSTITUTE OF REAL ESTATE MANAGEMENT
430 North Michigan Avenue
Chicago, IL 60611-9025
312-661-0004
Fax: 800-338-4736
http://www.irem.org

- *Careers in Real Estate Management.* ($5) 9 pages. Introduction to the wide array of career opportunities that exist today in the field of real estate management. Includes information on the IREM Real Estate Management Intern Program for college students.

422
INSTITUTE OF TRANSPORTATION ENGINEERS
525 School Street SW
Suite 410
Washington, DC 20024-2729
202-554-8050
Fax: 202-863-5486
http://www.ite.org

ITE's complete publications catalog with an electronic order form is available at the ITE home page.

- *Transportation Engineering and Planning: Moving into the 21st Century!* 8 pages. Outlines the various transportation careers, the required education, and prospective employment.

- *Additional Information on the Transportation Profession.* 4 pages. Describes the profession, careers, education, and prospective employers and includes additional sources of information

- *Survey Summary: 1995 Salaries and Benefits of Transportation Engineers in North America.* 8 pages. An *ITE Journal* reprint describing job level descriptions and salary information.

423
INSTRUMENT SOCIETY OF AMERICA
67 Alexander Drive
PO Box 12277
Research Triangle Park, NC 27709
919-549-8411
Fax: 919-549-8411
http://www.isa.org

- *Measurement and Control Careers: A Design for Your Future.* 6 pages. Describes the careers, the educational requirements, and personal qualifications.

424
INTEREXCHANGE
161 Sixth Avenue
New York, NY 10013
212-924-0446
Fax: 212-924-0575

- *Working Abroad.* 14 pages. Describes a number of work programs and au pair programs offered in Europe. Outlines eligibility, visas, and related topics.

425
INTERNATIONAL ASSOCIAITON OF WOMEN POLICE
PO Box 371008
Decatur, CA 30037

- *Law Enforcement: A Challenging and Rewarding Service Profession.* 6 pages. Tells how to begin a career in the field.

426
INTERNATIONAL ASSOCIATION FOR FINANCIAL PLANNING
Customer Service Department
5775 Glenridge Drive NE
Suite B-300
Atlanta, GA 30328-5364
800-945-4237 or 404-845-0011
Fax: 404-845-3660
http://www.iafp.org

- *Your Career in Financial Planning.* 8 pages. Provides information on the field, employment opportunities, compensation, education and training, skills and qualifications, and ethical standards.

427
INTERNATIONAL ASSOCIATION OF BUSINESS COMMUNICATORS
One Hallidie Plaza
Suite 600
San Francisco, CA 94102
415-433-3400
Fax: 415-362-8762
http://www.iabc.com

- *IABC Communication Bank Career Packet.* 31 pages. Contains background information on business communication and resource tips for career development.

428
INTERNATIONAL CHIROPRACTORS ASSOCIATION
1110 North Glebe Road
Suite 1000
Arlington, VA 22201-5722
703-528-5000
Fax: 703-528-5023

- *Information about Chiropractic Education Career Kit.* 6 pages. Includes information on undergraduate requirements, admission, licensure, and financial aid and scholarships. Lists CCE-accredited colleges and universities.

429
INTERNATIONAL COMMISSION ON HEALTHCARE PROFESSIONS
3600 Market Street
Philadelphia, PA 19104-2651
215-349-6721
Fax: 215-349-0026
admini@ichp.org

Contact for availability of new releases and updates regarding health care professions.

430
INTERNATIONAL FABRICARE INSTITUTE
12251 Tech Road
Silver Spring, MD 20904-1976

301-622-1900
http://www.ifi.org

- *Career Packet.* Includes a copy of *Fabricare* magazine, a copy of *Fabricare Resources*, an overview of a drycleaner usage and attitude study, several *Focus on Drycleaning* booklets, and other materials.

431
INTERNATIONAL FACILITY MANAGEMENT ASSOCIATION
One East Greenway Plaza
Suite 1100
Houston, TX 77046-0194
800-359-4362 or 713-623-4362
Fax: 713-623-6124
http://www.ifma.org

- *Recognized Programs and Friends of Education.* 7 pages. Information on educational institutions offering degrees or course work in or related to facility management.

432
INTERNATIONAL FOUNDATION OF EMPLOYEE BENEFIT PLANS
Publication Relations Department
18700 West Bluemound Road
PO Box 69
Brookfield, WI 53008-0069
414-786-6700
Fax: 414-786-8670
http://www.ifebp.org

- *Career Opportunities in Employee Benefits.* 8 pages. Describes the numerous roles of employee benefit professionals, getting started in the field, and sources of information.

433
INTERNATIONAL INSTITUTE OF MUNICIPAL CLERKS
1212 North San Dimas Canyon Road
San Dimas, CA 91773
909-592-IIMC
Fax: 909-592-1555

- *History of the Municipal Clerk.* 6 pages. Describes early history, development in England, and colonial development.

434
INTERNATIONAL JOINT PAINTING, DECORATING, AND DRYWALL APPRENTICESHIP AND MANPOWER TRAINING FUND
1750 New York Avenue NW, 8th Floor
Washington, DC 20006
202-783-7770
Fax: 202-637-0748

- *Big Questions.* 4 pages.

- *Reach Out for Tomorrow: Apprenticeship Training Pays Dividends in the Painting, Decorating and Drywall Finishing Industry.* 2 pages.

435
INTERNATIONAL MASONRY INSTITUTE
Apprenticeship and Training
823 15th Street NW
Suite 1001
Washington, DC 20005
202-383-3927
Fax: 202-783-0433
http://www.imiweb.org

- *The Trowel Trades: Crafts That Build Nations.* 6 pages. Contains answers to questions about the trowel trades.

436
INTERNATIONAL OCEANOGRAPHIC FOUNDATION
4600 Rickenbacker Causeway
Miami, FL 33149
305-361-4671
Fax: 305-361-4711

- *Training and Careers in Marine Science.* ($5) 11 pages. Describes a variety of oceanography-related careers, educational pathways, and sources of information.

437
INTERNATIONAL PERSONNEL MANAGEMENT ASSOCIATION
1617 Duke Street
Alexandria, VA 22314
703-549-7100
Fax: 703-684-0948
http://www.ipma-hr.org

Visit IPMA's web site for publications, training information, and job openings.

- *Let's Talk about...Careers in Human Resources.* 8 pages. Outlines the duties and responsibilities, educational and training requirements, and ways to get a job. Also discusses employment outlook, income ranges, and growth potential in the field.

438
INTERNATIONAL SOCIETY OF CERTIFIED ELECTRONICS TECHNICIANS
2708 West Berry Street
Fort Worth, TX 76109-2356
817-921-9101
Fax: 817-921-3741
http://www.iscet.org

- *Careers in the Electronics Industry.* 13 pages. Discusses the nature of the work, training and qualifications, employment outlook, earnings and working conditions for a variety of jobs in the field.

439
INTERNATIONAL SOCIETY OF PARAMETRIC ANALYSTS
478 Graywood Drive
Ballwin, MO 63011
314-527-2955

- *Careers in Cost Estimating in Construction.*

440
INTERNATIONAL TECHNOLOGY EDUCATION ASSOCIATION
1914 Association Drive
Reston, VA 20191
703-860-2100
http://www.iteawww.org

- *Directory of ITEA Institutional Members.* 4 pages. A list of institutions aiding individuals who are considering pursuing undergraduate or graduate degrees in technology education. Includes degrees offered and financial aid available.

441
INTERNATIONAL TRADEMARK ASSOCIATION
1133 Avenue of the Americas, 33rd Floor
New York, NY 10036
212-768-9887
http://www.inta.org

- *Careers in Trademark Law.* ($2.75) 12 pages.

442
INTERORGANIZATIONAL COUNCIL ON STUDENT AFFAIRS
c/o American Pharmaceutical Associates
2215 Constitution Avenue NW
Washington, DC 20037-2985
800-237-APHA
Fax: 202-783-2351
http://www.aphanet.org

- *Interorganizational Financial & Experiential Information Document.* 12 pages. A compilation of scholarships, loans, awards, grants, internships, residencies, research opportunities, and fellowships in the pharmaceutical sciences.

443
INTERSOCIETY COMMITTEE ON PATHOLOGY INFORMATION
4733 Bethesda Avenue
Suite 700
Bethesda, MD 20814

301-656-2944
Fax: 301-656-3179

- *Pathology as a Career in Medicine.* 12 pages. Describes the pathologist in patient care, as a teacher, and in research. Includes information on graduate medical education and career options.

444
IOWA WORKFORCE DEVELOPMENT
Research and Information Services Division
Labor Market Information Bureau
1000 East Grand Avenue
Des Moines, IA 50319-0209
800-562-4692 or 515-281-6642
Fax: 515-281-8203
http://www.state.ia.us/government/wd/lmi.htm

- *Merchandising Your Job Talents.* 16 pages. Offers tips for those just out of school—or those looking for a new position after years of experience—on carrying out a well-planned job search.

- *Conditions of Employment.* Analyzes Iowa's labor market and includes an occupational and industry outlook with wage and income information.

- *Iowa Licensed Occupations.* 97 pages. Provides career counselors and others with information concerning occupations in Iowa that require a license, certificate, or commission issued at the state level. Includes brief job descriptions for each listed occupation.

- *Iowa WorkNet.* A quarterly publication that analyzes the state's current economic condition.

- *Iowa Occupational Planning Guide.* Ranks occupations in the state by the number of expected openings, average wages, number of job applicants.

- *Iowa Statewide Occupational Projections.*

- *Iowa Wage Survey.*

- *Job Insurance Survey.* Tables, prepared monthly, showing the unemployment insurance benefits paid in each county in the state.

- *Labor Force Summary Tables.* Data outlining employment and unemployment statewide and for every county in Iowa, as well as the employment by industry. Prepared monthly.

- *Employment and Wages Covered by Unemployment Insurance.*

445
IOWA WORKFORCE DEVELOPMENT
Public Relations Department
1000 East Grand Avenue
Des Moines, IA 50319
515-281-8110
Fax: 515-281-4004

- *Iowa Licensed Occupations.* 50 pages.

- *Make the Most of What You've Got.* Advice on how to dress for the all-important interview.

- *Merchandising Your Job Talent.* 16 pages. Summarizes the application process, resume, and interview.

- *Self Appraisal.*

446
J.L. SCOTT MARINE EDUCATION CENTER AND AQUARIUM
PO Box 7000
Ocean Springs, Mississippi 39564-7000

- *Marine Education: A Bibliography of Education Materials Available from the Nation's Sea Grant College Programs.* ($2)

447
JEWELERS OF AMERICA, INC.
1185 Avenue of the Americas, 30th Floor
New York, NY 10036
212-768-8777

Fax: 212-768-8087
http://www.jewelers.org

- *Careers in Jewelry: Sales, Craftsmanship, Management.* 10 pages. Covers the working conditions, career opportunities, educational requirements, skills and personal qualifications, employment outlook, and how to get started in a jewelry career.

- *Jewelers' Circular-Keystone Directory of Schools.* 24 pages. Lists for each school the courses offered, course length, class size, tuition, and number of instructors.

448
JIST WORKS
720 North Park Avenue
Indianapolis, IN 46202
317-264-3720
Fax: 317-264-3709
http://www.in.net/JIST

Contact JIST Works for a resource directory listing materials on careers and job searches or visit their web site.

- *Effective Strategies for Career Success.* ($9.95) 160 pages. A workbook to help prepare for, find, and succeed on a job. Gives an overview of training options and how to apply and focus on study skills, time management, positive thinking, and assertiveness.

- *Pathfinder: Exploring Career and Educational Paths.* ($6.95) 112 pages. Written specifically to assist students in planning their career paths through high school and into postsecondary training. Helps both tech-prep and college-bound students develop Individual Career Plans (ICP), including a plan for high school courses.

- *Getting the Job You Really Want.* ($9.95) 222 pages. Covers career planning, job-seeking skills, resumes, applications, and interviewing.

- *How to Get a Job Now! Six Easy Steps to Getting A Better Job.* ($6.95) 128 pages. Covers the essentials to getting a better job.

- *La Busqueda Rapida de Trabajo-The Spanish Quick Job Search.* ($7.95) 60 pages. Includes English and Spanish on facing pages. Provides brief tips on career planning and job searching.

- *The Quick Job Search.* ($4.95) 36 pages. Contains brief tips on career planning and job searching.

449
JOCKEY'S GUILD, INC.
250 West Main Street
Suite 1820
Lexington, KY 40507
606-259-3211
Fax: 606-252-0938

- *So You Want to Be a Jockey...* 6 pages. Covers the qualifications, training, and expenses.

450
JOINT COMMISSION ON ALLIED HEALTH PERSONNEL IN OPHTHALMOLOGY
Communications Coordinator
2025 Woodlane Drive
St. Paul, MN 55125-2995
612-731-2944
Fax: 612-731-0410
jcapho@jcapho.org
http://www.jcapho.org

- *Ophthalmic Medical Assisting.* 6 pages. Explains who ophthalmic medical personnel are, what they do, what their qualifications are, what education is required, and why they must be certified.

- *Certification-Why and How.* 6 pages. Describes certification levels and exam.

- *Educational Programs for Ophthalmic Medical Personnel.* 8 pages. Lists accredited programs.

451
JOINT REVIEW COMMITTEE FOR RESPIRATORY THERAPY EDUCATION
1701 West Euless Boulevard
Suite 300
Euless, TX 76040
817-283-2835
Fax: 817-354-8519
staff@jointreview.com

- *Respiratory Therapy Educational Programs.* 26 pages. Lists programs in the United States.

452
JOINT REVIEW COMMITTEE ON EDUCATION IN CARDIOVASCULAR TECHNOLOGY
Attn: Executive Director
3525 Ellicott Mills Drive
Suite N
Ellicott City, MD 21043
410-418-4800
Fax: 410-418-4805

- *Accredited Cardiovascular Technology Programs.* 4 pages.

- *Essentials and Guidelines of an Accredited Educational Program for the Cardiovascular Technologist.* 18 pages.

453
JUNIOR ENGINEERING TECHNICAL SOCIETY
Guidance
1420 King Street
Suite 405
Alexandria, VA 22314-2794
703-548-5387
http://www.asee.org/jets

- *JET's Guidance Brochures* and *Brochures for Most Engineering Specialties* (both suitable for middle and high school students) may be reviewed at the web site. Titles include *Engineering and You, Engineering is For You, Engineering Technologists and Technicians, Biological Engineering, Electrical Engineering, Environmental Engineering, Mechanical Engineering,* and *Safety Engineering.*

454
KANSAS CAREERS
Kansas State University
2323 Anderson Avenue
Suite 248
Manhattan, KS 66502
913-532-6540
Fax: 913-532-7732
http://www-personal.ksu.edu/~dangle

Visit the web site for information on women in nontraditional occupations.

- *Kansas Career Transitions.* ($3) 16 pages. Aids adults in the job application process, as well as describing the outlook for various occupations in different parts of the state.

455
KANSAS DEPARTMENT OF HUMAN RESOURCES
Labor Market Information Services Division
401 SW Topeka Boulevard
Topeka, KS 66603-3182
913-296-5058
Fax: 913-296-5286
http://laborstats.hr.state.ks.us

- *Labor Market Information Catalog.* Lists career-related resources available from federal agencies, Kansas state offices, colleges and universities in Kansas, and private sources.

456
KANSAS STATE UNIVERSITY
Department of Grain Science and Industry
303 Shellenberger Hall
Manhattan, KS 66506-2201
913-532-6161
http://www.oznet.ksu.edu/dp_grsi/

- *Information Sheets.* 2 pages. each. Available disciplines: bakery science; feed science and management; grain science and industry; and milling science and management.

457
KENNEDY INFORMATION
Kennedy Place
Route 12 South
Fitzwilliam, NH 03447
603-585-6404

- *Job and Career Library Catalogue.* Lists some 70 books of interest to job-seekers.

458
KENTUCKY CABINET FOR HUMAN RESOURCES
Department for Employment Services
Research and Statistics, CHR Building 2W
Frankfort, KY 40621-0001

- *Kentucky Occupational Wage Data.*

459
KRAFT GENERAL FOODS
Choosing to Succeed
PO Box 23430
Kankakee, IL 60902

- *Choosing to Succeed.* A directory of 97 historically black colleges. Includes details on major programs, enrollment, and fees.

460
LAW SCHOOL ADMISSIONS COUNCIL
Box 2000
Newtown, PA 18940
215-968-1001
http://www.lsac.org

- *Thinking about Law School: A Minority Guide.* 82 pages. A handbook guiding minorities through the law school application process, law school, and choosing a career path.

461
LEARNING CENTER
PO Box 27616
San Francisco, CA 94127
415-873-6099
Fax: 415-873-7055

- *Career Success: Five Essential Steps to Career & Job Satisfaction.* ($10) 162 pages. Written as a guide for all ages from precareer high school students to career-changing senior citizens. Includes five tasks that contain a learner-tested formula for success.

- *Bridging the Gap: A Learner's Guide to Transferable Skills.* ($5) 32 pages. Contains exercises for self-directed learning.

- *76 Career-Transferable Skills.* ($2) 4 pages. Lists transferable skills.

462
LEARNING DISABILITIES ASSOCIATION OF AMERICA
4156 Library Road
Pittsburgh, PA 15234-1349
412-344-0224
Fax: 412-344-0224
http://www.ldanatl.org

- *College Students with Learning Disabilities.* 8 pages.

- *Colleges/Universities That Accept Students with Learning Disabilities.* ($5) 50 pages.

- *Helping Adolescents with Learning Disabilities Achieve Independence.* 6 pages.

- *A Learning Disabilities Digest for Literacy Providers.* ($3) 24 pages.

- *You Can Open a Door.* 8 pages.

463
LEGAL SUPPORT SYSTEMS, INC.
PO Box 709
Cambridge, MA 02139
617-864-6600
Fax: 617-876-5351

- *Public Interest Employer Directory.* Distributed free of charge to University of Chicago and University of Michigan law school students and to the placement office of every law school in the country approved by the American Bar Association. Lists employer information for government and publicly and privately funded nonprofit organizations.

464
LIFE SKILLS EDUCATION
314 Washington Street
Northfield, MN 55057-2025
800-783-6743, Department 199
Fax: 507-645-2995
http://www.lifeskillsed.com

The LSE provides 16-page career-skills pamphlets at $2.50 each. The following is a selection from the many pamphlets available. Contact the LSE for an order form listing all titles.

- *How to Choose a Career.* (#7001)

- *How to Choose a Vocational School.* (#7002)

- *How to Choose a College.* (#7003)

- *The Interview.* (#7004)

- *The Application.* ($7005)

- *The Resume.* (#7006)

- *The Cover Letter.* (#7007)

- *The Follow-up Letter.* (#7010)

- *The Summer Job Book.* (#7012)

- *Part-time Job Book.* (#7013)

- *The Mature Resume: A Resume with Experience.* (#7018)

- *The Informational Interview.* (#7019)

- *Changing Careers.* (#7023)

- *Your First Career.* (#7025)

- *Your First Resume.* (#7026)

- *Phone Interview.* (#7027)

- *Untangling the Internet.* (#7028)

- *Computerized Job Search.* (#7029)

465
LINGUISTIC SOCIETY OF AMERICA
1325 18th Street NW
Suite 211
Washington, DC 20036-6501
lsa@lsadc.org
http://www.lsadc.org

- *The Field of Linguistics.* Available at LSA's web site.

466
LOG CABIN PUBLISHERS
620 West Washington Street
Allentown, PA 18102-1606
610-434-2448

- *The College Admissions Guide-How to Prepare Applications, Essays, and Letters.* ($1.50) 21 pages.

467
LOUISIANA STATE UNIVERSITY SEA GRANT COLLEGE PROGRAM
Communications Office
Wetland Resources Building
Baton Rouge, LA 70803-7507
504-388-6710
Fax: 504-388-6331

- *Marine Science Careers: A Guide to Ocean Opportunities.* 40 pages. An introduction to a wide range of marine career fields and to people working in those fields.

468
LOYOLA UNIVERSITY OF CHICAGO
Office of Public Relations
Water Tower Campus

820 North Michigan Avenue
Chicago, IL 60611
312-915-6157

- *How to Survive Freshman Year: Tips from College Students Who've Been There.* 36 pages.

469
MAGAZINE PUBLISHERS OF AMERICA
919 Third Avenue
New York, NY 10022
212-872-3700

- *Guide to Careers in Magazine Publishing.* 14 pages.

- *MPA Fact Sheet.*

- *MPA Sheet of Related Career Materials.*

470
MANUFACTURERS' AGENTS NATIONAL ASSOCIATION
23016 Mill Creek Road
PO Box 3467
Laguna Hills, CA 92654-3467
714-859-4040

- *The Manufacturers' Agent.* 1 page. Describes the duties and responsibilities, personal qualifications, working conditions, education and training, earnings, and the employment outlook.

- *What is a Manufacturers' Representative?* 1 page. Explains what an agent's role is in the marketing process.

471
MANUFACTURING JEWELERS AND SILVERSMITHS OF AMERICA, INC.
1 State Street, 6th Floor
Providence, RI 02908-5035
800-444-MJSA or 401-274-3840
Fax: 401-274-0265
mjsa@internetmci.com
mjsa.polygon.net

- *Careers in Jewelry: Opportunities in the Retail Jewelry Field.* 10 pages. Discusses the retail jewelry business as a career choice for men and women.

- *Bench Jewelers.* 4 pages. Describes the work, education and training, employment outlook, related occupations, and more.

- *The Jewelry Industry.* 27 pages. Discusses the jewelry tradition, job opportunities, advantages and disadvantages of working in the industry, and future outlook.

- *Guide to Education Resources.* Contains a list of schools and universities that provide courses in jewelry training.

472
MARINE MAMMAL SCIENCE
PO Box 1897
Lawrence, KS 66044-8897
913-843-1221
http://www.bev.net/education/SeaWorld/Careers/mshome.html

- *Strategies for Pursuing a Career in Marine Mammal Science.* This publication is available at the Marine Mammal Science web site.

473
MARINE TECHNOLOGY SOCIETY
1828 L Street NW
Suite 906
Washington, DC 20036-5104
202-775-5966
Fax: 202-429-9417
mtspubs@aol.com

- *University Curricula in Oceanography and Related Fields.* ($6) 204 pages. Presents data (facilities, programs offered, faculty, student support, and contact information) on 266 colleges and universities, as well as 44 technical schools and institutions.

- *Ocean Opportunities: A Guide to What the Oceans Have to Offer.* ($3)

474
MARK O. HATFIELD MARINE SCIENCE CENTER
Cooperative Extension Service
Oregon State University
2030 South Marine Science Drive
Newport, OR 97365-5296
541-867-0257
http://www.hmsc.orst.edu/education/educat.html

- *Marine Careers.* 6 pages. Describes maritime careers and contains other sea information.

475
MARKETING DIRECTIONS INCORPORATED
PO Box 715
Avon, CT 06001-0715
800-562-4357
http://www.marketingdirections.com

- *The ABCs of Coping With Unemployment.* ($1.45) 28 pages. Contains ideas for how to overcome the negative emotions associated with unemployment.

- *The ABCs of Finding a Job.* ($3.50) 40 pages. Contains information on job-search skills, writing effective resumes and cover letters, determining proper salary, and using effective time-management techniques.

- *The ABCs of Finding Prospective Employers.* ($1.45) 32 pages. Offers information on searching for employment in areas other than help-wanted ads.

- *Advanced Interviewing Techniques.* ($1.45) 12 pages. Contains further information concerning successful interviewing techniques.

- *Effective Job-Search Telephone Techniques.* ($1.45) 20 pages. Describes techniques designed to make effective phone contacts with prospective employers.

- *Preparing for the Interview.* ($1.45) 20 pages. Contains information on strategies for preparing for job interviews.

- *Resumes That Get Jobs.* ($1.45) 20 pages. Contains tips on how to write an effective resume that gets results.

- *Successful Interviewing Techniques.* ($1.45) 20 pages. Contains information about proven techniques that lead to successful interviews.

- *Writing Persuasive Cover Letters.* ($1.45) 16 pages. Contains information on producing attention-getting cover letters.

476
MATHEMATICAL ASSOCIATION OF AMERICA
Service Center
PO Box 90973
Washington, DC 20090
800-331-1622 or 301-617-7800
http://www.maa.org

- *Careers in the Mathematical Sciences.* 8 pages. A discussion by professionals from diverse mathematical settings about their workday, challenges they encounter, and how mathematics directed them toward their careers.

- *More Careers in the Mathematical Sciences.* 8 pages. A discussion by professionals in the field about the variety of occupations open to those with bachelor's or master's degrees in mathematics.

- *Mathematical Scientists at Work.* ($3) 16 pages. Describes the work of the mathematical scientist.

477
MEDICAL LIBRARY ASSOCIATION, INC.
Professional Development Department
6 North Michigan Avenue
Suite 300
Chicago, IL 60602-4805
312-419-9094
http://www.kumc.edu/MLA

- *Careers in Health Sciences Information: The Health Sciences Librarian.* 6 pages. Describes duties and required education.

- *Careers in Health Sciences Information: The Health Sciences Library Technician.* 6 pages. Describes the work involved, the work environment, required education, salary, and employment opportunities.

- *Courses in Health Sciences Librarianship Offered by ALA-Accredited Library School Programs.* 15 pages.

- *Health Sciences Librarians.* 6 pages.

- *Library Technicians and Assistants.* 4 pages.

478
MERION PUBLICATIONS
650 Park Avenue West
PO Box 61556
King of Prussia, PA 19406-0956
800-355-1088 or 610-265-7812

- *ADVANCE for Medical Laboratory Professionals/Nurse Practitioners/Occupational Therapists/Physical Therapists/Physician Assistants/Radiologists/Speech-Language Pathologists and Audiologists.* These publications are free to licensed, registered, or certified professionals in the field and also list employment opportunities.

479
MICHIGAN STATE UNIVERSITY EXTENSION
MSU Bulletin Office
10-B Agriculture Hall
East Lansing, MI 48824-1039

- *Catalog of Publications, Videotapes, Software.* 37 pages.

480
MILITARY OPERATIONS RESEARCH SOCIETY
101 South Whiting Street
Suite 202
Alexandria, VA 22304
703-751-7290

- *Careers in Military Operations Research.* 8 pages.

481
MINE SAFETY AND HEALTH ADMINISTRATION
Office of Information and Public Affairs
U.S. Department of Labor
4015 Wilson Boulevard
Room 601
Arlington, VA 22203
703-235-1452
Fax: 703-235-1452
http://www.msha.gov

- *Catalog of Training Programs for the Mining Industry.* 115 pages. Discusses cement, mining, and underground coal, among other fields.

482
THE MINERALS, METALS & MATERIALS SOCIETY
Education Department
420 Commonwealth Drive
Warrendale, PA 15086-7514
412-776-9000
Fax: 412-776-3770
http://www.tms.org

- *Materials Science and Engineering: An Exciting Career Field for the Future.* 4 pages. Discusses the future of the field, job opportunities, typical duties, personal qualifications, and education and training. Lists the 80 accredited colleges and universities offering materials/metallurgical engineering programs.

483
MINING AND METALLURGICAL SOCIETY OF AMERICA
9 Escalle Lane
Larkspur, CA 94939
415-924-7441
Fax: 415-924-7463

- *Opportunities for a Career in Mining & Metallurgy.* 304 pages. Describes the career options in the industry and provides a complete, four-page profile of each educational institution offering a degree in materials/metallurgical engineering.

484
MISSISSIPPI-ALABAMA SEA GRANT CONSORTIUM
PO Box 7000
Ocean Springs, MS 39566-7000
601-875-9341
Fax: 601-875-0528
http://www.waidsoft.com/seagrant/

- *Marine Education: A Bibliography of Educational Materials Available from the Nation's Sea Grant Programs.* ($2.50) 51 pages. Lists Sea Grant programs and institutions and the materials they developed. Includes ordering instructions and information about materials available for free or at a nominal cost.

485
MODERN LANGUAGE ASSOCIATION OF AMERICA
10 Astor Place
New York, NY 10003-6981
212-475-9500
Fax: 212-477-9863

- *English: The Professional Major.* ($4.85) 31 pages.
- *Foreign Languages and Careers.* ($4.85) 32 pages.

486
MUSIC EDUCATORS NATIONAL CONFERENCE
1806 Robert Fulton Drive
Reston, VA 20191
703-860-4000

- *Careers in Music.* 4 pages. Provides an overview of music careers in 10 areas including teacher/supervisor, music therapist, and conductor and more than 50 specialties, as well as a chart covering earnings, personal qualifications, knowledge and skills required, recommended precollege training, and minimum college training required.

487
MUSIC LIBRARY ASSOCIATION, INC.
PO Box 487
Canton, MA 02021

- *Music Librarianship: Is It For You?* 5 pages. Provides an overview of the career of music librarian, including a description of employment opportunities, educational requirements, everyday duties, career prospects, and sources of additional information.

- *Directory of Library School Offerings in Music Librarianship* ($5.00). To obtain this publication, contact MLA Executive Secretary, Richard Griscom, Music Library, University of Louisville, Louisville KY 40292.

488
MUSKEGON COMMUNITY COLLEGE
Education Department
221 South Quarterline Road
Muskegon, MI 49442
616-773-9131

- *Care about Kids? Come Fly with Us into the World of Early Childhood Education.*
- *Career Choices in Early Childhood Education.*

489
MYCOLOGICAL SOCIETY OF AMERICA
Dr. Maren Klich, PO Box 19687
USDA Southern Regional Research Center
New Orleans, LA 70179
504-286-4364
Fax: 504-286-4367
mklich@nola.srrc.usda.gov

- *Careers in Mycology.* 14 pages. Discusses employment opportunities, education and training, personal qualifications, and other topics.

490
NATIONAL ACADEMY OF OPTICIANRY
10111 Martin Luther King Jr. Highway
Suite 112
Bowie, MD 20720-4299
301-459-8075

- *List of Accredited Schools in Opticianry.* 4 pages. Includes a description of the profession.

491
NATIONAL ACCREDITING COMMISSION FOR SCHOOLS AND COLLEGES OF ACUPUNCTURE AND ORIENTAL MEDICINE
1424 16th Street NW
Suite 501
Washington, DC 20036
202-265-3370

- *Accredited and Candidate Programs.*

492
NATIONAL ACCREDITING COMMISSION OF COSMETOLOGY ARTS AND SCIENCES
901 North Stuart Street
Suite 900
Arlington, VA 22203-1816
703-527-7600

- *List of Accredited Training Schools in Cosmetology Arts.*

- *Where Do I Go From Here?*

493
NATIONAL ACTION COUNCIL FOR MINORITIES IN ENGINEERING, INC.
3 West 35th Street, 3rd Floor
New York, NY 10001-2281
212-279-2626

- *Academic Gamesmanship: Becoming a Master Engineering Student.* ($1)

- *Design for Excellence: How to Study Smartly.* ($1)

- *Financial Aid Unscrambled: A Guide for Minority Engineering Students.* ($1) 24 pages. English or Spanish.

494
NATIONAL AERONAUTICS AND SPACE ADMINISTRATION (NASA)
Aerospace Education Services Program
Mail Code FEO-2
300 E Street SW
Washington, DC 20546

- *Astronaut Selection and Training.* [Information Summaries (PMS-019B JSC). 5 pages, includes 2 pages of photographs. Includes a brief history of astronaut selection, present-day training and educational requirements, and brief descriptions of the space shuttle crew positions.

- *Applications for the Astronaut Candidate Program* can be obtained by writing to the Astronaut Selection Office, Mail Code AHX, Johnson Space Center, Houston, TX 77058-3696.

495
NATIONAL AGRICULTURAL AVIATION ASSOCIATION
1005 E Street SE
Washington, DC 20003
202-546-5722
Fax: 202-546-5726

Information packet includes:

- *AG Aviation/AG-Pilot...A Career You Can Grow In.* 6 pages.

- *Agricultural Aviation Pilot Training.* 1 page. Lists organizations offering pilot training courses and schools offering a degree in agricultural aviation.

496
NATIONAL AGRICULTURAL LIBRARY
Alternative Farming Systems Information Center
U.S. Department of Agriculture
10301 Baltimore Avenue
Room 304
Beltsville, MD 20705-2351
301-504-5724
Fax: 301-504-6409
afsic@nal.usda.gov
http://www.nal.usda.gov/afsic

- *Educational and Training Opportunities in Sustainable Agriculture.* 49 pages. Includes a directory for institutions in the United States and Canada, as well as an international directory. Additional resources may be found on the internet.

497
NATIONAL AQUARIUM IN BALTIMORE
Educational Department, Pier 3
501 East Pratt Street
Baltimore, MD 21202-3120
http://www.aqua.org

- *Careers in Marine Biology: Preparation and Opportunities.* 2 pages. Contains educational guidelines to help prepare for the many different career opportunities in marine biology.

- *Ask the Aquarium: Careers in Aquatic and Marine Science.* 6 pages.

- *Ask the Aquarium: Student Opportunities at the National Aquarium in Baltimore.* 2 pages.

498
NATIONAL ARBORIST ASSOCIATION, INC.
The Meeting Place Mall
Route 101
PO Box 1094
Amherst, NH 03031-1094
800-733-2622 or 603-673-3311
Fax: 603-672-2613
http://newww.com/org/naa

- *Careers in Arboriculture.* 14 pages. Discusses career tracks in arboriculture, career preparation, and employment opportunities.

- *Database of Educational Institutions.* 8 pages. Lists colleges and universities offering arboriculture or related courses.

499
NATIONAL ARCHITECTURAL ACCREDITING BOARD, INC.
1735 New York Avenue NW
Washington, DC 20006
202-783-2007
Fax: 202-783-2822

- *Accredited Programs in Architecture.* 18 pages. Lists accredited programs and indicates program types by identifying the professional degree conferred upon completion of the program.

500
NATIONAL ART EDUCATION ASSOCIATION
1916 Association Drive
Reston, VA 20191-1590
800-299-8321 (Visa/Mastercard orders)
or 703-860-8000
Fax: 703-860-2960
http://www.naee-reston.org

- *Careers in Art.* ($2) Designed to help high school students match interests and talents with career possibilities in the visual art field.

- *Teaching Art as a Career.* ($2) Discusses the necessary skills and training to become an art teacher.

- *Your First Job Interview.* ($3.50) 17 pages. Advice for those wanting to teach art at an elementary or secondary school. Covers the application, resume, letters of recommendation, the interview, and more.

501
NATIONAL ASSOCIATION FOR GIRLS AND WOMEN IN SPORT
AAHPERD
PO Box 385
Oxon Hill, MD 20750-0385
800-321-0789 (customer service)
or 800-213-7193 (membership)
Fax: 301-567-9553

- *Leadership Skills for Women in Sport.* ($3)

- *NAGWS Guide to Internship: Climbing the Ladder.* ($5) 52 pages. Lists more than 75 organizations offering sport-related internship programs.

502
NATIONAL ASSOCIATION FOR LAW PLACEMENT
1666 Connecticut Avenue NW
Suite 325
Washington, DC 20009
202-667-1666
Fax: 202-265-6735

- *Guide to Small Firm Employment.* ($3.50) 8 pages. Addresses the advantages and disadvantages of working for a small firm, job search techniques, characteristics valued by small firms, cover letters and interviews.

- *NALP Pro Bono Guide for Law Students.* ($5) 26 pages. Discusses questions to ask prospective employers, the benefits of pro bono work, and related topics.

503
NATIONAL ASSOCIATION FOR MUSIC THERAPY, INC.
8455 Colesville Road
Suite 1000
Silver Spring, MD 20910
301-589-3300
Fax: 301-589-5175
http://www.namt.com/namt/

- *Baccalaureate Curriculum in Music Therapy.* 4 pages.

- *Music Therapy as a Career.* 6 pages. Describes the career of music therapy and includes an NAMT school directory.

- *Music Therapy Makes a Difference.* 6 pages. Describes the types of patients who benefit from music therapy, qualifications and skills, employment opportunities, and duties and responsibilities.

- *NAMT Fact Sheet.* 1 page.

504
NATIONAL ASSOCIATION FOR THE EDUCATION OF YOUNG CHILDREN
1509 16th Street NW
Washington, DC 20036-1426
800-424-2460 or 202-232-8777
Fax: 202-328-1846
http://www.naeyc.org/naeyc

- *Careers in Early Childhood Education.* ($.50) Looks at the role of early childhood educators, career options, educational preparation, and personal qualifications.

505
NATIONAL ASSOCIATION OF ADVISORS FOR THE HEALTH PROFESSIONS
PO Box 1518
Champaign, IL 61824-5018
217-355-0063
Fax: 217-355-1287

- *The Medical School Interview.* ($2) 24 pages. Applicable to anyone interviewing in a professional school admissions system.

- *Write for Success: Preparing a Successful Professional School Application.* ($5) 41 pages. Provides help in writing clearly for tasks related to the health professions application process. Includes suggestions, strategies, and examples.

506
NATIONAL ASSOCIATION OF ANIMAL BREEDERS
401 Bernadette Drive
PO Box 1033
Columbia, MO 65205
573-445-4406
Fax: 573-446-2279
http://www.naab-css.org

- *Exciting Career Opportunities in Artificial Insemination.* 7 pages. Lists various job titles for a number of areas.

507
NATIONAL ASSOCIATION OF BIOLOGY TEACHERS
11250 Roger Bacon Drive
Suite 19
Reston, VA 20190
703-471-1134
http://www.nabt.org

- *Careers in Biology: An Introduction.* 4 pages. Highlights research, technology, and educational opportunities in the biology profession.

- *Biotechnology-Careers for the 21st Century.* ($10) A videotape for middle and high school students. Explores the career opportunities in the field of biotechnology.

508
NATIONAL ASSOCIATION OF BROADCASTERS
1771 N Street NW
Washington, DC 20036-2891
800-368-5644 or 202-429-5373
Fax: 202-775-3515

- *Careers in Radio.* ($4)

- *Careers in Television.* ($4) Describes the key jobs found in radio and television, as well as the educational requirements and job-related experience required for each.

509
NATIONAL ASSOCIATION OF CHAIN DRUG STORES
413 North Lee Street
PO Box 1417-D49
Alexandria, VA 22313-1417
703-549-3001
Fax: 703-836-4869

- *Careers in Pharmacy.* 30 pages. Profiles the pharmacies of some of the big retailers, describes what chain pharmacists look for, and offers resume tips.

- *Focus on Pharmacy.* 6 pages. Outlines the necessary course work and skills needed for the field. Includes list of colleges and universities offering pharmacy majors.

- *The Pfizer Guide: Careers in Chain Pharmacy.* 45 pages. Focuses on opportunities in chain pharmacy.

- *Shall I Study Pharmacy?* 17 pages. Provides general information on the pharmacy profession. Includes a list of U.S. colleges and schools of pharmacy.

510
NATIONAL ASSOCIATION OF COLLEGE ADMISSION COUNSELORS
1631 Prince Street
Alexandria, VA 22314-2818
703-836-2222
Fax: 703-836-8015
http://www.nacac.com

- *A Guide to the College Admission Process.* ($6)

- *Facts about American Colleges.* ($6) Covers admission requirements, admission office contacts, deadlines, enrollment, degrees offered, costs, and phone numbers for more than 1,200 colleges and universities.

- *High School Planning for College-Bound Athletes.* ($6)

511

NATIONAL ASSOCIATION OF CONSERVATION DISTRICTS
509 Capitol Court NE
Washington, DC 20002
202-547-6223
Fax: 202-547-6450
nacdinfo@nacdnet.org
http://www.nacdnet.org

- *A Guide to Careers in Natural Resource Management.* 9 pages. Lists sources of career information in such fields as agriculture, biology, engineering, fisheries science, forestry, geology, landscape, marine science, range management, soil and water conservation, and wildlife management.

512

NATIONAL ASSOCIATION OF DENTAL ASSISTANTS
900 South Washington Street
Suite G-13
Falls Church, VA 22046
703-237-8616

- *Salary Survey.* ($7) 2 pages. Lists job titles, types of practice, and salaries by state.

513

NATIONAL ASSOCIATION OF DENTAL LABORATORIES, INC.
555 East Braddock Road
Alexandria, VA 22314-2199
703-683-5263
http://www.nadl.org

- *Dental Laboratory Technology.* 8 pages. Discusses duties and responsibilities, the advantages of a dental technology career, employment opportunities, education and training, certification, earning potential, and sources of additional information.

- *Dental Laboratory Technology Today.* 2 pages. Describes career possibilities in dental technology, the required education, and more.

- *Accredited Dental Laboratory Technology Educational Programs.* 2 pages.

514

NATIONAL ASSOCIATION OF ELEMENTARY SCHOOL PRINCIPALS
1615 Duke Street
Alexandria, VA 22314-3483
703-684-3345

- *Considering Becoming a Principal?* 10 pages. Discusses how to become a principal. Compares the duties, impact, salary, and career growth of teachers and principals.

515

NATIONAL ASSOCIATION OF EMERGENCY MEDICAL TECHNICIANS
102 West Leake Street
Clinton, MS 39056
601-924-7744
Fax: 601-924-7325
http://www.naemt.org

- *Emergency Medical Technicians Show Up at the Worst Times.* 6 pages. Describes the nature of the work, training and advancement, earnings, and job outlook.

516

NATIONAL ASSOCIATION OF EXECUTIVE SECRETARIES AND ADMINISTRATIVE ASSISTANTS
900 South Washington Street
Suite G-13
Falls Church, VA 22046
703-237-8616
Fax: 703-533-1153

- *Improving Communication in the Workplace.* ($7.95 plus $1.50 shipping) 54 pages. A how-to book for administrative professionals on improving communication in the workplace.

- *Biennial Salary Survey.* ($7) Lists salaries of executive secretaries and administrative assistants.

517
NATIONAL ASSOCIATION OF INDEPENDENT COLLEGES AND UNIVERSITIES
1025 Connecticut Avenue NW
Suite 700
Washington, DC 20036
202-785-8866
Fax: 202-835-0003

- *Independent Colleges and Universities: A National Profile.* 19 pages. Contains sections on minority students, family income, college costs, student financial aid, scholarships, degree completion rates, and a variety of other topics.

518
NATIONAL ASSOCIATION OF INDEPENDENT SCHOOLS
Assistant to the Director
Career Paths and Gender Equity Services,
1620 L Street NW, 11th Floor
Washington, DC 20036-5605
202-973-9700
Fax: 202-973-9790
http://www.nais-schools.org

- *Getting Started.* A packet containing the NAIS guide to finding the right independent school job, *Backgrounder: Teachers at Independent Schools,* and *NAIS School Leadership Group Resource List for Teacher Candidates,* which lists teacher placement agencies, available directories of schools, and more.

- *Teaching Abroad.* A packet containing employment sources for overseas teachers, overview of overseas teaching opportunities, listing of NAIS affiliated schools, and more.

- *Intern and Teaching Fellow Programs in Independent Schools.* 40 pages. List of schools.

519
NATIONAL ASSOCIATION OF LEGAL ASSISTANTS
1516 South Boston
Suite 200
Tulsa, OK 74119-4013
918-587-6828
Fax: 918-582-6772
http://www.nala.org

- *What is a Legal Assistant?* 6 pages. Discusses career and employment opportunities, education and training, and certification information.

- *How to Choose a Paralegal Education Program.* 8 pages. Describes paralegal education programs and lists paralegal schools approved by the American Bar Association.

520
NATIONAL ASSOCIATION OF LEGAL SECRETARIES
2250 East 73rd Street
Suite 550
Tulsa, OK 74136-6864
918-493-3540

- *Careers: Tracking the Industry.* 3 pages. A survey giving insight into what legal secretaries do, what they earn, and the skills and technologies they use.

- *Summary of Duties and Responsibilities.* 1 page. Summarizes a legal secretary's job duties and responsibilities.

521
NATIONAL ASSOCIATION OF LETTER CARRIERS
Information Center
100 Indiana Avenue NW
Washington, DC 20001
202-393-4695

- *Carrying the Mail: A Career in Public Service.* 8 pages. Addresses a carrier's duties, wages and benefits, and qualifications, as well as how to apply for a position.

- *Working for You, Your Letter Carrier.* 6 pages. Information about letter carriers and how they feel about their jobs.

522
NATIONAL ASSOCIATION OF LIFE UNDERWRITERS
Public Relations Department
1922 F Street NW
Washington, DC 20006-4387
202-331-6000
http://www.agents-online.com

- *Explore Your Future: A Career in Life Insurance Sales.* 6 pages. SASE.

- *Your Career Path: A Successful Plan for Professional Development in Life Underwriting.* 13 pages. SASE. Looks at education and training programs.

523
NATIONAL ASSOCIATION OF PEDIATRIC NURSE ASSOCIATES AND PRACTITIONERS
1101 Kings Highway North
Suite 206
Cherry Hill, NJ 08034
609-667-1773
Fax: 609-667-7187
http://www.napnap.org

- *Pediatric Nurse Practitioner School List.* 15 pages. Lists for each institution programs and degrees offered, the academic schedule, and the minimum prerequisites.

- *Scope of Practice.* ($2.50) Outlines basic functions and responsibilities of pediatric nurse associates and practitioners.

524
NATIONAL ASSOCIATION OF PLUMBING-HEATING-COOLING CONTRACTORS
NAPHCC Educational Foundation
180 S. Washington Street
PO Box 6808
Falls Church, VA 22046
800-533-7694
Fax: 703-237-7442

- *Your Pipeline to Hot Careers and Colds Cash* ($5.25) Includes a nine minute video and a sixteen-page booklet for those interested in the plumbing, heating, and cooling industry. The video features high school students asking common questions about opportunities in the field. Industry experts respond to these questions and their responses are illuminated further by background shots of hands-on work within the field. A single copy of the booklet alone costs $.35.

525
NATIONAL ASSOCIATION OF PROFESSIONAL BAND INSTRUMENT REPAIR TECHNICIANS
PO Box 51
Normal, IL 61761-0051
309-452-4257
Fax: 309-452-4825
http://www.ice.net/~napbirt

Information on band instrument repair and schools is available at NAPBIRT's web site or by mail or phone.

- *Survey of Musical Instrument Repair Schools.*

526
NATIONAL ASSOCIATION OF PROFESSIONAL INSURANCE AGENTS
400 North Washington Street
Alexandria, VA 22314
703-836-9340

- *People Who Work for Insurance Companies Do a Lot More Than Sell Insurance.* 8 pages. Describes career opportunities in the property and casualty insurance industry.

527
NATIONAL ASSOCIATION OF PURCHASING MANAGEMENT
2055 East Centennial Circle
PO Box 22160
Tempe, AZ 85285-2160
602-752-6276
Fax: 602-752-2299
http://www.napm.org

- *Golden Opportunities: A Resource for Careers in Purchasing.* 12 pages. Discusses duties and responsibilities, opportunities for advancement, salary, personal characteristics, and required education and training.

528
NATIONAL ASSOCIATION OF REALTORS
Library-Career Information
430 North Michigan Avenue
Chicago, IL 60611
312-329-8292
http://www.realtor.com

- *Careers in Real Estate.* 30 pages. Describes job advantages, required education, professional requirements, personal qualifications, and the duties, responsibilities, and work environments of various specialties in the field.

529
NATIONAL ASSOCIATION OF SCHOOLS OF ART AND DESIGN
Publications Department
11250 Roger Bacon Drive
Suite 21
Reston, VA 20190
703-437-0700
Fax: 703-437-6312

- *Brief Guide to Art and Design Studies.* SASE. Describes opportunities in the art and design field.

- *Guiding the Arts Student: Academic Advising, Career Counseling, and Mentoring.* ($3.00) Includes a bibliography of references for additional information.

- *Directory of Accredited Schools in Art and Design.* ($15).

530
NATIONAL ASSOCIATION OF SCHOOLS OF PUBLIC AFFAIRS AND ADMINISTRATION
1120 G Street NW
Suite 730
Washington, DC 20005
202-628-8965
naspaa@naspaa.org
http://www.unomaha.edu/~wwwpa/nashome.html

- *Annual Roster of Accredited Programs.* 16 pages.

- *Master of Public Administration for Careers in Public Service.* Summarizes the field along with profiles of some who work in it.

531
NATIONAL ASSOCIATION OF SCHOOLS OF THEATRE
11250 Roger Bacon Drive
Suite 21
Reston, VA 22090
703-437-0700

- *The Assessment of Graduate Programs in Theatre.* ($8) Designed to assist individuals making assessments about graduate degree programs.

- *The Assessment of Undergraduate Programs in Theatre.* ($8) Provides a framework for analyzing undergraduate theatre programs and curricula.

- *Directory.* ($10) Lists accredited institutions and major degree programs.

- *Handbook.* ($10) Includes NAST standards for non-degree-granting, baccalaureate, and graduate programs in theatre.

532

NATIONAL ASSOCIATION OF SCIENCE WRITERS, INC.
PO Box 294
Greenlawn, NY 11740
516-757-5664
http://www.nasw.org

- *A Guide to Careers in Science Writing.* 12 pages. SASE business size. Looks at the roles and duties of science journalists and public information writers. Discusses where they work, salaries, educational background, colleges and universities with programs in the field, and getting a job.

533

NATIONAL ASSOCIATION OF SECONDARY SCHOOL PRINCIPALS
1904 Association Drive
Reston, VA 20191-1598
703-860-0200
http://www.naasp.org

- *The Principalship as a Career.* 16 pages. Discusses the secondary school principal's duties and responsibilities, the rankings of ideal and actual allocation of time for high school principals, and the time log of a high school principal.

- *Profile of Administrators.* 1 page. Provides data on superintendents, high school principals, junior high and middle school principals, and elementary school principals in such categories as sex, ethnic background, assessment of job security, average hours worked per week, and highest degree earned.

- *Technomic School District-Generic Job Description: School Principal.* 4 pages. Analyzes the job in such areas as curriculum development, supervision, and evaluation; student assessment and monitoring; student and staff relations; establishment of an effective workplace; professional development; staff supervision and personnel evaluation; communications; decision making and problem solving; community relations; personal development; and record keeping and financial management.

534

NATIONAL ASSOCIATION OF SOCIAL WORKERS
750 First Street NE
Suite 700
Washington, DC 20002-4241
800-638-8779 or 202-408-8600
Fax: 202-336-8331
http://www.naswdc.org

- *Choices: Careers in Social Work.* 40 pages. Contains information on educational requirements and social work careers.

- *Social Work Brochures.* Discusses various subjects including social workers in child welfare, school social workers, clinical social workers, and social work with older people.

- *Student Financial Aid Guide.* 4 pages. Describes scholarship sources for high school students and doctoral candidates.

- *Licensed to Care.* 3 pages. A reprint from *In View* magazine, May/June 1991.

535

NATIONAL ASSOCIATION OF SPORT AND PHYSICAL EDUCATION
1900 Association Drive
Reston, VA 20191
703-476-3410
Fax: 703-476-8316
http://www.aahperd.org/naspe.html

- *Careers in Physical Education, Sports and Related Areas.* 5 pages. SASE. Lists various physical education and sport occupations, the educational requirements, the compensation range, and the occupational outlook.

536

NATIONAL ASSOCIATION OF STUDENT PERSONNEL ADMINISTRATORS
1875 Connecticut Avenue NW
Suite 418
Washington, DC 20009-5728
202-265-7500
http://www.naspa.org

- *Consider a Career in College Student Affairs.* ($7) 11 pages. Designed to assist college students in exploring the field of student affairs.

- *NASPA Salary Survey.* ($7) Compares salaries with other student affairs professionals. Provides a reference for planning budgets, marking salary trends, evaluating pay plans, and managing resources.

537

NATIONAL ASSOCIATION OF TEMPORARY SERVICES
119 South Saint Asaph Street
Alexandria, VA 22314-3119
703-549-6287

Add 15 percent of total for shipping and handling.

- *Discover the Advantage...Freedom, Flexibility, Choice, Control.* ($.80) Details the benefits of a career in temporary help.

- *Issues and Answers.* ($.80) Answers some of the most frequently asked questions about temporary help.

- *Temporary Jobs: Making Them Work for You.* ($.50) Discusses what to expect, evaluating a service, and interviewing with prospective companies.

538

NATIONAL ASSOCIATION OF UNDERWATER INSTRUCTORS
PO Box 14650
Montclair, CA 91763-1150
800-553-6284 or 909-621-5801

- *Guide to NAUI Membership.* 14 pages. Gives descriptions of and requirements for skin diving leader, assistant instructor, divemaster, and instructor.

- *Learn to Dive with NAUI: It's Fun!*

- *NAUI Affiliate Directory.* 19 pages. Includes SCUBA Educational Centers and Leadership Development Centers.

539

NATIONAL ATHLETIC TRAINERS' ASSOCIATION
2952 Stemmons Freeway
Suite 200
Dallas, TX 75247
214-637-6282
Fax: 214-637-2206
http://www.nata.org

- *Athletic Training Career Information.* 6 pages. Highlights typical employers, duties and responsibilities, and how to become certified.

- *The Certified Athletic Trainer.* 8 pages. Discusses education, certification, a typical day in the life of an athletic trainer, and female trainers.

- *Accredited Athletic Training Education Programs.* 8 pages.

- *Credentialing Information.* 23 pages. Discusses the entry-level eligibility requirements for an athletic trainer.

540

NATIONAL AUCTIONEERS ASSOCIATION
8880 Ballentine
Overland Park, KS 66214-1985
913-541-8084
naahq@aol.com

- *The Auction Profession.* 4 pages. Discusses the work, necessary personal traits, education and licensing, and earnings.

541

NATIONAL AUTOMOBILE DEALERS ASSOCIATION
8400 Westpark Drive
McLean, VA 22102-3591
703-821-7000
Fax: 703-821-7075
http://www.nadanet.com

- *Automotive Careers.* 12 pages. Explains administrative, service, parts, and sales careers, as well as how to prepare for a job.

542

NATIONAL AUTOMOTIVE TECHNICIANS EDUCATION FOUNDATION, INC.
13505 Dulles Technology Drive
Suite 2
Herndon, VA 20171-3421
703-713-0100
Fax: 703-713-3919

- *Career Opportunities in the Automotive Collision Repair and Refinishing Industry.* 10 pages. Contains information about the job, earnings, advancement opportunities, opportunities for women, and employment outlook.

- *Automotive Technician: A Challenging and Changing Career.* 10 pages. Discusses the job, areas of specialty, employers, certification, advancement, employment outlook, and opportunities for women and minorities.

- *Automobile Technician: Realize Your Dream.* 2 pages.

- *Autobody Technician: Realize Your Dream.* 2 pages.

- *Truck Technician: Realize Your Dream.* 2 pages.

543

NATIONAL BUSINESS ASSOCIATION
PO Box 700728
Dallas, TX 75370
800-456-0440
Fax: 972-960-9149
http://www.nationalbusiness.org

Available on diskette only, the following are part of the First Step Software Series.

- *First Step Review.* For PC or Macintosh. Assesses one's chance of receiving a loan backed by the Small Business Association (SBA).

- *First Step Balance Sheet.* ($5) For PCs only. Designed to help prepare balance sheets for general accounting purposes.

- *First Step Projected Profit or Loss Statement.* ($5) For PCs only. Offers an exact duplicate of the SBA Operating Plan Forecast form used by the SBA as part of the loan eligibility process.

- *First Step Cash Flow Analysis.* ($5) For PCs only. Helps estimate the expected profit or loss for the month or year.

- *First Step Business Plan.* ($5) For PCs only.

544

NATIONAL CABLE TELEVISION ASSOCIATION
1724 Massachusetts Avenue NW
Washington, DC 20036-3695
202-775-3550
Fax: 202-775-3675
http://www.ncta.com

- *Careers in Cable Television.* 36 pages. Discusses career opportunities with cable systems, multiple system operators, and cable programming networks. Provides information on job searching, education, and financial aid.

545

NATIONAL CARTOONISTS SOCIETY
PO Box 20267
Columbus Circle Station
New York, NY 10023
212-627-1550

- *NCS Occupation and Education Guide.* ($2) 18 pages. SASE. Discusses the history of cartooning, offers tips on assembling a portfolio and finding a job, lists schools.

546
NATIONAL CENTER FOR EDUCATION STATISTICS
Publications Office
U.S. Department of Education
Washington, DC 20208-5650

- *Mini Digest of Education Statistics.* 65 pages. Summary of the information on education today.

547
NATIONAL CENTER FOR RESEARCH IN VOCATIONAL EDUCATION
NCRVE Materials Distribution Center
Western Illinois University
46 Horrabin Hall
Macomb, IL 61455
800-637-7652
Fax: 309-298-2869

Offers a free 75-page catalog describing its various publications.

548
NATIONAL CENTER FOR THE EARLY CHILDHOOD WORK FORCE
733 15th Street NW
Suite 1037
Washington, DC 20005
202-737-7700
ncecw@ncecw.org

- *Questions and Answers about Entering the Child Care Profession.* 1 page.

549
NATIONAL CENTER FOR THE STUDY OF HISTORY
RR 1, Box 679
Limington, ME 04049
207-637-2873

- *Connecting Scholarships and Careers.* ($.40) 4 pages. Connects the research skills learned in the study of history to research used in business or government.

- *Resumes for Graduates in History & the Liberal Arts.* ($.40) 4 pages. A guide for resume preparation. Provides a sample resume, a resume worksheet, and tips on effective communication techniques.

- *Industry-Education Alliances in History.* Outlines the purpose and framework of alliances. Provides teachers with examples of advice and assistance that industry can give schools and colleges. Wall chart formats ($4.00 each) in two colors and heavy stock (14 high by 20 wide, fold to 10 x 7) and notebook charts ($.40 each) in one color (14 high x 20 wide, fold to 10 x 7)

- *Careers for Graduates in History.* Guides history students through the process of considering advanced education or choosing a career in private, public, or nonprofit sectors. Cites numerous specific career opportunities.

- *Careers in Information Management.* Illustrates the roles for liberal arts and history graduates in archives, libraries, museums, and the research and informational field. Lists duties, requirements, and job titles.

- *Business & History.* Identifies the corporate opportunities for history graduates and relates studies to typical business career tracks.

- *Insurance & History.* Relates duties in insurance industry positions to the study of history education.

- *Historic Preservation Family Tree.* Provides a broad view of the heritage preservation field. A two-page chart graphically represents career opportunities and the decision-making process for selecting careers.

- *Value History!* Corrects the misconception that history is an impractical, for academics-only subject. Illuminates the benefits that knowledge of history brings to personal, civic, and professional lives.

550
NATIONAL CHRISTIAN COLLEGE ATHLETIC ASSOCIATION
PO Box 1312
Marion, IN 46952
765-674-8401
Fax: 765-674-1364
nccaa@bright.net
http://www.bright.net/~nccaa

- *NCCAA Membership Directory.* ($5) 33 pages. Lists member schools, coaches, and sports offered and provides geographic breakdowns.

551
NATIONAL CLEARINGHOUSE FOR ESL LITERACY EDUCATION
Product Orders
1118 22nd Street NW
Washington, DC 20037-1214
202-429-9292, ext. 200
Fax: 202-659-5641
ncle@cal.org
http://www.cal.org/ncle

An organization focusing on literacy education for adults and out-of-school youth learning English as a second language. For a complete publications list and order form, call, write, or send an e-mail request.

- *Learning to Work in a New Land: A Review and Sourcebook for Vocational and Workplace ESL.* ($7) 165 pages.

- *The Vocational Classroom: A Great Place to Learn English.* ($4) 31 pages.

ERIC Digest, ERIC Q&A, and annotated bibliography topics include but are not limited to:

- *Access to Literacy Education for Language Minority Adults.*

- *English Plus and Official English: Linguistic Diversity in the United States.*

- *Language and Literacy Education for SE Asian Refugees.*

- *Current Terms in Adult ESL Literacy.*

- *Improving ESL Learners' Listening Skills: At the Workplace and Beyond.*

- *Creating a Professional Workforce in Adult ESL Literacy.*

- *Union Sponsored Workplace ESL Instruction.*

552
NATIONAL CLEARINGHOUSE FOR PROFESSIONS IN SPECIAL EDUCATION
Council for Exceptional Children
1920 Association Drive
Reston, VA 20191-1589
800-641-7824 or 703-264-9476 (voice)
or 703-264-9480 (TDD)
Fax: 703-264-1637
ncpse@cec.psed.org
http://www.cec.sped.org

Below is a list of a some of the publications available. For a complete publications list and order form, call, write, or send an e-mail request.

- *Professions that Provide Services to Students With Disabilities.* (#9.95) Identifies many of the professions involved in providing special education, related services, and early intervention to infants, toddlers, children, and youth with disabilities. Also describes career opportunities in those professions.

- *Career Advancement for Paraprofessionals.* (#20.96) Encourages the paraprofessional to consider becoming a special education teacher. Describes the advantages of a career, the diverse professional settings, and how to begin a professional career.

- *VOLUNTEER! Find Out More about Careers in Special Education.* (#26.96) Describes options for volunteering to help individuals with disabilities and tips for finding volunteer opportunities.

- *Career Resources.* (#70.96) Lists information for individual states. You may request information for a maximum of three states.

- *Special Education Recruiters.* (#75.97) A list of special educators who have volunteered to talk to individuals interested in a career in special education.

- *State Licensing Agencies.* (#76.96) A list of state offices responsible for licensing teachers, including special education teachers in each of the 50 states.

- *Higher Education Programs for Personnel Preparation in Special Education.* (#10.95) Lists colleges and universities that offer programs in special education fields for each of the 50 states. You may request information for a maximum of three states.

- *Clearinghouse Mailbox: How to Choose a Graduate School.* (#98.94) Describes some factors to consider when selecting a graduate school in special education.

- *Clearinghouse Mailbox: Job Search Strategies.* (#65.93) Describes strategies the job seeker may want to use when looking for a special education position.

- *Heroes Have a Thousand Faces.* (#HS.BR, brochure, #HS.POS, poster) Targeted to high school and junior college students. Provides a brief introduction to special education as a career option.

- *You Can Prepare for a Diverse Career in Physical Education.* (#52.96) Describes the field of adapted physical education.

- *Educational Therapy.* (#95.94) An overview of a career as an educational therapist.

- *Financial Resource Guide.* (#17.97) Provides information on finding financial assistance for pursuing preparation in special education and related service professions.

- *Colleges and Universities That Have Programs Meeting CEC's Accreditation Standards.* (#69.96)

Career flyers include an overview of each career; a description of the work, work settings, and educational requirements; and a practitioner profile. Titles available:

- *Early Childhood Special Educator.* (#90.93)

- *Special Education Resource Teacher/Elementary Level.* (#91.93)

- *Special Education and Related Services.* (#108.95)

- *Adapted Physical Education Teacher.* (#113.96)

- *Secondary Special Education Teacher.* (#114.96)

- *Occupational Therapist.* (#115.96)

- *Physical Therapist.* (#116.96)

- *Speech-Language Pathologist.* (#117.96)

553
NATIONAL CLEARINGHOUSE ON CAREERS AND EMPLOYMENT IN SPECIAL EDUCATION
Council for Exceptional Children
CEC Publications
1920 Association Drive
Reston, VA 20191
800-CEC-READ or 703-620-3660
cecpubs@cec.sped.org
http://www.cec.sped.org/ericec.htm

For a catalog and order form of CEC publications, call, write, or send an e-mail request. *ERIC Digests* ($1 each) are short reports providing a basic overview, plus pertinent references, on topics of interest to the broad educational community. Among the many titles are:

- *College Planning for Gifted and Talented Youth.* (E490)

- *College Planning for Students with Learning Disabilities.* (R466)

- *Bilingual Special Education.* (E496)

- *Preparing Children with Disabilities for School.* (E503)

- *ADHD and Children Who Are Gifted.* (E522)

- *Assistive Technology for Students with Mild Disabilities.* (E529)

- *National and State Perspectives on Performance Assessment.* (E532)

554
NATIONAL COALITION FOR CHURCH VOCATIONS
1603 South Michigan Avenue
Suite 400
Chicago, IL 60616
312-663-5453
Fax: 312-663-5030

The following 32-page booklets cost $2 each:

- *Brother.*

- *Diocesan Priest.*

- *Lay Minister.*

- *Missionary.*

- *Religious Priest.*

- *Sister.*

555
NATIONAL COLLEGIATE ATHLETIC ASSOCIATION
NCAA Publishing
PO Box 7347
Overland Park, KS 66207-0347
913-339-1900
Fax: 913-339-1900
http://www.ncaa.org

- *NCAA Guide for the College-Bound Student-Athlete.* 15 pages. Addresses academic eligibility, core-course requirements, financial aid, recruiting, the national letter of intent, professionalism, agents, and other topics.

- *NCAA Guide for the 2-Year College Student-Athlete.* 23 pages. Discusses academic eligibility, general eligibility requirements, recruiting, the national letter of intent, and amateurism.

556
NATIONAL COMMISSION FOR COOPERATIVE EDUCATION
360 Huntington Avenue
Boston, MA 02115
617-373-3770
Fax: 617-373-3463
ncce@lynx.neu.edu

- *Advantages of Cooperative Education.* 6 pages. Lists advantages of cooperative education to the student, society, employers, and educational institutions. Briefly describes cooperative education.

- *Choosing Your College for Today...For the Future...A Student/Parent Guide to Cooperative Education.* 12 pages. Includes a list of 345 colleges with cooperative education programs.

- *Where Do You Plan to Be Five Years after You Graduate from College?* 4 pages. Applicable to college freshmen. Features career success stories from outstanding graduates, as well as information about professional employment opportunities.

557
NATIONAL COMMITTEE ON PAY EQUITY
1126 16th Street NW
Suite 411
Washington, DC 20036
202-331-7343
Fax: 202-331-7406
ncpe@essential.org

For a complete publications and materials list and order form, call, write, or send an e-mail request.

- *Background on the Wage Gap.* ($2) 5 pages. Clarifies some common misconceptions about the wage gap and provides information about earnings by age, education, sex, and race/ethnicity.

- *Pay Equity Bibliography and Resource List.* ($4) 16 pages. More than 100 citations of books, articles, and other publications on pay equity.

- *Bargaining for Pay Equity: A Strategy Manual.* ($9) 120 pages. A collection of stories of union struggles for pay equity. Serves as a how-to manual for developing winning pay equity campaigns.

- *Job Evaluation: A Tool for Pay Equity.* ($7) A basic introduction to job evaluations. Includes definitions, brief descriptions of different types of systems, and suggestions on working with consultants.

- *Closing the Wage Gap: An International Perspective.* ($2) 16 pages. An overview of pay equity policies and activity in more than 20 international jurisdictions.

- *Fair Pay Action Kit.* ($10) 48 pages. Contains fact sheets, background information on pay equity, and suggestions for organizing to eliminate sex- and race-based wage discrimination.

The following factsheets (1995-1997) are available:

- *Questions & Answers on Pay Equity.*

- *The Wage Gap: 1995.*

- *Information on the Fair Pay Act.*

- *The Contingent Workforce.*

- *Work & Retirement.*

- *Women, Family, Future Trends: A Selective Research Overview.*

558
NATIONAL COMMUNICATION ASSOCIATION
5105 Backlick Road
Building F
Annandale, VA 22003
703-750-0533
Fax: 703-914-9471
http://www.scassn.org

- *Pathways to Careers in Communication.* ($2) 18 pages. Looks at different fields entered by people with a communication degree, as well as the outlook and salary for a number of positions.

- *Careers in Communication.* A colorful poster listing a variety of careers in communication, such as speech writer, anchorperson, and politician.

- *Speaking, Listening and Media Literacy Standards for K through 12 Education.* ($2.50) 8 pages. Concentrates on speaking, listening, and media literacy standards; their importance; the criteria for selecting them; and their implementation.

- *Speaking & Listening Competencies.* ($3.50) 12 pages. Assists elementary schools in developing and evaluating oral communication programs by identifying essential speaking and listening skills for elementary school children.

559
NATIONAL COMMUNITY EDUCATION ASSOCIATION
3929 Old Lee Highway
Suite 91-A
Fairfax, VA 22030-2401
703-359-8973
Fax: 703-359-0972
ncea@ncea.com

- *Guide to Community Education Resources.* 27 pages. Lists community education resources by state, national community education agencies and special projects, and international community education agencies and centers. Describes community education.

560
NATIONAL CONFERENCE OF EDITORIAL WRITERS
6223 Executive Boulevard
Rockville, MD 20852-3906
301-984-3015
http://www.ncew.org/

- *So You Want to Know about Editorial Writing: Some Questions and Answers...* 6 pages. SASE business-size. Describes how to become an editorial writer, what editorial writers do, and how to prepare for an editorial writing career.

561
NATIONAL CONSORTIUM FOR GRADUATE DEGREES FOR MINORITIES IN ENGINEERING AND SCIENCE, INC.
PO Box 537
Notre Dame, IN 46556
219-631-7771
Fax: 219-297-1486
http://www.nd.edu/~gem/

- *Making the Grade in Graduate School: Survival Strategy 101.* ($2.50)

- *Minority Student Graduate School Information Kit.* ($3.50)

- *Successfully Negotiating the Graduate School Process: A Guide for Minority Students.* ($2)

- *Your Internship Is As Good As You Make It: A Practical Guide to Student Internships.* ($2)

562
NATIONAL COSMETOLOGY ASSOCIATION, INC.
3510 Olive Street
St. Louis, MO 63103
800-527-1683 or 314-534-7980
Fax: 314-534-8618
nca-now@primary.net
http://www.nca-now.com

- *Barbers and Cosmetologists.* 6 pages. Describes the nature of the work, working conditions, employment outlook, training and qualifications, and earnings.

- *Cosmetology: The Career of a Lifetime.* 2 pages.

563
NATIONAL COUNCIL FOR ACCREDITATION OF TEACHER EDUCATION
2010 Massachusetts Avenue NW
Suite 500
Washington, DC 20036-1023
202-466-7496
Fax: 202-296-6620
http://www.ncate.org

- *List of Professionally Accredited Schools, Colleges, and Departments of Education.* 4 pages. Contains the names of institutions whose professional education units (schools, departments, or colleges of education) or programs have been accredited by NCATE.

- *Professionally Accredited Non-Traditional Routes to Teaching.* 8 pages. Lists accredited schools of education that offer teacher training to students with a bachelor's degree.

- *Quality Assurance for the Teaching Profession.* 16 pages. Describes the NCATE, necessary skills for teaching, and professional accreditation.

564
NATIONAL COUNCIL OF LA RAZA
810 First Street NE
Suite 300
Washington, DC 20002
202-785-1670

- *Hispanics in the Labor Force: A Chartbook.* ($3) Provides information on 13 occupational categories.

565
NATIONAL COUNCIL OF TEACHERS OF ENGLISH
1111 West Kenyon Road
Urbana, IL 61801-1096
800-369-6283 or 217-328-3870
Fax: 217-328-0977
http://www.ncte.org

Career Packet includes:

- *Average Annual Salaries of Classroom Teachers.* 3 pages.

- *The College Major in English and English Education.* 4 pages. Suggestions on how English majors can better market (and prepare) themselves for the real world.

- *Bibliography of Books for Beginning Teachers' Professional Libraries.* 3 pages.

- *Careers for English Majors: Where Are They and How Can Departments Help?* 4 pages. Discusses various careers for English majors and assistance in seeking them.

- *Careers for Liberal Arts Majors.* 4 pages. Lists resources from ERIC and other sources.

- *The College Board: Guide to 150 Popular College Majors.* 5 pages. Discusses preparation programs, postgraduate certification, opportunities in teaching, and exploration of teaching.

- *Don't Leave Teaching-Examine Other Teaching Related Careers.* 3 pages. Suggestions for teaching careers outside the typical classroom.

- *Pointers for Teachers.* 1 page. Lists 17 personality questions for teachers to consider.

- *ERIC Clearinghouse on Adult, Career, and Vocational Information.* Digests 37 and 46, 5 pages. Looks at jobs of the future and education for high-technology jobs.

- *Technical Writing As a Career.* 5 pages. Provides an overview of technical writing as a career and information that a teacher can use to counsel students about the field. Information is divided into origins, job opportunities, salaries, training and experience, and types of work available.

- *Training.* 1 page. Describes training, program length, and transfer credits for various degree levels.

- *What Can You Do with an English Major?* 4 pages. Discusses the connection between majoring in English and working in the real world from several perspectives.

- *NCTE Affiliates.* 2 pages. Lists state, regional, and local affiliates of NCTE.

566
NATIONAL COUNCIL OF TEACHERS OF MATHEMATICS
1906 Association Drive
Reston, VA 20191
800-235-7566 (orders only) or 703-620-9840
Fax: 800-220-8483 (fax on demand) or 703-476-2970
orders@nctm.org
http://www.nctm.org

Career Information Packet includes:

- *Career Information in the Mathematical Sciences: A Resource Guide.* 25 pages.

- *Careers, Grants, Scholarships: A Resource Guide.* 2 pages.

- *Shape the Future: A Career as a Mathematics Teacher.*

- *State Licensing Agencies.* 1 page.

- *Going the Alternate Route.* 1 page.

- *Tech Prep.* 2 pages. Contains background information and resources.

- *Jobs Online.* 4 pages. Available at NCTM's web site.

567

NATIONAL COUNCIL OF THE CHURCHES OF CHRIST IN THE USA
Professional Church Leadership
475 Riverside Drive
Room 812
New York, NY 10115
212-870-2144

- *List of Seminaries,* from the *Yearbook of American and Canadian Churches.* 5 pages.

- *Ministry Options.* 8 pages. Lists church-related vocations, applicable personality types, and work-setting preferences.

- *What Are You Going to Do with the Rest of Your Life?* 8 pages. Discusses how to choose your life work, describes what church leaders do, and offers suggestions for further reading.

568

NATIONAL COUNCIL ON REHABILITATION
c/o Garth Eldredge
Department of Special Education and Rehabilitation
Utah State University
Logan, UT 84322-2890

- *The Growing Profession of Rehabilitation Counseling.*

- *Rewarding Opportunities in Rehabilitation Counseling.*

569

NATIONAL COURT REPORTERS ASSOCIATION
Membership and Marketing Department
8224 Old Courthouse Road
Vienna, VA 22182-3808
800-272-NCRA
Fax: 703-556-6291
703-556-6289 (TDD)
http://www.ncraonline.org

- *Court Reporting: It's Your Move.* 8 pages. Provides a basic overview of the field.

- *What Career Combines...* Includes general information about the field and the training required.

- *NCRA List of Approved Court Reporter Education Programs.* Lists programs and selected articles describing the field.

570

NATIONAL FEDERATION OF LICENSED PRACTICAL NURSES, INC.
1418 Aversboro Road
Garner, NC 27529
919-779-0046
Fax: 919-779-5642
http://www.nflpm.com

- *A Profile of Practical Nursing.* 6 pages. Describes what LPNs actually do, where they work, and what they earn. Also discusses the education required, school selection, licensure, continuing education, and general information about NFLPN.

571

NATIONAL FEDERATION OF MUSIC CLUBS
1336 North Delaware Street
Indianapolis, IN 46202
317-638-4003

Competition and Awards Chart. ($1). Lists prizes in various categories of music

572

NATIONAL FEDERATION OF THE BLIND
Job Opportunities for the Blind (JOB)
1800 Johnson Street
Baltimore, MD 21230
800-638-7518 (12:30-5:00 p.m. EST)
or 410-659-9314
http://www.nfb.org

The following are some of the many publications distributed free to the legally blind (others are available by writing or calling for a JOB order form).

- *JOB Sample Package.* Contains the latest issue of *JOB Recorded Bulletin,* the latest *JOB National Seminar* (cassette tapes), the JOB Applicant Registration Form, the JOB Publication Order Form and A List of Jobs Found by JOB Applicants.

- *Assessing Your Job Readiness: Remarks by Dick Rapages.* Cassette tape.

- *What's a Job Seeker to Do?* Practical tips on finding a job.

- *Focus on Success by Gary Wunder.* Cassette tape.

- *Getting Chosen: The Job Interview and Before.* Cassette tape.

- *Job Seeking Skills Handbook.* Cassette tapes.

- *Merchandising Your Job Talents.* Cassette tape.

- *Networking.* Cassette tape.

- *Blind Americans at Work National Seminars.* Cassette tapes. Taped annual seminars (1993 to date) featuring national speakers on a variety of topics for the blind.

- *CAREERS: Job Searching and Success.* An annotated bibliography of career information.

- *Math and Computer Jobs Held by Blind Persons.* An annotated bibliography of interviews in JOB bulletins (1992 to date).

- *Checklist for Going into Business.* Small Business Administration braille pamphlet.

- *Some Ideas for Persons Considering the Establishment of a Small Business.* Cassette tape.

- *Making Points When an Interviewer Asks Tough Questions.* Print and cassette tape. Recommended for counselors and teachers.

- *A Blind Co-Worker! What Do I Do Now?* 4 pages. Tips for worried co-workers.

- *If Blindness Comes.* 248 pages. Provides information about where to get things and how to learn new techniques for a person faced with blindness.

- *Making Hay.* 116 pages. A collection of short stories depicting experiences and lives of people.

573
NATIONAL FFA ORGANIZATION
National FFA Center
5632 Mt. Vernon Memorial Highway
PO Box 15160
Alexandria, VA 22309-0160
703-780-5600
Fax: 800-366-6556
http://www.ffa.org

- *Agriculture: An Industry Too Big to Ignore.* ($1.50) 4 pages. Describes the numerous career opportunities in agriculture available to youth.

- *Discovering an Agricultural Biotechnology Career That May Be for You.* ($1.50) 4 pages. Discusses necessary skills for a career in agricultural biotechnology.

- *Open Door.* ($1.40) 14 pages. Discusses agricultural career opportunities.

- *Think about It.* ($.50) 8 pages. Highlights more than 200 agricultural careers.

574
NATIONAL FUNERAL DIRECTORS ASSOCIATION
11121 West Oklahoma Avenue
Milwaukee, WI 53227-4096
414-541-2500
Fax: 414-541-1909
http://www.nfda.org

- *Are You Interested in: Helping Others? The Human Biological Sciences? Community Involvement? A Business Environment? Have You Considered Funeral Service?* 6 pages. Describes the duties and responsibilities, educational requirements, and career opportunities of a funeral service professional. Includes a list of mortuary science programs.

- *Schools of Mortuary Science.* 4 pages. Lists of ABSFE accredited mortuary colleges and programs.

- *State Funeral Service Boards and Licensing Requirements.* 7 pages. Lists by state the type of license required, educational and apprenticeship requirements, and state board addresses.

- *Funeral Service Scholarships.* 7 pages. Lists scholarships available for funeral service students.

575
NATIONAL HEALTH COUNCIL
1730 M Street NW
Suite 500
Washington, DC 20036-4505
202-785-3910
Fax: 202-785-5923

- *200 Ways to Put Your Talent to Work in the Health Field.* ($6) 35 pages. Lists job descriptions and educational requirements for health professions ranging from art therapists and clinical chemists to nurse practitioners and physicians. Also lists sources of information on training schools and financial aid programs for health professions.

576
NATIONAL INSTITUTE OF GOVERNMENTAL PURCHASING, INC.
11800 Sunrise Valley Drive
Suite 1050
Reston, VA 22091-9733
703-715-9400

- *Business Occupations: Purchasing Agents.* 2 pages.

577
NATIONAL JOB CORPS ALUMNI ASSOCIATION
607 14th Street NW
Suite 610
Washington, DC 20005
800-733-JOBS

- *The Faces of Job Corps.* 6 pages. Includes information on the skills needed, life on campus, and job training.

578
NATIONAL MANAGEMENT ASSOCIATION
2210 Arbor Boulevard
Dayton, OH 45439
937-294-0421
Fax: 937-294-2374
http://www.cris.com/~nmal/index.shtml

- *Management as a Career.* 6 pages. Describes the roles and duties of managers, careers in the field, and keys to success.

579
NATIONAL MUSEUM OF NATURAL HISTORY
Anthropology Outreach Office
NHB, MRC 112, Smithsonian Institution
Washington, DC 20560
202-357-1592
kaupages.ann@nmnh.si.edu

- *Summer Fieldwork Opportunities.* 5 pages. Suggests ways teachers, students, and the general public can become personally involved in the field of anthropology through field schools and research organizations.

- *Smithsonian Programs.* 1 page. Information on Smithsonian programs for research grants, fellowships, internships, and other visiting faculty appointments.

- *Smithsonian Opportunities.* 1 page. Information on job opportunities, volunteer opportunities, and internships at the Smithsonian Institution.

- *Anthropological Materials Available from the Smithsonian Institution.* 10 pages.

580
NATIONAL MUSEUM OF NATURAL HISTORY
Department of Vertebrate Zoology
Room 369, MRC 109, Smithsonian Institution
Washington, DC 20560
202-357-2740

- *Sources for Information on Careers in Biology, Conservation, and Oceanography.* 4 pages.

581
NATIONAL OCEANIC AND ATMOSPHERIC ADMINISTRATION
Office of Public Affairs
1315 East-West Highway
Silver Spring, MD 20910
301-713-0677 (Employee Information Line)
http://www.rdc.noaa.gov
or, http://www.usajobs.opm.gov

Call for NOAA's employee information line or visit NOAA's web site for current job opportunities (updated weekly).

582
NATIONAL PARALEGAL ASSOCIATION
PO Box 406
Solebury, PA 18963-0406
215-297-8333

- *Local Paralegal Club Directory.* ($5) Lists over 200 local paralegal clubs.

- *Paralegal Information Packet.* SASE $.75 postage. Contains information about the profession.

- *Paralegal Schools: State Listings.* ($2.50 each; $3.50 each for New York and California) Each state listing includes universities, vocational schools, proprietary institutions, community colleges, and correspondence schools; ABA-approved programs are earmarked.

583
NATIONAL PARK SERVICE
U.S. Department of the Interior
Public Information Office
PO Box 37127
Washington, DC 20013-7127
202-208-5228
http://info.er.usgs.gov/doi/avads/index.html

- *Careers in National Park Service.* 20 pages. Contains information about the National Park Service; describes career opportunities in the field; covers employment benefits and the application and hiring process; and lists Federal job information/testing offices.

584
NATIONAL PEST CONTROL ASSOCIATION
8100 Oak Street
Dunn Loring, VA 22027
703-573-8330

- *The Structural Pest Control Industry.* 4 pages.

585
NATIONAL PRESS PHOTOGRAPHERS ASSOCIATION, INC.
3200 Croasdaile Drive
Suite 306
Durham, NC 27705
919-383-7246

Information Packet includes:

- *Careers in News Photography.* 4 pages. Addresses the necessary skills, personal attributes, required education, employment opportunities, and employment outlook.

- *National Press Photographers Association.* 12 pages. Describes NPPA, member benefits, activities, and education and student programs.

- *NPPA Membership Application.*

586
NATIONAL RECREATION AND PARK ASSOCIATION
22377 Belmont Ridge Road
Ashburn, VA 20148
703-858-0784
http://www.nrpa.org

- *About Therapeutic Recreation.* 14 pages. Suitable for use as an introductory informational handout.

- *Consider a Career in Therapeutic Recreation.* 6 pages. Discusses the role of professionals, employment opportunities, and professional resources. Suitable for high schools, colleges, universities, and therapeutic recreation agencies.

- *Preparing for a Career in Therapeutic Recreation.* ($7.50) 21 pages. Describes the continuum of service within therapeutic recreation and standards for certification. Lists colleges and universities offering therapeutic recreation programs, including those accredited by the NRPA/AALR Council on Accreditation.

587
NATIONAL REHABILITATION COUNSELING ASSOCIATION
8807 Sudley Road
Suite 102
Manassas, VA 20110-4719
Fax: 703-361-2489
http://www.ed.wright.edu/cehs/nrca/nrcahome.html

- *The Growing Profession of Rehabilitation Counseling.* 13 pages. Analyzes the demand for rehabilitation counseling services, as well as the roles and responsibilities, the scope of services, academic preparation, financial assistance, certification and licensure, salary, and career and employment opportunities.

588
NATIONAL RESEARCH COUNCIL
Fellowship Office
2101 Constitution Avenue NW
Washington, DC 20418
202-334-2000
http://felowships.nas.edu

- *Ford Foundation Postdoctoral Fellowships for Minorities.* 4 pages.

- *Ford Foundation Predoctoral and Dissertation Fellowships for Minorities.* 6 pages.

- *Howard Hughes Medical Institute Predoctoral Fellowships in Biological Sciences.* 12 pages.

- *United States Department of Energy Integrated Manufacturing Predoctoral Fellowships.* 4 pages.

- *NASA Administrators Fellowship Program.* 6 pages.

- *Humanities Doctorates in the United States.* Useful information, attractively presented.

589
NATIONAL RETAIL FEDERATION
325 7th Street
Suite 1000
Washington, DC 20004
800-NRF-HOW2 or 202-783-7941
http://www.nrf.com

- *Careers in Retailing.* 11pages. Covers many retailing topics, including opportunities available and career preparation. Also lists colleges and universities offering degrees in retailing, retail management, retail merchandising, retail marketing, retail sales, and fashion/apparel merchandising.

590
NATIONAL RIFLE ASSOCIATION OF AMERICA
Hunter Services Division
1600 Rhode Island Avenue NW
Washington, DC 20036-3268
202-828-6029

- *A Wildlife Conservation Career for You.*

591
NATIONAL SAFETY COUNCIL
Publications Marketing Department
PO Box 558
Itasca, IL 60143-0558
800-621-3433 or 708-285-1121
Fax: 630-285-1315
http://www.nsc.org

- *Evaluating Your Workplace: Hands and Arms-Stretching and Toning.* ($6.15) 15 pages.

- *Evaluating Your Workplace: Lifting.* ($6.15) 10 pages.

- *Emergency First Aid Guide.* 64 pages. ($5.50)

592
NATIONAL SCHOLARSHIP TRUST FUND OF THE GRAPHIC ARTS
200 Deer Run Road
Sewickley, PA 15143
412-741-6860
Fax: 412-741-2311
http://www.gatf.lm.com

- *Directory of Technical Schools, Colleges, and Universities Offering Courses in Graphic Communications.* 90 pages. Spans all degree levels for technology, management, and education.

- *A Counselor's Guide: Careers in Graphic Communications.* 13 pages.

- *Scholarship Application For National Scholarship Trust Fund.* Suitable for graphics arts students.

593
NATIONAL SCHOOL TRANSPORTATION ASSOCIATION
PO Box 2639
Springfield, VA 22152-0639

- *Career Information Packet.*

594
NATIONAL SCIENCE FOUNDATION
Forms and Publications Unit
4201 Wilson Boulevard
Arlington, VA 22230
703-306-1234
703-306-0890 (TDD)
info@nsf.gov
http://www.nsf.gov/

- *Shaping the Future: New Expectations for Undergraduate Education in Science, Mathematics, Engineering, and Technology.*

- *Gaining the Competitive Edge.* Addresses critical issues in science and engineering technician education.

595
NATIONAL SCIENCE TEACHERS ASSOCIATION
1840 Wilson Boulevard
Arlington, Virginia 22201-3000
703-243-7100
http://www. nsta.org

- *You Can Teach Science.* Available in an elementary version and an adult version. Highlights the teaching profession, salaries, and related topics.

596
NATIONAL SOCIETY OF ACCOUNTANTS
1010 North Fairfax Street
Alexandria, VA 22314-1574
703-549-6400
Fax: 703-549-2984
http://www.nsacct.org

Career Information Packet includes:

- *A Special Opportunity in Accounting for You.* 6 pages. Includes information on small business practice and entering the field.

- *THE NSPA Annual Scholarship Awards.* 6 pages.

- *Accountants and Auditors.* 2 pages. Reprint from the *Occupational Outlook Handbook.*

597
NATIONAL SOCIETY OF GENETIC COUNSELORS, INC.
233 Canterbury Drive
Wallingford, PA 19086-6617

- *Is a Career in Genetic Counseling in Your Future?*

598
NATIONAL SPELEOLOGICAL SOCIETY
2813 Cave Avenue
Huntsville, AL 35810-4431
205-852-1300
Fax: 205-851-9241
http://www.caves.org

- *Caving Basics.* ($10) 50 pages. Covers the basics of caving and the equipment required.

599
NATIONAL STUDENT NURSES' ASSOCIATION, INC.
555 West 57th Street
Suite 1327
New York, NY 10019
212-581-2211
http://www.nsna.org

- *Is Nursing for You?* 4 pages. Describes the various specialties, accreditation, how to choose a degree program, and personal requirements.

600
NATIONAL TECHNICAL ASSOCIATION
PO Box 7045
Washington, DC 20032-7045
202-829-6100

- *Careers in Science and Technology.* 98 pages.

601
NATIONAL THERAPEUTIC RECREATION SOCIETY
22377 Belmont Ridge Road
Ashburn, VA 20148
800-626-6772
ntrsnrpa@aol.com
http://www.nrpa.org

- *About Therapeutic Recreation.* 16 pages.

- *Consider a Career in Therapeutic Recreation.* 6 pages. Discusses various settings and career opportunities.

- *Prep for a Career in Therapeutic Recreation.* ($7.50) Details therapeutic recreation careers.

602
NATIONAL TOURISM FOUNDATION, INC.
546 East Main Street
PO Box 3071
Lexington, KY 40596-3071
800-682-8886 or 606-226-4251
Fax: 606-226-4414
http://www.ntaonline.com

- *Internship List.* 30 pages. Listing by state of tour operator, tour supplier, and destination marketing organization internship programs.

- *Schools List.* 71 pages. Alphabetical list by state or province of U.S. and Canadian certificate programs, as well as institutions with associate, bachelor's, master's, and doctoral degree programs in travel/tourism.

- *Scholarships.* 4 pages. Annual list of the general requirements and application information for the foundation's nearly 30 scholarships, grants, and awards.

- *Tour Operators, Tour Managers, and Guides.* 8 pages. Describes the work performed in each position, working conditions, hours and earnings, education and training, certification, personal qualifications, employment outlook, entry methods and advancement, related occupations, and sources of additional information.

- *Tour Managers, Escorts and Guides.* 1 page. A partial list of colleges, universities, and proprietary schools offering courses in tour guiding or escorting.

603
NATIONAL TRAINING FUND FOR THE SHEET METAL AND AIR CONDITIONING INDUSTRY
Edward F. Carlough Plaza
601 North Fairfax Street
Suite 240
Alexandria, VA 22314

- *Careers in Sheet Metal.* 24 pages.

604
NATIONAL TRAPPERS ASSOCIATION
PO Box 3667
Bloomington, IL 61702
309-829-2422
Fax: 309-829-7615
http://www.nationaltrappers.com

- *NTA Trapping Handbook.* ($8 plus shipping) 206 pages. Contains an introduction to trapping in the United States and covers furbearer management objectives, laws, responsibilities, harvesting, and safety. Special rate available for libraries.

605
NATURE CONSERVANCY
1815 North Lynn Street
Arlington, VA 22209
703-841-5300
Fax: 703-841-7292
http://www.tnc.org

- *Careers at the Nature Conservancy.* 7 pages. Discusses career areas and how to apply for employment opportunities.

- *The Nature Conservancy Nation-Wide Internships/Short Term Positions.* 20 pages. Lists and describes typical internships and short-term positions that recur annually.

606
NAVY OPPORTUNITY INFORMATION CENTER
U.S. Department of the Navy
PO Box 9406
Gaithersburg, MD 20898-6006

- *Today's Navy.* 25 pages. Explores various career opportunities with the U.S. Navy. Call or visit your local Navy recruiter for a copy.

607
NAVY RECRUITING COMMAND
U.S. Department of the Navy
4015 Wilson Boulevard
Arlington, VA 22203
800-USA-NAVY

- *Navy Campus.* 8 pages.

- *The Navy College Fund Program.* 6 pages.

- *The Navy Experience.* 12 pages.

- *Navy: How You Can Join.* 28 pages.

- *Navy-Marine Corps ROTC College Scholarship Bulletin.* 20 pages.

- *Today's Navy.* 24 pages.

- *Navy Officer Dental Corps.* 6 pages.

- *Navy Officer Medical Corps.* 13 pages.

- *Navy Officer Medical Service Corps.* 16 pages.

- *Navy Officer Nurse Corps.* 12 pages.

608
NEDA (NATIONAL ELECTRONIC DISTRIBUTORS ASSOCIATION) EDUCATION FOUNDATION
35 East Wacker Drive
Suite 1100
Chicago, IL 60601

312-558-9114
Fax: 312-558-1069
http://www.nedassoc.org

- *Careers in Electronic Distribution.* ($1) 4 pages. Discusses career opportunities in the field.

609
NELLIE MAE
50 Braintree Hill Park
Braintree, MA 02184
800-634-9308
http://www.nelliemae.org

- *Steps to Success-A Comprehensive Guide to Preparing and Paying for College: For High School Students and Their Parents.* 21 pages. Nellie Mae is the largest non-profit provider of student loan funds in the country. This booklet provides a helpful financial aid instructional timeline for students and their parents, as well as financial aid guidelines, types of financial aid, and helpful telephone numbers.

610
NEVADA DEPARTMENT OF EMPLOYMENT, TRAINING AND REHABILITATION
Research and Analysis Bureau
Labor Market Information Unit
500 East Third Street
Carson City, NV 89713
702-687-4550
Fax: 702-687-1063
http://www.state.nv.us/detr/detr.html

- *Employment Guide: Nevada Job Finding Techniques.* 66 pages. Provides students and other job seekers with steps to be taken in preparing for employment; in-depth analysis on seeking jobs, including how to complete a resume and application form; and advice on employment testing job interviews.

611
NEW HAMPSHIRE DEPARTMENT OF EMPLOYMENT SECURITY
Economic and Labor Market Information Bureau
32 South Main Street
Concord, NH 03301-4857
603-228-4124
Fax: 603-228-4172
http://www.nhes.state.nh.us

- *How to Look for a Job.* 12 pages. Includes a checklist and information on techniques and time management for job searching.

- *Job Search Letters.* 12 pages. Offers tips on writing cover letters and letters of application.

- *Job Interviewing Techniques.* 20 pages. Suggests how to organize and prepare for an interview and effectively present yourself and your skills.

- *Job Applications.* 12 pages. Includes tips for completing a job application, information on state applications, and sample application forms.

- *Preparing a Resume.* 12 pages. Helpful tips on resumes.

- *Economic Conditions in New Hampshire.* 8 pages. A monthly report discussing economic conditions in New Hampshire.

- *New Hampshire Employment Projections by Industry and Occupation 1994 to 2005.* 86 pages. Includes the results of a long-term forecast of employment in New Hampshire in the year 2005.

- *New Hampshire Job Outlook and Locator Occupation by Industry: Base Year 1994 to Projected Year 2005.* 274 pages. Lists the primary industries providing employment for occupational categories in New Hampshire.

- *A User's Guide to Labor Market Information.* 26 pages. Provides labor market information and lists available publications.

- *New Hampshire Works.* 10 pages. Information on the electronic bulletin board, which provides a meeting place for job seekers and employers.

612
NEW HAMPSHIRE OCCUPATIONAL INFORMATION COORDINATING COMMITTEE
64 Old Suncook Road
Concord, NH 03301
603-228-3349
Fax: 603-228-3209
soiccnh@aol.com
http://www.state.nh.us/soicchp.htm

- *New Hampshire JOB NOTES.* ($1) 36 pages. A career tabloid providing varied and useful career information.

- *H.S. Graduate v. H.S. Dropout.* A bookmark showing employment and financial differences of a high school graduate compared with a high school dropout.

613
NEW JERSEY DEPARTMENT OF LABOR
Division of Labor Market and Demographic Research
CN 388, 5th Floor
Trenton, NJ 08625-0388
609-984-2593
http://www.wnjpin.state.nj.us

- *Industry and Occupational Employment Projections for New Jersey: 1994 to 2005.* ($5)

614
NEW JERSEY OCCUPATIONAL INFORMATION COORDINATING COMMITTEE
Labor and Industry Building
CN 057, 5th Floor
Trenton, NJ 08625-0057
609-292-2682
Fax: 609-292-6692
http://wnjpin.state.nj.us/onestopcareercenter/soicc

- *Labor Demand Occupations.* ($5) 45 pages.

615
NEW MEXICO DEPARTMENT OF LABOR
Economic Research and Analysis Bureau
PO Box 1928
Albuquerque, NM 87103
505-841-8455
http://www.state.nm.us/dol

- *Look to the Future.* 6 pages. Provides basic information for middle school youth. Sections include Chart Your Goals, Chart Your Destination, What Courses Should You Take? and What Skills Do You Need?

- *Area Job Market Flyers.* 6 pages. Provide job hunting information and tips. Available for the state of New Mexico and the cities of Albuquerque, Santa Fe, and Las Cruces.

- *Industries-Companies-Occupations.* 17 pages. Lists the occupations employed by local companies; available for Albuquerque, Santa Fe, and Las Cruces.

- *New Mexico Jobs for Graduates.* 55 pages. For graduates of universities, community colleges, technical institutes, and junior colleges; provides direction to in-state graduates seeking employment in their fields and shows hiring plans for 153 of New Mexico's largest employers.

- *Large Employers in New Mexico by County.* 80 pages. Lists contact information for employers of 25 or more workers by county, excluding Bernalillo County (the Albuquerque area).

- *Large Employers in the Albuquerque Area.* Lists contact information for employers of 50 or more workers in the Bernalillo County area.

- *New Mexico 2005 Job Outlook—in Brief.* 3 pages. Presents information about the New Mexico job market and economy into the next century. Contains graphs and tables detailing the industries and occupations that will have an impact on the state's economic outlook through the year 2005.

- *New Mexico 2005, Economic Projections.* 86 pages. Designed to meet the needs of students, counselors, and job seekers for information about career opportunities in New Mexico. Includes information on nearly 600 occupations, as well as data and analysis of occupational employment from 1993 to 2005.

- *Wage Surveys.* Shows entry-level, average, and high and low wage rates for various cities and areas in the state, including Albuquerque, Las Cruces, Santa Fe, and the Combined Metro Area (Albuquerque, Santa Fe, and Las Cruces).

616

NEW MEXICO STATE OCCUPATIONAL INFORMATION COORDINATING COMMITTEE
PO Box 1928
Albuquerque, NM 87103
505-841-8455
Fax: 505-841-9007

- *New Mexico Labor Market Information Directory.* 10 pages. Lists the free publications available through the New Mexico Department of Labor.

- *Focus on the Future.* 20 pages. Provides basic information for young people just entering the work force on the job search, application process, and interviews.

- *Job Hunter's Guide.* 32 pages. Topics covered include directing the job search, applications and resumes, cover letters, the interview, government jobs, vocational technical programs, selecting or changing careers, cost of living, the regional job market, large employers in New Mexico, and sources of information.

- *New Mexico's Job Hunter's Guide: Inside Edition.* 20 pages. Designed to help adult and youthful ex-offenders find employment in New Mexico. Answers questions and highlights specific programs.

- *New Mexico Veteran's Employment Guide.* 18 pages. Designed to help veterans find employment in New Mexico. Describes programs available and lists agencies and organizations that offer assistance to veterans.

- *Prospects: Career and Educational Opportunities in New Mexico.* 27 pages. An annual tabloid containing information about New Mexico's economy and job market.

- *Your Job...Will You Keep It...or Lose It?* 12 pages. In English or Spanish. Lists some of the ways you can lose your job or keep it.

- *New Mexico Jobs for Graduates.* 58 pages. Provides direction to in-state graduates seeking employment in their fields. Describes hiring plans for 153 of New Mexico's largest employers by occupation, general economic structure and outlook for the state, how to use the Internet to assist in job hunting (includes a sample list of employment related web sites), and how to prepare a resume and cover letter.

617

NEW WAYS TO WORK
785 Market Street
Suite 950
San Francisco, CA 94103

- *Looking for Work in San Francisco: A Bay Area Guide to Employment Resources.*

618

NEW YORK STATE DEPARTMENT OF LABOR
Division of Research Statistics
Publications Unit
Room 401
State Campus Building 12
Albany, NY 12240
518-457-1130
Fax: 518-457-3652
rs.pubs@dol.mailnet.state.ny.us
http://www.labor.state.ny.us

- *Occupational Guides, Tips For Choosing Your Future Career.* 6 pages. Contains 25 individual guides covering a range of careers, including but not limited to auto mechanic, child care worker, home health aide, loan & credit clerk, paralegal, police officer, and travel agent.

- *NYS Labor BBS Brochure.* Describes how to access and download computer files from its regional electronic bulletin board system. Files pertain to job openings, employment prospects, occupational wages, county profiles, labor laws, and other topics.

- *Median Wages by Occupation.* 9 pages. For individuals planning a career or considering a job change. Lists median weekly wage rate for selected occupations in the United States.

- *Is Your Resume a Dinosaur?* Describes how to reformat the traditional resume in order to make it compatible with the types of resume scanning software increasingly used by employers.

- *The Jobseeker.* Source of information for young jobseekers. Provides students with information on work skills, career selection, and job-seeking strategies.

- *Job Clips.* Supplement to the above publication. Gives overviews of 175 occupations.

- *Suggestions for Career Exploration and Jobseeking.* In English and Spanish. Offers advice on where to get help in looking for a job and describes how to go about a job search.

- *Vision, a Teenager's Guide to Career Development.* Introduces the subject of career exploration and discusses adjusting to a work environment and understanding the role work plays in a society.

- *What Next? The Road to a New Job.* Aims to assist unemployed workers by outlining job search strategies, offering advice on handling financial difficulties, and suggesting methods to reduce stress and improve mental and physical health. Not intended for youth.

- *Your Winning Edge.* Provides tips on how to prepare a resume; includes sample resumes.

- *LMI, A Tool for Making Sense of the World.* Explains what labor market information is and how it can be used to accomplish job and career-related goals.

Other career-related information and region-specific publications are available. Call or write for a publications order form. A wide range of materials is also available at the web site.

619
NEWSLETTER PUBLISHERS FOUNDATION
1501 Wilson Boulevard
Suite 509
Arlington, VA 22209
703-527-2333
Fax: 703-841-0629

- *Newsletter Career Guide.* 8 pages.

620
NEWSPAPER ASSOCIATION OF AMERICA FOUNDATION
The Newspaper Center
1921 Gallows Road
Suite 600
Vienna, VA 22182-3900
703-902-1600
Fax: 703-902-1735
http://www.naa.org

- *Newspaper—What's in It for Me? Your Complete Guide to Newspaper Careers.* 26 pages. Covers the various departments (advertising, circulation, etc.), highlights opportunities for minorities and women, discusses how to get started and find a job, and provides salary information.

- *Newspapers, Diversity & You.* 48 pages. Takes a look at diversity in the newspaper industry, the various roles of journalists, salaries, academic preparation, and job hunting tips. Lists scholarship and grant information, internship and special training programs, and recruiters.

621
NEWSPAPER GUILD
501 Third Street NW
Washington, DC 20001-2797
http://www.newsguild.org

- *Gentlefolk and Scholars of the Press.* 4 pages. Describes the history of how reporters organized.

- *Professional Specialty Occupations.* 11 pages. Covers the nature of the work, working conditions, training, job outlook, and earnings for a number of occupations in the field, including reporters.

622
NORTH AMERICAN ASSOCIATION FOR ENVIRONMENTAL EDUCATION
Publications Department
6840 State Road 718
Pleasant Hill, OH 45359-9705
jthoreen@igc.apc.org

- *List of Colleges and Universities with Programs Related to EE.* ($6 plus $3.95 shipping) 35 pages. Lists by state the names and addresses of colleges and universities offering environmental education programs.

623
NORTH AMERICAN STUDENTS OF COOPERATION
PO Box 7715
Ann Arbor, MI 48107
313-663-0889
Fax: 313-663-5072
http://www.umich.edu/~nasco

- *Guide to Cooperative Careers.* ($3) 30 pages. Analyzes the many opportunities in producer-owned, worker-owned, consumer-owned, and other cooperatives.

- *Starting Out Right: Guidelines for Organizing a New Retail Cooperative.* ($5) 79 pages.

- *Twelve Challenges: Guidelines for Developing Food Co-ops in the Inner City.* ($3) 25 pages.

624
NORTHEASTERN STATE UNIVERSITY
Center for Tribal Studies
Tahlequah, OK 74464
918-456-5511 ext. 4350
Fax: 918-458-2073

- *Scholarships for American Indian Students.* ($10) 76 pages. Lists scholarships available to American Indians and contact information by subject matter e.g., education, medicine/health-related fields, art/literature/library/liberal arts, science/math/engineering/computer science).

625
THE OCEANOGRAPHY SOCIETY
4052 Timber Ridge Drive
Virginia Beach, Virginia 23455-7017
757-464-0131

- *Careers in Oceanography and Marine-Related Fields.*

626
OCTAMERON ASSOCIATES
PO Box 2748
Alexandria, VA 22301
Fax: 703-836-5650
http://www.octameron.com

For the following publications, postage equals five percent of the total order and handling is $3. Write for a catalog.

- *College.Edu: On-Line Resources for the Cyber-Savvy Student.* ($8) 108 pages. Provides an overview of Internet basics and useful sites on financial aid and admission, including bulletin boards and newsgroups.

- *Campus Daze: Easing the Transition from High School to College.* ($5) 40 pages. Contains anecdotes and practical advice. Describes what to expect and how to minimize any difficulties.

- *The Winning Edge: The Student Athlete's Guide to College Sports.* ($8) 144 pages. For all students interested in college athletics. Shows students how to use their athletic skills to increase their chances for financial aid and admission at the schools of their choice. Practical advice from coaches, information on scholarship opportunities, and a summary of NCAA rules and regulations.

- *College Opportunities for Students with Learning Differences.* ($5) 44 pages. Advises LD students on what questions to ask when selecting a school, how to prepare for a more rigorous academic schedule, and how and when to get special assistance. This book does not deal with physical handicaps, nor does it describe specific LD programs.

- *Don't Miss Out: The Ambitious Student's Guide to Financial Aid.* ($8) 144 pages. A how-to guide for parents and students. Explains how to lower their expected contribution to college costs; get the most money possible from federal, state, and collegiate sources; and develop short- and long-range planning strategies.

- *The A's and B's of Academic Scholarships.* ($7.50) 168 pages. Lists about 100,000 scholarships at 1,200 schools in the United States. Includes the names of awards, amounts, eligibility criteria, renewability options, and application deadlines.

- *Loans and Grants From Uncle Sam: Am I Eligible and for How Much?* ($6) 72 pages. Contains simple explanations and handy worksheets to help readers determine amount of federal student aid, the difference between lenders, and repayment options.

- *SAT Savvy: Last Minute Tips and Strategies.* ($6) 88 pages. Helps students build their test-taking confidence, brush up on math and verbal skills, and refine logic and reasoning techniques.

- *Earn & Learn: The Competitive Guide to Cooperative Education* ($5) 36 pages. Shows how to link up with cooperative education programs at more than 765 colleges in all 50 states.

- *College Match: A Blueprint for Choosing the Best School for You!* ($8) 132 pages. Combines easy-to-use worksheets with loads of practical advice to give students control over the entire college admission process.

- *Do-It Write: How to Prepare a Great College Application.* ($5) 40 pages. Shows students how to get started and gives hints for writing essays. Answers questions about the rest of the application process.

- *Campus Pursuit: Making the Most of Your Visit and Interview* ($5) 32 pages. Discusses what to look for during campus visits and how to survive interviews.

- *Our Counseling Service.* Describes a range of services helpful in finding money for college, selecting a college, and applying to college.

627
OFFICE FOR BASEBALL UMPIRE DEVELOPMENT
Major League Baseball Umpire Development Program
PO Box A
201 Bayshore Drive SE
St. Petersburg, FL 33731
813-823-1286
Fax: 813-823-7212
http://www.minorleaguebaseball.com/udp/

- *Making the Call: Becoming a Professional Baseball Umpire.* 6 pages. Describes the training, work, and compensation of professional baseball umpires.

628

OFFICE OF JOB CORPS
Employment and Training Administration
U.S. Department of Labor
200 Constitution Avenue NW
Room N4510
Washington, DC 20210
202-219-8550
Fax: 202-219-5183
http://www.jobcorp.org

- *Train for Skills and Success: A Directory of Job Corps Centers and Courses.* 66 pages. Lists vocational courses at 112 Job Corp centers nationwide.

629

OHIO SEA GRANT COLLEGE PROGRAM
Ohio State University1314 Kinnear Road
Columbus, OH 43212-1194
614-292-8949
Fax: 614-292-4364
http://www.ohiosg.osc.edu/ohioseagrant

- *Is Aquaculture for You?* 2 pages. Describes aquaculture and includes a checklist to help determine whether an aquaculture career is for you.

- *Marine-Related Careers: Options and Resources.* (FS-012) 2 pages. Lists marine career categories and job titles and other contact sources.

630

OKLAHOMA DEPARTMENT OF VOCATIONAL AND TECHNICAL EDUCATION
1500 West Seventh Avenue
Stillwater, OK 74074-4364
405-377-2000

- *Career Directions.* 24 pages. Provides information on hot careers as well as how to prepare for them, describes vocational education training opportunities, and includes a career interest test. Write to the above address care of Public Information.

- *Career Stuff: Counseling & Teaching Materials.* 85 pages. Write to the above address care of Career Information Division.

- *Through the Jungle: A Job Search Guide.* ($4) Covers interviewing, resume preparation, and other topics. Write to the above address care of the Customer Service Division.

- *Life Work Portfolio.* ($7.00 plus $3.00 shipping) Developed to help adults store the information they need to plan career moves and to document their own personal employment history and qualifications.

631

OKLAHOMA EMPLOYMENT SECURITY COMMISSION
Directory of Labor Market Publications
Economic Research and Analysis Division
Room 515
Will Rogers Memorial Office Building
PO Box 52003
Oklahoma City, OK 73152-2003
http://www.oesc.state.ok.us

- *Handbook of Employment Statistics.* Contains historical data about nonagricultural employment and selected industries in Oklahoma. Also includes hours and earnings data.

- *Oklahoma Economic News.* Presents data from a variety of sources on Oklahoma's economy, labor force, demographics, and government programs.

- *Oklahoma State Employment Service Job Openings and Applicants.* A quarterly publication covering occupations most frequently listed with the Employment Service and those with the most applicants. Also lists supply and demand ratios for major occupational categories. Contains a statewide list of applicants, openings, and average wage offered.

- *Oklahoma Wage Surveys.* Contain results of wage surveys by occupation and labor market area.

- *Oklahoma Labor Force Projections.* Provides information and forecasts about the labor force and employment for the state, for the metropolitan statistical areas, and for each county from 1994 to 2005.

632
ONCOLOGY NURSING SOCIETY
Oncology Nursing Press
Department 1889
Pittsburgh, PA 15278-8847
412-921-7373
Fax: 412-921-6565

ONS offers a wide variety of publications related to careers in oncology nursing. Write for their publications catalog (Publication #PBCT9702). Some of the titles available include:

- *Oncology Nurses Make a Difference—An Introduction to A Career in Oncology Nursing* (ONMD9101) ($1.25).

- *The Master's Degree With a Specialty in Advanced Practice Oncology Nursing.* (JRMD9401). ($4).

- *Continuing Education Activities: A Planning Manual.* (IMCE9401) ($12).

- *Graduate Programs in Cancer Nursing.* (FMGP9601)

- *ONS Career Resource Kit.* (FMRK9601). This kit offers tips on developing a resume, honing interview skills, and highlights various ONS products that are helpful to oncology nurses in their career development.

- *1997 Oncology Nursing Certification Testing Bulletin* (FMC19601).Provides resources on test study and application materials for the oncology nursing certification tests

633
ONTARIO INSTITUTE FOR STUDIES IN EDUCATION
Guidance Centre
712 Gordon Baker Road
Toronto, Ontario
Canada M2H 3R7
416-502-1262

- *The Educational Planner.* ($1) 32 pages. Contains a 138-question survey to match interests and abilities to major areas of study; summarizes admission requirements and programs for Canadian institutions.

634
OPTICIANS ASSOCIATION OF AMERICA
10341 Democracy Lane
Fairfax, VA 22030

- *What is a Dispensing Optician?*

- *What Does a Dispensing Optician Do?*

635
OREGON STATE UNIVERSITY
Indian Education Office
Snell Hall
Room 330
Corvalis, OR 97331-1634
541-737-4383
indimed@ccmail.orst.edu
http://www.orst.edu/dept/indianed

- *Financial Aid Resource Guide.* (Also available on a 3.5-inch computer disk). Information on scholarships provided for Native American students at Oregon State University, as well as federal and national corporate scholarships.

636
OREGON STATE UNIVERSITY
College of Oceanic and Atmospheric Sciences
Oceanography Administration Building 104
Corvallis, OR 97331-5503
541-737-5190

- *Careers in Oceanography.* 6 pages. Describes oceanography and other marine fields, basic qualifications, undergraduate preparation, working conditions, employment outlook and opportunities, and salary. Lists schools offering graduate work in marine science.

637
ORGANIZATION FOR EQUAL EDUCATION OF THE SEXES, INC.
PO Box 438
Blue Hill, ME 04614-0438
207-374-2489

- *Women at Work.* 4 pages. Details the organization's career-related, 11 x 17 posters, including *Money, Jobs & Women, Science Jobs, Women in the Trades, Who Says There Are No Women Firefighters,* and *Dentistry* (posters are $4 each).

638
ORGANIZATION OF AMERICAN HISTORIANS
112 North Bryan Street
Bloomington, IN 47408-4199
812-855-7311
http://www.indiana.edu/~oah

- *Careers for Graduates in History.* A one-page chart depicting career opportunities for history graduates in the nonprofit, private, and public sectors.

- *Career Information.* 1 page. Lists historical organizations and books that provide information about jobs for historians.

639
OUTWARD BOUND U.S.A.
National Headquarters
Route 9D, R2 Box 280
Garrison, NY 10524-9757
800-243-8520 or 914-424-4000
http://www.outwardbound.org

- *Outward Bound National Course Catalog.* 46 pages. Describes Outward Bound and provides information on instructors, the various programs, courses for young teens, international courses, tuition, enrollment, and financial aid.

640
PACE INTERNATIONAL
209 Prairie Avenue
PO Box 1557
Morgantown, WV 26507-1557
304-296-8444

- *Careers in Cost Engineering and Related Industry Specialties.* 9 pages. Describes the field of cost engineering, the duties, and education and training. Lists industries that typically employ cost engineers.

641
PEACE CORPS OF THE UNITED STATES OF AMERICA
1990 K Street NW
Washington, DC 20526
800-424-8580
http://www.peacecorp.gov

Peace Corps information is available by phone or at the web site.

642
PENNSYLVANIA DEPARTMENT OF LABOR AND INDUSTRY
Bureau of Research and Statistics
300 Capitol Associates Building
Harrisburg, PA 17120-0034
717-787-6466
Fax: 717-772-2168

- *Employment Outlook in Pennsylvania Industries and Occupations.* 50 pages. Compares employment in Pennsylvania in 1990 with employment projections for the year 2000. Includes industry employment tables and occupational data as well as data on the average annual number of job openings for approximately 50 occupations.

- *Pennsylvania Workforce 2000.* Contains concise analytical texts, summary tables and charts on population, labor force, and industrial and occupational employment.

643

PETERSON'S
Orders
PO Box 2123
Princeton, NJ 08543-2123
800-338-3282
http://www.petersons.com

- *Peterson's Pamphlets.* ($2.35 per pamphlet plus shipping) 12 pages. Available titles include *Choosing a College; The College Application Essay; The College Interview; The College Recommendation; The College Visit; Financial Aid: Graduate and Professional Education; Graduate School; Selecting Colleges: Getting In;* and *Selective Colleges: How to Manage the High Cost.*

644

PHOTO MARKETING ASSOCIATION INTERNATIONAL
3000 Picture Place
Jackson, MI 49201-8898
517-788-8100

- *Photo Industry Careers: A Lifelong Commitment to Excellence and Creativity.* 4 pages. Discusses job availability, salaries, benefits, career opportunities, and schools offering a photofinishing curriculum.

645

PILOT BOOKS
127 Sterling Avenue
PO Box 2102
Greenport, NY 11944
800-79-PILOT or 516-477-1094
Fax: 516-477-0978
http://www.pilotbooks.com

Call or write for a complete publications list and order form.

- *The Directory of Home-Based Business Resources.* ($7.95) Includes information on starting and running a successful home-based business, as well as resources for information on the home-based business.

- *How to Get That Job.* ($8.95) Filled with unusual insights, important tips, and wise advice for first-time job seekers, women going back to work after raising a family, and those who want to change careers.

- *Evaluating an Overseas Job Opportunity.* ($5.95) Covers employer/employee contracts, family considerations, and financial factors, problems in living overseas and returning home, taxation, and other considerations.

- *Guide to Cruise Ship Jobs.* ($7.95) Provides information on planning your job search, what positions are available, and necessary qualifications and how to make your experience and education fit them. Includes a list of major cruise lines and recruiting firms for cruise ship companies.

- *The Bare-Bones Guide to Better Business Writing.* ($7.95) Answers questions about proper grammar, punctuation and word choice, and offers suggestions on how to improve business and personal writing.

- *Look Before You Look into Business.* ($5.95) Provides checklists to help assess strengths and weaknesses of potential businesses before any money is invested.

646

POPULATION ASSOCIATION OF AMERICA
721 Ellsworth Drive
Suite 303
Silver Spring, MD 20910
301-565-6710
Fax: 301-565-7850

- *Careers in Population.* 16 pages. Topics covered include Why the Study of Population Matters, What the Study of Population Involves, Where Population Specialists Work, and Training To Be a Population Specialist. Also includes a list of other contact resources.

647
POULTRY SCIENCE ASSOCIATION, INC.
1111 North Dunlap Avenue
Savoy, IL 61874
217-356-3182
Fax: 217-398-4119
psa@assochq.org
http://www.psa.uiuc.edu

- *A Poultry Career Is Waiting for You.* 14 pages. For high school and undergraduate students. Describes opportunities in the poultry industry and explains degree options for the field.

648
PRECISION MACHINED PRODUCTS ASSOCIATION
6700 West Snowville Road
Brecksville, OH 44141-3292
216-526-0300
Fax: 216-526-5803
http://www.pmpa.org

- *Your Future in the Precision Machined Products Industry.* 6 pages. Describes career opportunities, skills required, future outlook, and earnings.

649
PRESBYTERIAN CHURCH (USA)
Office of Financial Aid for Studies
100 Witherspoon Street
Louisville, KY 40202-1396
502-569-5745

- *Financial Aid Programs for Higher Education Studies.* 12 pages.

650
PRESCRIPTION FOOTWEAR ASSOCIATION
9861 Broken Land Parkway
Suite 255
Columbia, MD 21046-1151
800-673-8447 or 410-381-7278

- *Pedorthics: Providing Footwear and Related Service to Aid in the Care of the Foot.* 8 pages. Discusses specialization within the field, certification, and educational opportunities.

- *Pedorthists.* Chronicle Guidance brief, 4 pages.

651
PRESIDENT'S COMMITTEE ON EMPLOYMENT OF PEOPLE WITH DISABILITIES
1331 F Street NW
Washington, DC 20004-1107
202-376-6200 or 202-376-6205 (TDD)
http://www.pcedp.gov

- *Career and Business Information.* Available online at the web site (see Publications and Business Focus) or by mail. Several fact sheets and brochures are available. Titles include:

- *Employment Checklist for Hiring People with Disabilities*

- *Guidelines for Conducting a Job Interview*

- *Interviewing Tips for the Job Applicant*

- *High School/High Tech: Promoting Science, Engineering and Technology Careers for Students with Disabilities*

652
PRIESTS OF THE SACRED HEART
Vocation Central
PO Box 206
Hales Corner, WI 53130-0206
414-529-4255
Fax: 414-529-3377

Call or write for a complete vocation resource catalogue.

- *A Student's Guide: Priest, Brother, Sister.* (#1601) ($.25) For teachers, parents, and pastors. Provides answers to the questions children ask about the priesthood and religious life.

- *A Parent's Guide: Priest, Brother, or Sister.* (#1608) ($.25 each) Brochures addressing questions parents may have about their child's pursuit of a vocation to the priesthood or religious life.

- *Religious Life: A Life of Prayer and Shared Service in Community.* (#1602)

- *The Brother: A Life of Service, Community and Prayer.* (#1603)

- *Today's Sister: Living a Life of Loving Service.* (#1604)

- *The Priest: Called to Serve and Proclaim.* (#1605)

- *The Contemplative Life.* (#1606)

- *The Deacon: A Ministry of Service in the Church.* (#1607)

653
PRINCETON REVIEW
2315 Broadway
New York, NY 10024
800-995-5565
Fax: 212-874-0775

- *College Admissions Roadmap: A Guide for the College-Bound Traveler.*

- *Graduate School Admissions Roadmap: A Guide for the College Graduate.*

654
PRINT RESOURCE GROUP, INC.
1682 Shelby Oaks Drive North
Suite 6
Memphis, TN 38134

- *Power of the Printed Word.* 28 pages. Famous writers, comedians, and others share their knowledge in this collection of two-page briefs on such topics as How to Write a Business Letter by Malcolm Forbes, How to Improve Your Vocabulary by Tony Randall, How to Read Faster by Bill Cosby, and How to Write with Style by Kurt Vonnegut.

655
PRINTING AND GRAPHIC COMMUNICATIONS ASSOCIATION
7 West Tower
1333 H Street, NW
Washington, DC 20005

- *The Printing Industry: An Exciting and Colorful Career.* Describes such jobs as estimator, bindery technician, press operator, graphic designer, customer sales representative, and film assembler.

656
PRINTING INDUSTRIES OF AMERICA
100 Daingerfield Road
Alexandria, VA 22314
703-519-8100
Fax: 703-548-3227
http://www.printing.org

- *Directory of Technical Schools, Colleges & Universities Offering Courses in Graphic Communications.* 90 pages. Lists by state or province the schools offering accredited programs in technology, management, and education. Provides contact information and degrees offered (certificate, associate's, bachelor's, master's, and doctoral).

657
PRO-PAK, INC.
527 Dundee Road
Northbrook, IL 60062
847-272-0408
http://homepage.interaccess.com/~propak

- *Off to College.* 2 pages. SASE. Includes a What to Take to College checklist.

658
PROFESSIONAL BOWLERS ASSOCIATION
1720 Merriman Road
PO Box 5118
Akron, OH 44334-0118
330-836-5568

Fax: 330-836-2107
http://www.pba.org

- *PBA Tour: Guidelines to a Professional Image.* 6 pages. Answers what it means to be a professional bowler, how to deal with the media, and how to promote yourself.

659
PROFESSIONAL GROUNDS MANAGEMENT SOCIETY
120 Cockeysville Road
Suite 104
Hunt Valley, MD 21031
410-584-9754
Fax: 410-584-9756

- *The Professional Grounds Manager.* 4 pages. Briefly describes what a ground manager is, areas of responsibility, areas of expertise, and suggested educational requirements.

660
PROFESSIONAL SECRETARIES INTERNATIONAL
10502 Northwest Ambassador Drive
PO Box 20404
Kansas City, MO 64195-0404
816-891-6600

- *Charting the Career of the Professional Secretary.* 5 pages.

- *Facts about Today's Secretaries.* 1 page.

- *Secretaries.* Occupational Outlook Handbook reprint, 2 pages.

661
PROFESSIONAL TRUCK DRIVER INSTITUTE OF AMERICA, INC.
2200 Mill Road
Alexandria, VA 22314
703-838-8842
Fax: 703-836-6610

- *Schools with PDTIA Certified Courses Listed by State.* 6 pages.

662
PROTOTYPE CAREER PRESS
626 Armstrong Avenue
St. Paul Minnesota 55102
800-368-3197
Fax: 612-224-5526
http://www getajob

The *Pocket Job Series* consists of 7 titles. ($2.95 each):

- *Cracking the Hidden Job Market* offers advice about tapping the unadvertised job market, which comprises nearly 95 percent of all jobs. Provides sample cold-calls, follow-up letters, and contact sheets.

- *Financial Survival Between Jobs* offers information on budgeting, dealing with creditors, and maintaining an upbeat attitude.

- *Five Steps to Your Next Job* offers tips for success in today's competitive job market.

- *Job Interviews: 10 steps to success* offers tips on salary negotiation, six types of interview styles, the four basic parts of an interview, and follow-up strategy.

- *Job Search Over 40: Selling to your strengths* offers tips on how to combat age bias, and facts and myths about workers over age 40.

- *Job Search Problem-Solving Companion* addresses issues job seekers face daily such as overcoming rejection, targeting a job search, and seeking out support groups.

- *Resumes Etc.* offers instructions for resumes (4 styles), cover letters, follow-up letters, and applications.

663
PUBLIC HEALTH SERVICE
U.S. Department of Health and Human Services
Bureau of Health Professions
Division of Nursing
Room 9-35
5600 Fishers Lane
Rockville, MD 20857

301-443-6333
http://www.hrsa.dhhs.gov/bhpr/bhpr.html

The Division of Student Assistance (301-443-4776) has information on health professions student loans. The grants management officer (301-443-6857) has information on professional anesthetist traineeships and professional nurse traineeships.

- *Fact Sheets on the Division of Nursing Grant Programs.* Titles include Advanced Nurse Education Grants, Nurse Practitioner/Nurse-Midwifery Program Grants, Nursing Education Opportunities for Individuals from Disadvantaged Backgrounds, Nursing Special Projects, Professional Nurse Traineeships, Nurse Anesthetist Traineeships, Nurse Anesthetist Education Programs, and Nurse Anesthetist Faculty Fellowships.

664
PUBLIC RELATIONS SOCIETY OF AMERICA, INC.
Educational Affairs Department
33 Irving Place, 3rd Floor
New York, NY 10003-2376
212-995-2230
http://www.prsa.org

- *Careers in Public Relations.* ($3.50) 8 pages. Discusses the field today, salaries, types of duties public relations professionals perform, personal qualifications, academic preparation, and employment opportunities.

665
PUBLIC/PRIVATE VENTURES
Communications Department
One Commerce Square
2005 Market Street
Suite 900
Philadelphia, PA 19103
215-557-4400
Fax: 215-557-4469
http://www.epn.org/ppv

Call or write for a complete catalog. Prepayment is required by check or money order to cover printing and postage costs.

- *Skills, Standards and Entry-Level Work: Elements of a Strategy for Youth Employability Development.* ($6) 74 pages.

- *Replication: A Strategy to Improve the Delivery of Education and Job Training Programs.* ($7) 50 pages.

- *YouthSources: An Employment Training Bibliography.* ($8.50) 96 pages.

- *College Students as Mentors for At-Risk Youth: A Study of Six Campus Partners in Learning Programs.* ($6) 56 pages.

- *Finding One's Way: Career Guidance for Disadvantaged Youth.* ($2) 63 pages.

- *Seniors in National and Community Service: A Report Prepared for the Commonwealth Fund's American Over 55 at Work Program.* ($6) 79 pages. An executive summary available free of charge.

- *Youth and the Workplace: Second Chance Programs and the Hard-to-Employ.* ($6) 55 pages.

666
RADIO-TELEVISION NEWS DIRECTORS ASSOCIATION
1000 Connecticut Avenue NW
Suite 615
Washington, DC 20036-5302
202-659-6510
Fax: 202-223-4007
http://www.rtnda.org

- *Careers in Radio and Television News.* ($5) 24 pages. Discusses qualifications, responsibilities, and how to prepare for and get a job.

667
RADIOLOGICAL SOCIETY OF NORTH AMERICA
2021 Spring Road
Suite 600
Oak Brook, IL 60521
630-571-7817

Written request on letterhead required to obtain the following materials.

- *Career Encounters: Radiology.* 28-minute video offering a detailed look at support careers in major subspecialties of radiology.

- *Medicine's New Vision.* 178 pages. Provides career information on major subspecialties in radiology.

668
RECRUITING NEW TEACHERS, INC.
385 Concord Avenue
Suite 100
Belmont, MA 02178
800-45-TEACH or 617-489-6407

Call or write for a complete RNT Educational Materials and Products list.

- *Careers in Teaching Handbook.* ($9.95) 122 pages. A comprehensive guide to pursuing a career in teaching. Provides information, resources, and advice to aspiring and novice teachers from all educational and professional backgrounds and experience (including college students, GED recipients, and business and technical professionals). Identifies topics of primary concern to would-be teachers, such as finding the right teacher education program, making a career transition, and funding.

- *What it Takes to Teach* brochure. ($1.50) 10 pages.

669
REFRIGERATION SERVICE ENGINEERS SOCIETY
1666 Rand Road
Des Plaines, IL 60016-3552
708-297-6464

- *Become a Refrigeration, Heating & Air Conditioning Service Engineer...a Rewarding Career Opportunity for the One without Four Years of College.* 4 pages. Describes the nature of the work, earnings, working conditions, and advancement potential.

670
RITTNERS FLORAL SCHOOL
345 Marlborough Street
Boston, MA 02115
617-267-3824
Fax: 617-267-3824
stevert@tiac.net
http://www.tiac.net/users/stevert/index.html

- *Floral Designing: The Now Profession.* ($.50) 8 pages. Covers working conditions, pay, preparation, and job outlook.

671
ROBERT HALF INTERNATIONAL
565 Fifth Avenue
New York, NY 10017
212-983-1800 or 212-687-7878
Fax: 212-682-7749
http://www.roberthalf.com

- *How to Get Ahead in Accounting, Finance and Banking.* 5 pages. Contains numerous tips on resume preparation and interviewing.

- *Salary Guide.* 28 pages. Annual source for reliable hiring and compensation data. Provides an in-depth look at employment factors affecting each geographic region of the United States, as well as cost-of-living variances for major cities.

- *The Robert Half Way to Get Hired in Today's Job Market.* 100 pages.

672
RURAL CLEARINGHOUSE FOR LIFELONG EDUCATION AND DEVELOPMENT
Kansas State University
111 College Court
Manhattan, KS 66506-6001
913-532-5560

- *Guide to Organizations, Consortia, and Networks That Provide Classes at a Distance.* ($5) 6 pages.

673
SALES AND MARKETING EXECUTIVES INTERNATIONAL
Statler Office Tower
Suite 977
Cleveland, OH 44115
800-999-1414 or 216-771-6650
Fax: 800-385-9178 or 216-771-6652
http://www.smei.org

- *Opportunities in Selling.* 12 pages. Describes the duties of different types of salespeople, personal characteristics, and education and training.

674
SCIENCE SERVICE, INC.
1719 N Street NW
Washington, DC 20036
202-785-2255
Fax: 202-785-1243
http://www.tss-inc.com/sciserv/

- *Directory of Student Science Training Programs for Precollege Students.* 61 pages. Lists 490 programs and internships for high school students in science, mathematics, and engineering throughout the United States and abroad. Points out more than 130 programs specifically targeted to minorities, women, and other groups traditionally underrepresented in the sciences.

675
SEA GRANT COLLEGE PROGRAM
Sea Grant Publications
1716 Briar Crest
Suite 603
Bryan, TX 77802
409-862-3770
Fax: 409-862-3789
http://texas-sea-grant.tamu.edu/staff.html

- *Questions about Careers in Oceanography.* 18 pages. Directed toward high school and college students, teachers, and guidance counselors with questions about careers in oceanography. Addresses what an oceanographer is, where to study oceanography, who hires oceanographers, who supports oceanographers, and where to obtain further information.

- *Vocational-Technical Marine Career Opportunities in Texas.* 24 pages. Covers the maritime transportation industry (merchant marines, inland marine transportation, and offshore supply and transportation); the offshore mineral, oil, and gas industry; commercial diving; commercial fisheries; and shipbuilding.

676
SEA GRANT COLLEGE PROGRAM
University of Puerto Rico
UPR-RUM
PO Box 5000
Mayaguez, Puerto Rico 00681-5000
787-834-4726

- *Coast Notes.* 2 pages. each. SASE business size. A series discussing six marine careers. Briefly explains the nature of the work, education required, and specific careers in the field. Choose from Technical Careers; Careers in Ocean Engineering; Careers in Physical and Chemical Oceanography; Careers in Resource Management, Planning, Policy Making, and Law; Careers in Marine Biology; and Marine Careers in Medicine and Health.

677
SEA WORLD OF FLORIDA
Education Department/Book Orders
7007 Sea World Drive
Orlando, FL 32821-8097
407-363-2207
Fax: 407-363-1457
http://www.seaworld.org

Sea World's Education Department offers more than 75 marine science educational resources (booklets, posters, and teacher's guides) designed for K-12 students and teachers. Write for a complete list and order form.

678
SELF HELP FOR HARD OF HEARING PEOPLE, INC.
Publications
7910 Woodmont Avenue
Suite 1200
Bethesda, MD 20814
301-657-2248 or 301-657-2249 (TTD)
Fax: 301-913-9413
http://www.shhh.org

For the following publications, add $.75 in postage and handling for orders up to $2 or $1.75 for orders of $2.01 to $5. Call, write, or visit the web site for a publications catalog.

- *College-Bound Students.* ($2.25)

- *Employment Discrimination: How to Recognize It and What to Do About It.* ($1.75)

- *Getting Help with a Job: Exploring Vocational Rehabilitation.* ($1.75)

- *Putting You in the Successful Employment Picture* (Series). ($6.50)

- *What Employers Want to Know about Assistive Technology in the Workplace.* ($2.25)

679
SHOE SERVICE INSTITUTE OF AMERICA
Educational Library
5024-R Campbell Boulevard
Baltimore, MD 21236-5974
410-931-8100
Fax: 410-931-8111

- *Career Kit of Materials in the Shoe Service Industry.* Lists shoe repair schools in the United States, as well as educational library books, pamphlets, and videos. Includes the latest issue of *Shoe Service Magazine.*

680
SMITHSONIAN INSTITUTION
Center for Museum Studies, MRC 427
Washington, DC 20560
202-357-3102
Fax: 202-357-3346
SIINTERN@SIVM.SI.EDU
http://www.si.edu/cms

- *Internship Opportunities at the Smithsonian Institution.* ($5) 129 pages. A guide to the work of the Smithsonian Institution and where to fit in as an intern. Describes projects to participate in, skills necessary, and how to apply for internships. Includes quotes from former Smithsonian interns as well as information on the Smithsonian Minority Internship Program and the Native American Internship Program.

- *The Internships and Fellowships Brochure.* Lists Smithsonian museums and offices that offer internships.

681
SOCIAL SECURITY ADMINISTRATION
U.S. Department of Health and Human Services
Room G-122, West High Rise
6401 Security Boulevard
Baltimore, MD 21235
800-772-1213

- *Disability.* (05-10029) 17 pages. Discusses the various kinds of disability benefits available, as well as who is eligible and how to apply.

- *If You Are Blind: How Social Security and SSI Can Help.* (05-10052) 1 page.

- *Medicare.* (05-10043) 20 pages.

- *Retirement.* (05-10035) 17 pages.

- *SSI.* (05-11000) 1p. Explains the Supplemental Security Income program, which provides a basic income to people with limited resources who are 65 or older, disabled, or blind.

- *Survivors.* (05-10084) 12 pages. Outlines the benefits available when a family breadwinner dies.

- *Understanding Social Security.* (05-10024) 40 pages.

- *When You Get Social Security Disability Benefits: What You Need to Know.* (05-10153) 24 pages.

- *When You Get Social Security Retirement or Survivors Benefits: What You Need to Know.* (05-10077) 27 pages.

- *When You Get SSI: What You Need to Know.* (05-11011) 1 page.

- *Working While Disabled: How Social Security Can Help.* (05-10095) 1 page.

Write or call for other available materials.

682
SOCIETY FOR AMERICAN ARCHAEOLOGY
900 Second Street NE
Suite 12
Washington, DC 20002-3557
202-789-8200
Fax: 202-789-0284
http://www.saa.org

- *Participate in Archaeology.* 16 pages. Describes the field of archeology and lists archeology contacts.

683
SOCIETY FOR ETHNOMUSICOLOGY, INC.
Morrison Hall 005
Indiana University
Bloomington, IN 47405-2501
812-855-6672
Fax: 812-855-6673
sem@indiana.edu
http://www.indiana.edu/~ethmusic

- *Guide to Programs in Ethnomusicology in the United States and Canada.* ($4 plus $2 shipping) 74 pages. Provides information about a variety of academic programs in ethnomusicology. Lists undergraduate and graduate programs.

684
SOCIETY FOR HISTORICAL ARCHAEOLOGY
PO Box 30446
Tucson, AZ 85751-0446
520-886-8006

- *Opportunities in Historical Archaeology.* 8 pages.

685
SOCIETY FOR HUMAN RESOURCE MANAGEMENT
606 North Washington Street
Alexandria, VA 22314
800-283-7476 or 703-548-3440
http://www.shrm.org

- *Careers in Human Resource Management.* 8 pages. Covers the many career options and specializations, required educational background and experience, personal characteristics, and salaries.

686
SOCIETY FOR IMAGING SCIENCE AND TECHNOLOGY
7003 Kilworth Lane
Springfield, VA 22151
703-642-9090
Fax: 703-642-9094
info@imaging.org
http://www.imaging.org

- *Make the Right Choice...Join IS&T.* 8 pages. Information on IS&T, honors and awards, and IS&T chapters as well as a publications list.

687

SOCIETY FOR INDUSTRIAL AND APPLIED MATHEMATICS
3600 University City Science Center
Philadelphia, PA 19104-2688
800-447-7426 or 215-382-9800
Fax: 215-386-7999
service@siam.org
http://www.siam.org

- *SIAM Report on Mathematics in Industry.* 41 pages. Describes the purposes of the SIAM study, roles of mathematics, working environments, and perceptions of graduate education.

688

SOCIETY FOR MINING, METALLURGY, AND EXPLORATION (SME), INC.
PO Box 625002
Littleton, CO 80162-5002
800-763-3132 or 303-973-9550
Fax: 303-973-3845
smenet@aol.com
http://www.smenet.org

- *Careers for Engineers in the Minerals Industry.* 13 pages. Describes the duties and responsibilities for a number of career options, employment opportunities, and accredited programs in minerals fields leading to degrees in engineering or engineering technology.

- *Career Planning Workshops.* ($5) Contains presentations made at annual career planning workshops.

689

SOCIETY FOR RANGE MANAGEMENT
1839 York Street
Denver, CO 80206
303-355-7070
Fax: 303-355-5059
srmden@ux.netcom.com
http://cnrit.tamu.edu/srm

- *Careers in Range Science and Range Management.* 12 pages. Discusses career and employment opportunities and educational preparation. Lists schools offering programs in management or range science in the United States and Canada.

690

SOCIETY FOR TECHNICAL COMMUNICATION
901 North Stuart Street
Suite 904
Arlington, VA 22203-1854
703-522-4114
Fax: 703-522-2075
http://www.stc-va.org

- *Careers in Technical Communication.* 6 p. Describes career opportunities and education requirements. Lists colleges and universities offering programs in technical communication.

691

THE SOCIETY OF ACTUARIES
475 North Martingale Road
Suite 800
Schaumburg, IL 60173
847-706-3500
Fax: 847-706-3599
http://www.soa.org

- *Actuaries Make a Difference.* 22 pages. Explains what actuaries do and where they work by highlighting several real-life actuaries who describe how they became an actuary, what they do on the job, and what they most enjoy.

- *Actuarial Training Programs.* 29 pages. Lists programs in the United States and Canada, as well as contact information, salary range, types of employment, employment requirements, and general program information.

- *Associateship and Fellowship Catalog.* 114 pages. Includes general information; lists requirements for admission, a schedule for examinations, and course descriptions; and provides order forms and application for exams.

- *Canadian and U.S Schools Offering Actuarial Science Courses Including Actuarial Mathematics.* 2 pages. Lists schools in Canada and the United States that offer actuarial science courses, including regularly scheduled classes covering substantially all the topics in the Society of Actuaries (SOA) Course 150, Actuarial Mathematics.

- *Canadian and United States Schools Offering a Pre-Actuarial Curriculum.* 8 pages. Lists schools in Canada and the United States that offer an actuaria-related curriculum.

692
SOCIETY OF AMERICAN ARCHIVISTS
Education Officer
600 South Federal Street
Suite 504
Chicago, IL 60605
312-922-0140
Fax: 312-347-1452
http://www.archivists.org

- *Directory of Archival Education in the United States and Canada.* 16 pages. Describes the archival profession and archival education, contains guidelines for the development of a curriculum for a master of archival studies degree, and lists archival education programs grouped geographically.

693
SOCIETY OF AMERICAN FLORISTS
1601 Duke Street
Alexandria, VA 22314
800-336-4743 or 703-836-8700
Fax: 703-836-8705
http://www.safnow.org

- *Careers in Floriculture.* Describes the field, education, and horticulture therapy for the disabled.

- *Careers in Floriculture: Catalog of Schools.* 44 pages. Lists degree and certificate programs in floriculture, horticulture, and floral design, as well as contact information.

- *Grow a Great Life.* 8 pages. Discusses the field, education, and related work experience.

694
SOCIETY OF AMERICAN FORESTERS
5400 Grosvenor Lane
Bethesda, MD 20814-2198
301-897-8720
Fax: 301-897-3690
http://www.safnet.org

- *So You Want to Be in Forestry.* 16 pages. SASE 9 x12 envelope. Explains the roles and duties of foresters, their education and training, career opportunities, and related fields.

The following publications are in the *Forestry Career Packet.* SASE 9 x 12 envelope:

- *Accredited Professional Forestry Degree Programs.* 2 pages. Lists institutions with SAF-accredited curricula and SAF-recognized curricula in the United States and Canada.

- *Forestry Career Information Question and Answer Sheet.* 2 pages. Contains the most frequently asked questions about the profession of forestry.

- *Job Seekers' Guide.* 2 pages. Lists contact information of forestry employers.

695
SOCIETY OF AUTOMOTIVE ENGINEERS, INC.
400 Commonwealth Drive
Warrendale, PA 15096-0001
412-776-4841
http://www.sae.org

- *Automotive Engineering: A Moving Career.* 6 pages. Describes the field and educational requirements and provides information on schools.

- *SAE Collegiate Chapters.* 27 pages. Lists student chapters and contact information.

696
SOCIETY OF COSMETIC CHEMISTS
120 Wall Street
Suite 2400
New York, NY 10005-4088
212-668-1500

- *Career Opportunities in Cosmetic Science.* 14 pages.

697
SOCIETY OF DIAGNOSTIC MEDICAL SONOGRAPHERS
12770 Coit Road
Suite 708
Dallas, TX 75251
972-239-7367
Fax: 972-239-7378

- *Diagnostic Medical Sonography Career Information.* 6 pages. Discusses the various specialties in the field, as well as duties, education, advancement, and salary.

- *Directory of Education in Diagnostic Medical Sonography.* ($5) Provides detailed information on programs in diagnostic medical sonography in the United States and Canada.

- *Job Profile.* ($3) Describes the staff, management, and educational staff within the sonography profession.

698
SOCIETY OF EXPLORATION GEOPHYSICISTS
PO Box 702740
Tulsa, OK 74170-2740
918-493-3516
Fax: 918-497-5557
http://www.seg.org

- *Catch the Wavelet: 21st Century Careers in Exploration Geophysics.* 6 pages. Briefly describes geophysics, how to prepare for a career in the field, and scholarship opportunities.

- *Women Exploring the Earth.* 8 pages. Brief biographies on five women in the field.

699
SOCIETY OF FIRE PROTECTION ENGINEERS
One Liberty Square
Boston, MA 02109-4825
617-482-0686
Fax: 617-482-8184
http://www.wpi.edu/academics/depts/fire/sfpe.html

- *Fire Protection Engineering.* 6 pages. Describes the personal qualifications and skills required, as well as career and employment opportunities.

- *Fire Service Careers for the Fire Protection Engineer.* 6 pages. Describes the field and how to prepare for a fire service related career.

- *Schools Offering Courses in Fire Protection Engineering.* 2 pages.

700
SOCIETY OF MANUFACTURING ENGINEERS
Education Department
One SME Drive
PO Box 930
Dearborn, MI 48121-0930
800-733-4SME or 313-271-1500
Fax: 313-271-2861
http://www.sme.org

- *Adventures in Manufacturing.* 8 pages.

- *Junior Engineering Technical Society: Exploring the World of Tomorrow...Today.* 10 pages.

701
SOCIETY OF MOTION PICTURE AND TELEVISION ENGINEERS
595 West Hartsdale Avenue
White Plains, NY 10607-1824

914-761-1100
Fax: 914-761-3115
http://www.smpte.org

Several publications are available on career opportunities for engineers in television, film, and the production and postproduction fields. Contact the society or visit the web site for a current list of publications.

702
SOCIETY OF NAVAL ARCHITECTS AND MARINE ENGINEERS
601 Pavonia Avenue
Suite 400
Jersey City, NJ 07306
201-798-4800
Fax: 201-798-4975
http://www.sname.org

- *Careers in the Maritime Industry: Naval Architecture, Marine Engineering, Ocean Engineering.* 24 pages. Discusses the future of the maritime industry; the roles of naval architects, marine engineers, and ocean engineers; and employers. Lists accredited institutions offering bachelor's degrees in engineering or engineering technology and provides scholarship information.

703
SOCIETY OF NUCLEAR MEDICINE
1850 Samuel Morse Drive
Reston, VA 20190-5316
703-708-9000

- *Joint Review Committee on Educational Programs in Nuclear Medicine Technology: Accredited Programs.* 18 pages.

- *Nuclear Medicine Technology: A High-Tech Career for Today and Tomorrow.* Takes a look at the technologist's role and responsibilities, employment outlook and opportunities; salary, career alternatives, educational programs, and certification.

704
SOCIETY OF PETROLEUM ENGINEERS
Book Order Department
PO Box 833836
Richardson, TX 75083-3836
972-952-9452
Fax: 972-952-9435
http://www.spe.org

- *Explore a World of Unlimited Opportunities: Careers in Petroleum Engineering.* 12 pages. Describes various careers in the field.

- *Petroleum Engineering & Technology Schools.* 6 pages. An international list of schools.

- *United States Petroleum Engineering & Technology Schools.* 4 pages. List of schools in the United States.

705
SOCIETY OF PLASTICS ENGINEERS, INC.
14 Fairfield Drive
Brookfield, CT 06804-0403
203-775-0471
Fax: 203-775-8490
http://www.4spe.org

- *Plastics As an Engineering Career.* 6 pages.

- *Professional Careers in the Polymer/Plastics Industries.* 9 pages.

706
SOCIETY OF RANGE MANAGEMENT
1839 York Street
Denver, CO 80206

- *Careers in Range Science and Range Management.* Describes the field and lists schools which offer special training programs for it.

707
SOCIETY OF SYSTEMATIC ZOOLOGY
c/o National Museum of Natural History
10th and Constitution Avenues
Washington, DC 20560

- *Careers in Biological Systematics.*

708
SOCIETY OF TOXICOLOGY
1767 Business Center Drive
Suite 302
Reston, VA 20190-5332
703-438-3115
Fax: 703-438-3113
http://www.toxicology.org

- *Resource Guide to Careers in Toxicology.* 147 pages. Discusses duties and responsibilities, employment opportunities, regional distribution of toxicology jobs, salaries, and preparation; profiles the schools offering toxicology programs.

709
SOCIETY OF WOMEN ENGINEERS
120 Wall Street, 11th Floor
New York, NY 10005-3902
212-509-9577
Fax: 212-509-0224
http://www.swe.org

- *Is Engineering for You?* 4 pages. Explains college entrance requirements and what women engineers do.

710
SOCIETY OF WOOD SCIENCE AND TECHNOLOGY
One Gifford Pinchot Drive
Madison, WI 53705
608-231-9347

- *Careers in Wood Science and Technology: the Material Science of the Forest Products Industry.* 6 pages.

- *SWST Directory: North American Schools Offering Baccalaureate and Graduate Programs of Study in Wood Science and Technology.* 15 pages.

711
SOIL AND WATER CONSERVATION SOCIETY
7515 Northeast Ankeny Road
Ankeny, IA 50021-9764
800-THE-SOIL or 515-289-2331
Fax: 515-289-1227
pubs@swcs.org
http://www.swcs.org

- *Consider a Career in Soil and Water Conservation.* 4 pages. Discusses the various roles of conservationists, salary, how to enter the field, and educational requirements.

- *Fact Sheet: Careers for the Future.* 1 page. Describes what careers are available in the Natural Resources Conservation Service.

712
SOLAR ENERGY INDUSTRIES ASSOCIATION
122 C Street NW, 4th Floor
Washington, DC 20001-2109
202-383-2600

- *Renewable Energy.* 12 pages. Discusses the field and its various specialties. Defines each specialty and lists its applications and potential.

713
SOURCE EDP
2 Pen Plaza
Suite 1176
New York, NY 10121
212-760-2200
Fax: 212-760-2222
http://www.experienceondemand.com

- *Salary Survey and Career Planning Guide.* 20 pages. Highlights the latest trends in the information technology industry and provides detailed compensation data on a wide range of positions.

714
SPECIAL LIBRARIES ASSOCIATION
1700 18th Street NW
Washington, DC 20009-2514
202-234-4700
Fax: 202-265-9317
http://www.sla.org

- *Careers in Special Libraries.*

715
SPIE-THE INTERNATIONAL SOCIETY FOR OPTICAL ENGINEERING
PO Box 10
1000 20th Street
Bellingham, WA 98227-0010
206-676-3290

- *Optics Education: SPIE's Annual Guide to Optics Programs Worldwide.* 135 pages. Includes a detailed entry for each program. Lists contact information, degrees granted, number of students specializing in optics or related fields, academic and research specialties, research facilities, continuing education, and industry/university cooperative programs, tuition, application deadline and admission requirements, financial assistance information, and a description of the department/program.

716
SPORTING GOODS MANUFACTURERS ASSOCIATION
200 Castlewood Drive
North Palm Beach, FL 33408
561-842-4100
Fax: 561-863-8984
http://www.sportlink.com

- *Sports Instructors.* 4 pages. Discusses nature of the work, requirements, advancement, employment outlook, earnings, working conditions, and sources of additional information.

717
STUDENT CONSERVATION ASSOCIATION, INC.
1800 North Kent Street
Suite 1260
Arlington, VA 22209-2104
703-524-2441

- *Conservation Career Development Program.* 5 information sheets. This program trains ethnic minorities and women at both the high school and college level for careers with natural and cultural resources management organizations.

- *Resource Assistance Program: Volunteer Positions.* 82 pages. Lists volunteer opportunities by state for a wide range of natural and cultural resource assistance programs.

- *The Student Conservation Association: Making a Difference.*

718
SUBURBAN NEWSPAPERS OF AMERICA
401 North Michigan Avenue
Chicago, IL 60611-4267
312-644-6610
Fax: 312-527-6658
http://www.suburban-news.org

- *Suburban Newspaper Careers.* A brief description of newspaper careers.

719
SUN FEATURES INCORPORATED
PO Box 368
Cardiff, CA 92007
619-431-1660

- *Internships: Rocket into a Career You Choose.* ($5.95) Written by popular national career columnist Joyce Lain Kennedy, this is packed with useful information about how to make internships work for you. It not only includes her excellent advice but also lists the major directories which cite thousands of opportunities.

- *The College Financial Aid Emergency Kit.* ($6.95) 41 pages. Cowritten by Dr. Herm Davis, one of the nation's top student aid authorities, and Joyce Lain Kennedy, this handy guide offers tips and resources to students and their families who need to find a way to finance their college education. The guide is broken down into four time frames for obtaining college funds. The first three frames address the need for urgent immediate college cash. The fourth time frame offers tips to those who have lead time of a year or so before their education begins. This digest covers grants, loans, scholarships, and many other resources. A helpful list of printed resources and internet resources are also provided.

720
TAPPI
Technology Park
PO Box 105113
Atlanta, GA 30348-5113
Fax: 770-209-7329
http://www.tappi.org

- *An Invitation to Students Interested in Math/Science/Engineering Careers from the Pulp and Paper Industry.* 8 pages. Describes technical career opportunities in the pulp and paper industry and the academic programs that lead to them.

721
TEN SPEED PRESS
PO Box 7123
Berkeley, CA 94707

Offers a variety of career titles.

- *Job Hunting on the Internet*, by Richard Nelson Bolles. ($4.95) 110 pages. Essentially a pocket directory of Web sites useful for those selecting a career or searching for a job.

722
TENNESSEE OCCUPATIONAL INFORMATION COORDINATING COMMITTEE
Executive Director
11th Floor, Davy Crockett Tower
500 James Robertson Parkway
Nashville, TN 37245-1600
615-741-6451
Fax: 615-532-9434

- *The Tennessee Career Guide: The Sky's the Limit.* A guide for high school juniors and seniors that discusses careers, educational requirements, and job-hunting tips.

723
TEXAS HEALTH CAREERS
PO Box 15587
Aus. , TX 78761

- *Directory of Financial Aid and Educational Programs.*

- *Health Careers in Texas.*

724
TEXAS HIGHER EDUCATION COORDINATING BOARD
Division of Student Services
PO Box 12788, Capitol Station
Austin, TX 78711-2788
800-735-2988 or 512-483-6340

- *Financial Aid for Texas Students.* 50 pages.

725
TINSLEY COMMUNICATIONS, INC.
100 Bridge Street
Suite A-3
Hampton, VA 23669
757-723-4499
Fax: 757-723-8727

- *The Minority Guide to Scholarships and Financial Aid.* ($7.98) 32 pages. Lists close to 200 undergraduate and graduate programs and, for each, a program sponsor, an award amount, eligibility requirements and restrictions, and the deadline.

726
TOOLING AND MANUFACTURING ASSOCIATION
1177 South Dee Road
Park Ridge, IL 60068-9809
847-825-1120
Fax: 847-825-0041
http://www.tmanet.com

Contact TMA for other available materials or visit the web site.

- *How Valuable Is Your Future? This Short Quiz Could Make Your Career Dreams Come True.* 10 pages. Describes the duties of precision metalworkers, as well as interning, education, salary, and advancement opportunities.

- *The Tooling & Machinery Industry.* 7 pages. Discusses the industry as well as its customers, benefits, and opportunities.

- *Why Metalworking Careers Are Very Attractive.* 2 pages. Compares the metal trades to construction using 25 different criteria.

- *Apprentice Training Courses in Related Classroom Instruction.* 23 pages. Contains registration information, entrance and testing requirements, attendance requirements, and course descriptions.

727
TRUCKLOAD CARRIERS ASSOCIATION
2200 Mill Road
Alexandria, VA 22314
703-838-1950
Fax: 703-836-6610

- *Careers in Trucking.* 64 pages. A recruitment magazine for anyone interested in working for the trucking industry. Contains information from over 600 member companies of the Truckload Carriers Association.

728
U.S. NEWS & WORLD REPORT
Best Colleges
2400 N Street NW
Washington, DC 20037-1196
Fax: 215-579-8589
http://www.usnews.com

- *America's Best Colleges.* ($3) A reprint of an annually produced report that ranks the nation's accredited four-year colleges and universities.

- *America's Best Colleges.* ($5.95) 280 pages. A guide book available by calling 800-523-5948. Lists by state the colleges and universities offering baccalaureate degrees. Contains information on choosing a school, how to get in, application procedures, paying for college, and grants and loans.

- *America's Best Graduate Schools.* ($5.95) 164 pages. A guide book available by calling 800-523-5948. Contains exclusive ranking for schools of business, law, medical, engineering, and other disciplines.

The web site contains helpful information about colleges and career solutions and is a comprehensive tool for anyone planning to go to college or grad school. Sections include choosing a college, finding financial aid, pursuing graduate school or a career, and learning about aspects of college life outside the classroom.

729
UNITED BROTHERHOOD OF CARPENTERS AND JOINERS OF AMERICA
Apprenticeship and Training Department
101 Constitution Avenue NW
Washington, DC 20001
202-546-6206

- *You Can Become a Tile, Marble, Terrazzo and Dimensional Stone Installer.* ($.12) 6 pages.

- *The Carpenter.* 2 pages. Describes a career as a carpenter.

730

UNITED FARM WORKERS OF AMERICA
PO Box 62
La Paz
Keene, CA 93531
805-822-5571
Fax: 805-822-6103
http://www.ufwlatinoweb.com-ufw

Visit the web site to see additional publications.

- *Jobs for Dignity: Volunteer a Little of Your Life to Help Save Lives.* 6 pages.

731

UNITED FOOD AND COMMERCIAL WORKERS INTERNATIONAL UNION
Education Office
1775 K Street NW
Washington, DC 20006-1598
202-223-3111
Fax: 202-466-1587
http://www.ufcw.org

- *UFCW Occupational Briefs.* 6 pages. Available in English or Spanish for the following careers: barber and cosmetologist, footwear worker, insurance sales professional, nursing aide, packinghouse worker, pharmacist, registered nurse, retail clerk, retail meat cutter, and seafood worker.

732

UNITED METHODIST CHURCH
Board of Higher Education and Ministry
PO Box 871
Nashville, TN 37202-0871
615-340-7406
Fax: 615-340-7377
http://www.umc.org/gbhem/dhehome.html

- *Certification in Youth Ministry.* ($.05) 8 pages. Discusses the personal, spiritual, professional, and academic requirements.

- *Foundational Studies for Diaconal Ministries.* 2 pages.

- *God's Call and Your Vocation: A Look at Christian Calls and Church Operations.* ($3) 47 pages.

- *Graduate and Theological Schools for Diaconal Ministry and Certification Studies.* 2 pages.

- *Steps into Certification: Christian Education, Youth Ministry, Evangelism, Music Ministry.* ($.05) 6 pages. A Korean version and Spanish version are available free of charge.

- *Varieties of Diaconal Ministry.* ($.05) 6 pages. Describes the profession, necessary experience, and training. Includes Certification As a Chaplain, Diaconal Minister Serving in Gerontology, Diaconal Minister Serving in Peace and Justice, Diaconal Minister as Parish Nurse, and United Methodist Diaconal Pastoral Counselor.

- *Why I Am A...* 6 pages each. A series of brochures containing career information on particular fields from a personal perspective. Available for the following career disciplines: pastoral counselor, air force chaplain, navy chaplain, national guard chaplain, prison chaplain, nursing home chaplain, mental health chaplain, and hospital chaplain.

- *Serving in Extension Ministries: Chaplains and Pastoral Counselors.* 8 pages. Discusses chaplains and their responsibilities in different settings.

- *United Methodist Pastors and the Armed Forces Reserve/Guard Program.* 6 pages. Questions and answers about pastors in the armed forces.

- *Pastoral Care/Counseling/Education.* 2 pages. Lists organizations offering education for, information about, and certification for pastoral care in specialized settings.

- *College Bound: Featuring Loan and Scholarship Information for Undergraduate and Graduate Students.* (HE5001) 24 pages. Includes information such as fall enrollment figure, percentage of students receiving financial aid, required admissions tests and financial aid forms, undergraduate tuition and fees, and programs and degrees offered.

• *Schools, Colleges, and Universities of the United Methodist Church, U.S.A.* 8 pages. Lists schools of theology, professional schools, senior colleges and universities, two-year colleges, and college preparatory schools of the United Methodist Church, U.S.A. Also includes a map showing the location of the institutions.

• *Handbook of the United Methodist-Related Schools, Colleges, Universities and Theological Schools with a Guide to United Methodist Loans and Scholarships.* (#740534) ($5) 338 pages. Designed as a resource for students, families, and pastors. Describes educational opportunities available through United Methodist-related educational institutions and includes information about selecting a college, financing a college education, and United Methodist loans and scholarships

For information on the following materials, contact the UMC and/or order directly from Cokesbury Customer and Distribution Services at 800-672-1789

• *The Christian as a Minister.* (#804294) ($4) 104 pages. Chapters include Servant Ministry, The Settings for Servant Leadership, and Steps into Servant Ministries. Contains an index of United Methodist schools for theology.

• *United Methodist Schools of Theology.* (#806910) 27 pages. Lists and describes the 13 United Methodist seminaries.

• *Steps into Ordained Ministry.* (#741436) 4 pages. Describes seven steps for ordination as a deacon or an elder in the United Methodist Church.

• *Are You Ready?* (#789847) ($.50) 8 pages. Information on ordained ministry. Serves as a recruitment piece for young audiences.

733
UNITED NEGRO COLLEGE FUND, INC.
Program Services Department
8260 Willow Oaks Corporate Drive
PO Box 10444
Fairfax, VA 22031-4511
703-205-3538 or 800-331-UNCF

• *College Guide: 39 Places to Expand Your Mind.* 47 pages. Lists and describes the 39 historically black colleges and universities.

• *Student Handbook.* 16 pages. Advises on how to choose a college; and includes a directory of UNCF's member schools and the types of programs offered.

734
UNITED STATES COAST GUARD
14180 Dallas Parkway
Suite 326
Dallas, TX 75240-4373
800-GET-USCG
http://www.gov/dotinfo/uscg

• *Get M.O.R.E. Out of Life.* 8 pages. Describes the Minority Officer Recruiting Effort.

• *Get to the Top Faster: Become a United States Coast Guard Officer.* 10 pages.

• *Missions of the United States Coast Guard.* 8 pages.

• *Montgomery G.I. Bill: Get up to $14,998 for College, Plus a Whole Lot More.* 6 pages.

• *Officer Candidate School: How Do You Get to the Top Faster?* 10 pages.

• *Opportunities for Action: Enlisted Career Guide.* 43 pages.

• *Things to Remember When You Visit Your Coast Guard Recruiter.* 6 pages.

• *United States Coast Guard: Ready for Action?* 10 pages.

• *United States Coast Guard: Unique Education, Unique Opportunity.* 8 pages.

- *United States Coast Guard Academy: This Is More than 4 Years in the Classroom.* 10 pages.

- *United States Coast Guard Reserve: Want to See Some Action This Weekend?* 10 pages.

735
UNITED STATES COMMISSION ON CIVIL RIGHTS
Publications
624 Ninth Street NW
Washington, DC 20425
202-376-8128
Fax: 202-376-7597
http://www.usccr.gov

- *Catalog of Publications.* 13 pages. Lists various reports and studies on national, regional, and local civil rights matters.

- *Civil Rights Journal.* A magazine published quarterly by the U.S. Commission on Civil Rights. Available from the Superintendent of Documents, Government Printing Office, Washington, DC 20402. Features a variety of articles on civil rights issues.

- *Civil Rights Update.* A quarterly pamphlet containing a selection of timely articles about civil rights matters.

736
UNITED STATES DEPARTMENT OF AGRICULTURE
Office of Personnel
Recruitment and Employment Division
Attn: Summer Internship Program
Room 301
West Administrative Building
1400 Independence Avenue SW
Washington, DC 20250-0002
202-447-2791

- *Summer Internship Program.* Offers paid internships that may be administrative, professional, scientific, or technical, depending on the agency.

737
UNITED STATES DEPARTMENT OF EDUCATION
Office of the Secretary
400 Maryland Avenue SW
Washington, DC 20202-0001
202-708-5366

- *A Teacher's Guide to the United States Department of Education.* 94 pages. A resource guide for teachers about the support programs, services, and publications available from the Department of Education. Provides a general description of programs and their relative location within the department, as well as a reference to which teachers can turn for specific needs or questions.

738
UNITED STATES DEPARTMENT OF EDUCATION
Information Resource Center
400 Maryland Avenue SW
Washington, DC 20202
800-USA-LEARN or 800-872-5327
http://www.ed.gov

- *Community Update.* A monthly newsletter, also available at the web site, containing timely articles on community involvement in education.

- *Preparing Your Child for College: A Resource Book for Parents.* 57 pages. Designed to help parents explore college options with their child and their child's teachers and guidance counselors, prepare their child academically for the rigors of college, and plan financially for the costs of a college education.

739
UNITED STATES DEPARTMENT OF ENERGY
National Energy Information Center
PO Box 62
Oak Ridge, TN 37831
202-586-8800
Fax: 202-586-0727
http://www.eia.doe.gov

- *Energy Education Resources.* Provides free or low-cost energy-related educational materials to kindergarten through 12th grade students and educators.

- *Learning about Renewable Energy.* Suitable for middle and high school students. Includes inserts on transportation alternatives, recycling, conservation activities for the classroom, solar heating, and saving energy as well as an energy reading list.

740
UNITED STATES DEPARTMENT OF LABOR
Employment and Training Administration
200 Constitution Avenue NW
Room N4700
Washington, DC 20210
202-219-6871
Fax: 202-273-4793
http://www.doleta.gov

- *Tips for Finding the Right Job.* 27 pages. Offers information on resumes, cover letters, and interviewing.

741
UNITED STATES DEPARTMENT OF LABOR
Assistant Secretary of Policy
Washington, DC 20210
202-219-6197
http://www.dol.gov/dol/asp/public/programs/handbook/main.htm

- *The Small Business Handbook: Laws, Regulations and Technical Assistance Services.* Available at the web site and at local libraries. Includes such topics as minimum wage, child labor, alien workers, occupational safety and health, employment benefit plans, whistle-blower protection, veterans, plant closings, lie detector tests, and family and medical leave.

742
UNITED STATES DEPARTMENT OF STATE
Student Programs
Recruitment Division
PO Box 9317
Arlington, VA 22219
703-875-7490
http://www.state.gov

Visit the web site for Foreign Service and Civil Service career information.

743
UNITED STATES FISH AND WILDLIFE SERVICE
Office of Public Affairs
U.S. Department of the Interior
Washington, DC 20240
202-208-5611
Fax: 202-208-7409

- *A Challenge and an Adventure.* A video describing career opportunities with the Fish and Wildlife Service. To borrow a copy, contact your regional office or the Office of Public Affairs (202-208-5611) to find the branch nearest you.

- *Careers with the U.S. Fish and Wildlife Service.* 20 pages. More color photos than text, this book highlights the problems addressed by the service (pollution, deforestation, wildlife habitat), and describes the academic background required for its jobs.

744
UNITED STATES GOVERNMENT PRINTING OFFICE
Superintendent of Documents
PO Box 371954
Pittsburgh, PA 15250-7954
202-512-1800
Fax: 202-512-2250
http://www.access.gpo.gov/su_docs/

Call, write, or visit the web site for a current list of GPO career sales publications and subscriptions.

745–749 Free and Inexpensive Career Materials

- *Tips for Finding the Right Job.* ($1.25) (029-014-002445) 27 pages. Filled with advice on things which can make the job search successful.

745

UNITED STATES INFORMATION AGENCY
Fulbright Teacher Exchange Program
301 Fourth Street SW
Room 353
Washington, DC 20547
800-726-0479 or 202-619-4556
Fax: 202-401-1433

- *Fulbright Teacher Exchange Program.* 22 pages. Describes the exchange opportunities for U.S. university faculty, as well as secondary and elementary school teachers and administrators, to teach abroad; lists available positions by country; and includes application form.

746

UNITED STATES INFORMATION AGENCY
Office of Academic Programs
301 Fourth Street SW
Room 234
Washington, DC 20547
202-619-4360
exchange@usia.gov
http://www.usia.gov./education/1 eburus.htm

- *Fulbright Scholar Program.* 167 pages. Lists and describes the specific Fulbright senior scholar awards available for U.S. faculty, professionals, teachers, and students. Includes application for grants.

747

UNITED STATES MILITARY ENTRANCE PROCESSING COMMAND
2500 Green Bay Road
North Chicago, IL 60064
800-323-0513

- *Military Careers: A Guide to Military Occupations and Selected Military Career Paths.* 427 pages. A collection of military occupational, training, and career information. Used as a reference source for educators and students to aid in learning about the diverse opportunities available to young people in the military. Contains descriptions of 152 enlisted and officer occupations.

748

UNITED STATES OFFICE OF PERSONNEL MANAGEMENT
Washington Area Service Center
1900 E Street NW
Washington, DC 20415
202-606-1000
http://www.usajobs.opm.gov

OPM's self-service system for employment information, described below, provides a list of the latest federal worldwide job openings, state and local government jobs, and private industry jobs, as well as access to application materials.

- *Career America Connection (CAC).* Dial 912-757-3000 or 912-744-2299 (TDD) to request full-text vacancy announcements and receive complete information about the job and application process.

- *USA JOBS Web Site.* Lets you tailor your job search, view daily updated listings, and receive other employment information.

- *Turn on Your Computer and Dial Up.* Access the Federal Job Opportunities Board (FJOB) from a personal computer by dialing 912-757-3100. You can also access FJOB by Telenet at fjob.opm.gov or file transfer protocol at ftp.fjob.opm.gov.

749

UNITED STATES PATENT AND TRADEMARK OFFICE
U.S. Department of Commerce
Public Affairs, Crystal Park 2
Suite 0100
Washington, DC 20231

703-305-8341
Fax: 703-308-5258
http://www.uspto.gov/

- *Basic Facts about Patents.* 7 pages. Answers some of the most frequently questions about getting a patent.

- *Basic Facts about Trademarks.* 32 pages. Contains instructions and forms for registering a trademark for a product or service.

- *Internet Information.* 3 pages. Describes U.S. patent and trademark information available on the Internet.

750
UNITED STATES SMALL BUSINESS ADMINISTRATION
Publications, Mc 7111
409 Third Street SW
Washington, DC 20416
202-205-6666
http://www.sba.gov

- *Planning and Goal Setting for Small Business.* (#MP06) ($3) Lists management techniques for planning.

- *Checklist for Going into Business.* (#MP12) ($3) Also available in Spanish (#MP12s). Highlights the important factors in reaching a decision to start a business.

- *How to Buy or Sell a Business.* (#MP16) ($3) Lists several techniques for determining the best price to buy or sell a small business.

- *Handbook for Small Business.* (#MP31) ($4) Information for getting started in a new business. Developed by SBA's Service Corps of Retired Executives (SCORE).

- *Ideas into Dollars.* (#P101) ($3) Identifies the main challenges in product development and provides a list of resources to help investors and innovators take their ideas into the marketplace.

- *Avoiding Patent, Trademark and Copyright Problems.* (#P102) ($3) Tips on how to avoid infringing upon the rights of others and how to protect your own rights.

- *Resource Directory for Small Business Management.* 6 pages. A list of SBA publications and videotapes for starting and managing a successful small business.

751
UNITED STATES SMALL BUSINESS ADMINISTRATION
Investment Division, MC 7940
409 Third Street SW
Washington, DC 20416
202-205-7589
Fax: 202-205-6013

- *Directory of Small Business Investment Companies.* 100 pages.

752
UNIVERSITY AVIATION ASSOCIATION
Resource Center Manager
3410 Skyway Drive
Opelika, AL 36801
205-844-2434

- *Federal Aviation Administration (FAA) Aviation Career Series.* Titles in this series of brochures include *Pilots and Flight Engineers, Flight Attendants, Airline Non-Flying Careers, Aircraft Manufacturing, Aviation Maintenance and Avionics, Aviation Safety Inspector, Air Traffic Control Specialist, Airport Careers, Government Careers, Women in Aviation,* and *Your Career in Aviation: The Sky's the Limit.*

753
UNIVERSITY OF CALIFORNIA
Department of Anthropology
Berkeley, California 94720-3710
510-642-3616
http:/ls.berkeley.edu/dept/anth/handbook.html

- *Anthropology: A Handbook for Undergraduate Majors.* Provides career information.

754
UNIVERSITY OF CALIFORNIA
Environmental Design Library
210 Wurster Hall, #6000
Berkeley, California 94720-6000
510-642-4818
http://www.lib.berkeley.edu/ENVI/jobs.html

- *Job Hunting.* Selectively annotated guide to help job seekers in the professions of city and regional planning, architecture, and landscape architecture. Highlights useful information on job hunting, researching prospective employers, creating resumes and portfolios, interviewing for jobs, and negotiating for salaries.

755
UNIVERSITY OF DELAWARE SEA GRANT COLLEGE PROGRAM
Marine Communications Office
Newark, DE 19716-3530
302-831-8175
Fax: 302-831-2005
http://www.udel.edu/cms/seagrant

- *Marine Careers.* 4 pages. Covers educational requirements and outlook for marine science careers, including marine biologist, marine chemist, marine geologist, physical oceanographer, and ocean engineer. Also contains sources of additional marine career information.

756
UNIVERSITY OF ILLINOIS AT URBANA-CHAMPAIGN
Department of Agricultural Engineering
338 Agricultural Engineering Science Building
1304 West Pennsylvania Avenue
Urbana, IL 61801
217-333-3570
Fax: 217-244-0323
http://www.age.uiuc.edu

- *A Challenging and Rewarding Career: Agricultural Engineering at the University of Illinois.* 8 pages.

- *Food and Bioprocess Engineers: People in Demand.* 8 pages. A promotional brochure for the school containing some good, general information on the field.

757
UNIVERSITY OF ROCHESTER
Center for Work and Career Development
107 Administration Building
Rochester, NY 14627
http://www.rochester.edu/student-srvcs/cwcd/

- *Thinking about a Career in Law.* 1 page. SASE. Suggests the educational route for undergraduate students to follow in preparation for law school.

758
UNIVERSITY/RESIDENT THEATRE ASSOCIATION, INC.
1560 Broadway
Room 1307
New York, NY 10036
212-221-1130
Fax: 212-869-2752
urta@aol.com

- *U/RTA Theatre Directory of Member Training Programs and Associated Theatres.* ($5) 50 pages. Lists professional training programs (contact information, type of programs offered, period of engagement, stipends available, degree programs, and planned productions for the season) and provides similar details on U/RTA producing companies.

759
USA TODAY
Education Partnerships
1000 Wilson Boulevard, T1-19
Arlington, VA 22229
http://www.usatoday.com

- *Careers: A Lifetime Journey.* ($5) A teaching guide that provides educators with real-world tools and information to assist students in life-long career planning. Leads students through self-assessment activities and introduces them to role models.

Many other educational materials are available. Write for a *Connect Your Curriculum to the World* catalog featuring *USA Today* educational programs and materials.

760
VINCENT/CURTIS
224 Clarendon Street
Boston, MA 02116
617-536-0100

- *Vincent/Curtis Educational Register.* 235 pages. Lists by region day and boarding schools, camps, and summer study programs.

761
VIRGINIA EMPLOYMENT COMMISSION AND VIRGINIA OCCUPATIONAL INFORMATION COORDINATING COMMITTEE
Economic Information Services Division
Labor Market and Demographics Analysis Section
Room 213
PO Box 1358
Richmond, VA 23218-1358
804-786-8223
Fax: 804-371-0412

- *Mid-Atlantic Guide to Information on Careers (MAGIC).* 24 pages. Contains occupational information from educators, state employment offices, administrators, counselors, students, businesses, and job seekers. Includes sections on career planning, training and education, financial aid, occupations, job searching, applying for a job, job interviews, and budgeting.

- *Apprenticeship Occupations in Virginia.*

- *Covered Employment & Wage Data.* Specify statewide, county, or city.

- *Industry and Occupational Employment Projections: 1994-2005, Virginia-Statewide.*

- *Labor Market Information Directory.*

- *Licensed and Certified Occupations in Virginia.*

762
VIRGINIA VIEW
Virginia Polytechnic Institute
205 West Roanoke Street
Blacksburg, VA 24061-0527
540-231-7571
Fax: 540-231-4979
http://vaview.vavu.vt.edu/

- *Career Hunt.* 56 pages. An annual newspaper providing educational and occupational information, including brief descriptions of 300 occupations. Lists Virginia approved two- and four- year public and private institutions and private career schools, and more.

- *VIEWStart.* A tabloid designed for elementary and middle school students. Takes a lighter approach to discussing career development.

- *Interactive VIEW.* ($5.50) A software program that contains the complete Virginia VIEW career information database. Uses approximately 10MB of storage and is available for Macintosh and PCs.

- *Career Information Hotline.* Call 800-542-5870 (toll free in Virginia). Provides access to up-to-date career information and a list of software programs, print materials, and resources on the Internet. Discusses occupational outlook, work requirements, salaries, postsecondary education, military training, apprenticeships, licensure and other topics. Hotline hours are 9 a.m. to 9 p.m. Monday through Friday and 10 a.m. to 2 p.m. on Saturday.

763
VISTA MAGAZINE
999 Ponce de Leon Boulevard
Suite 600
Coral Gables, FL 33134
800-521-0953 or 305-442-2462

- *The Scholarship Guide for Hispanics: College Financial Assistance Opportunities.* 95 pages. *Vista Magazine,* together with Chrysler Corporation compiled this book, which is distributed by Montemayor y Asociados, 70 Northeast Loop 410, Suite 870, San Antonio, TX 78216.

764
VOCATIONAL BIOGRAPHIES, INC.
Attn: LA6
PO Box 31
Sauk Center, MN 56378-0031
800-255-0752
Fax: 320-352-5546
VocBio@aol.com

- *Vocational Biographies.* Choose from 875 titles. Each four-page brief discusses careers ranging from the traditional to the newly emerging and talks about real-life experiences of actual people. Call or write for a complete *Vocational Biographies Career Library Index.*

765
WATER ENVIRONMENT FEDERATION
601 Wythe Street
Alexandria, VA 22314-1994
703-684-2400
http://www.wef.org

- *Test the Waters! Careers in Water Quality.* 8 pages. SASE. Highlights career and employment opportunities, as well as the required training and skills for a number of jobs.

766
WEED SCIENCE SOCIETY OF AMERICA
PO Box 1897
Lawrence, KS 66044-8897
800-627-0629
Fax: 913-843-1274
http://www.uiuc.edu/ph/www/wssa/

- *Career Opportunities in Weed Science.* 6 pages. Describes the field, scope of the work, employment opportunities, and educational requirements.

767
WEST VIRGINIA BUREAU OF EMPLOYMENT PROGRAMS
Office of Labor and Economic Research
112 California Avenue
Charleston, WV 25305-0112
304-558-2600

- *Employment and Earnings Trends.*

- *Employment and Wages.*

- *Industrial and Occupational Wage Survey.*

- *Licensed Occupations in West Virginia.*

- *Occupational Employment in West Virginia Businesses and Industries.*

- *Special Report: West Virginia Women in the Workforce.*

- *Special Report on Veterans: State of West Virginia.*

- *West Virginia County Profiles.* County-by-county description of basic economic, employment, and demographic data.

- *West Virginia Economic Summary.* Monthly data on employment, unemployment, industry, and civilian labor force.

- *West Virginia Occupational Projections.*

- *West Virginia Youth and the Labor Market.*

768
WEST VIRGINIA OCCUPATIONAL INFORMATION COORDINATING COMMITTEE
West Virginia Department of Education
Barron Drive
PO Box 487
Institute, WV 25112-0487
304-766-2687
Fax: 304-766-2689

- *Job Openings for West Virginia.* 4 pages. Lists the annual average number of job openings for various job clusters.

- *West Virginia Careers.* 36 pages. A tabloid containing valuable career information geared toward the high school and college student. Provides insights into the job market, identifies growing job fields, discusses required education, and lists additional resources for information.

769
WIDER OPPORTUNITIES FOR WOMEN
815 15th Street NW
Suite 916
Washington, DC 20005
202-638-3143

- *Fact Sheets.* ($1.50 each) Available titles include *Overview: Women in the Workforce; Women and Nontraditional Work; Women, Work and Age; Women, Work and Child Care; Women, Work and Family; Women, Work and the Future;* and *Women, Work and Health Insurance.*

770
WILDLIFE SOCIETY
5410 Grosvenor Lane
Bethesda, MD 20814-2197
301-897-9770
Fax: 301-530-2471
tws@wildlife.org

- *A Wildlife Conservation Career for You.* 12 pages. Describes careers in wildlife management, related opportunities, education needed, and personal requirements.

- *Universities and Colleges Offering Curricula in Wildlife Conservation.* 6 pages. North American campuses that have special curricula related to the fields of wildlife conservation and management.

771
WISCONSIN CAREER INFORMATION SYSTEM
Center on Education and Work
University of Wisconsin at Madison
Room 1074, Educational Sciences Unit I
1025 West Johnson Street
Madison, WI 53706
800-442-4612 or 608-263-2725

- *Wisconsin Careers.* 8-16 pages. A tabloid newspaper published twice a year.

772
WISCONSIN DEPARTMENT OF WORKFORCE DEVELOPMENT
Employment and Training Library
PO Box 7944
Madison, WI 53707-7944
608-266-2832
Fax: 608-266-5887

- *Labor Market Planning Information.* 80 pages. A statewide report providing a general economic picture of Wisconsin (employment, population, and income).

773
WOMEN'S BUREAU
Office of the Secretary
U.S. Department of Labor
200 Constitution Avenue NW
Washington, DC 20210
800-827-5335
http://www.dol.gov/dol/wb/

- *Worth More than We Earn; Fair Pay for Working Women.*

774
WOMEN'S EDUCATIONAL EQUITY ACT
Education Development Center, Inc.
55 Chapel Street
Newton, MA 02158-1060
800-225-3088 or 617-969-7100
Fax: 617-332-4318

WEEApub@EDC.org
http://www.edc.org/ceec/weea

- *Women in School Administration: Overcoming the Barriers to Advancement.* 6 pages.

775
WOMEN'S SPORTS FOUNDATION
Eisenhower Park
East Meadow, NY 11554
800-227-3988 or 516-542-4700
Fax: 516-542-4716
http://www.lifetimetv.com/wosport

- *Women's Athletic Scholarship Guide.* ($3)

- *Women's Guide to Coaching.* ($3)

- *Award, Grant & Scholarship Summary.*

- *Parent's Guide to Girls' Sports.* More materials are available. Call or write for a resource order form.

776
WORLD SPORTS MEDICINE ASSOCIATION OF REGISTERED THERAPISTS
206 Marine Avenue, Box 5527
Balboa Island, CA 92662-5527
818-574-1999

- *Sports Medicine Therapist.*

Section V

Career Sites on the World Wide Web

Following is a sampling of career sites on the World Wide Web. Professional associations, Internet clearinghouses of job information, employment services, online career centers, and other sites are represented. This will give you an idea of the variety of career information available for free on the Internet. For a more in-depth list of resources, look for *Ferguson's Guide to the Best Career Resources on the Web,* which will be published in the spring of 1998.

AMERICAN ASSOCIATION OF COLLEGES OF NURSES (AACN)
http://www.aacn.nche.edu/index.html

The AACN describes itself as the national voice for nursing education programs. Its extremely well-organized site includes a schedule of upcoming conferences and seminars.

AMERICA'S JOB BANK
http://www.ajb.dni.us

Operated by the U.S. Department of Labor, this computerized network links the 1,800 local offices of state Employment Service programs and provides the largest selection of job opportunities available on the Internet.

BEST BETS FROM THE NET
http://www.lib.umich.edu/chdocs/employment/

This guide collects the Net's best sources for job openings and career development information, with a description and evaluation of each resource.

CAREER MAGAZINE
http://www.careermag.com

With daily job updates, profiles of employers, discussion groups, classified ads, and news articles, this is a comprehensive career resource for job seekers and employers.

CAREER MOSAIC
http://www.careermosaic.com

This site offers job listings, employer profiles, job fairs, and a career resource center, which provides tips on job-hunting and resume writing, as well as links to professional and industry associations.

CAREERNET
http://www.careers.org

A comprehensive site for job listings and information, CareerNet offers links to jobs and employers, as well as to business, education, and career service professionals on the Internet.

CAREER PATH
http://www.careerpath.com

This is a World Wide Web employment service with job listings from six major city newspapers.

CAREER RESOURCES HOMEPAGE, RENSSELAER POLYTECHNIC INSTITUTE
http://www.rpi.edu/dept/cdc/homepage.html

Career Sites on the World Wide Web

This site contains an index of Internet career resources, including the Internet Job Surfer which provides access to various commercial job databases on the Internet.

THE CATAPULT, NATIONAL ASSOCIATION OF COLLEGES AND EMPLOYERS
http://www.jobweb.org/catapult/catapult.htm

This clearinghouse contains references to career guides and library resources, job postings, professional associations, and college career centers.

COLOSSAL LIST OF CAREER LINKS
http://www.emory.edu/CAREER/Links.html

This is a clearinghouse of career resources on the Internet.

COOLWORKS
http://www.coolworks.com/showme

CoolWorks quickly links you up to a mass of information about seasonal employment at dozens of national and state parks, preserves, monuments, and wilderness areas.

EMPLOYMENT OPPORTUNITIES AND RESOURCES PAGE
gopher://cwis.usc.edu/11/other_Gopher_and_Information_Resources/Gophers_by_Subject/Gopher_Jewels/stuff/employment

This site offers job postings, resume postings, and an entire section on academic job openings.

EMPLOYMENT RESOURCES ON THE INTERNET
http://member.iguest.net/~swlodin/jobs/

This site lists career articles and books, career-based employment companies, contract employment and consulting opportunities, professional recruiters, and more.

ENGINEERING: YOUR FUTURE
http://www.asee.org/pre/pre.html

Sponsored by the American Society for Engineering Education, this web site supplies excellent information for "precollege engineers."

ENVIRONMENTAL CAREERS ORGANIZATION
http://www.eco.org

Founded in 1972 as an experimental internship program in Massachusetts, the Environmental Careers Organization (ECO) has developed into a national, nonprofit organization offering career advice, career products, and numerous environmental internships across the country.

ENVIRONMENTAL PROFESSIONAL'S HOMEPAGE
http://www.clay.net

Sponsored by GZA GeoEnvironmental Technologies, this home page for environmental professionals provides a straightforward index to a wealth of factual data and information. It's fast, reliable, and will link you to original source documents from the EPA and other agencies.

ERISS
http://www.eriss.com

This is a list of sites focusing on job listings, resumes, career resources, government agencies, and job search software sources.

E-SPAN'S INTERACTIVE EMPLOYMENT NETWORK
http://www.espan.com

Register at this site-free-and E-Span's search system automatically emails you appropriate job openings.

GOOD WORKS
http://www.tripod.com/work/goodworks/search.html

This is a great source of information on careers in social change.

HEALTHWEB: NURSING
http://www.lib.umich.edu/hw/nursing.html

An impressive, collaborative effort of the Taubman Medical Library, the School of Nursing at the University of Michigan, and the HealthWeb project, this site is a heavyweight of nursing information.

HUMAN RESOURCE PLANNING SOCIETY
http://www.hrsp.org

This professional association's site offers networking opportunities for human resource and business executives.

INTERNATIONAL HOMEWORKER'S ASSOCIATION
http://www.homeworkers.com

This web site offers career information and job postings for people who work out of their homes.

INTERN-NET
http://www.vicon.net/~internnet

Intern-NET is a new and growing database for students seeking internships. From the home page you can search for an internship by selecting a category, then choosing a region of the United States where you want to work.

JOB HUNT, STANFORD UNIVERSITY
http://rescomp.stanford.edu/jobs.html

This site contains job postings, classified ads from major newspapers, and other job search resources and services.

JOBLIST
http://asae.org/jobs/

This is an alphabetical list of employment resources on the Internet.

JOBTRAK
http://www.jobtrak.com

A huge job listing service, with special links to more than 350 college and university career centers nationwide, this site focuses on services to employers seeking new or recent college graduates and on students seeking job and career information.

JUNIOR ENGINEERING TECHNICAL SOCIETY (JETS)
http://www.asee.org/jets/

The mission of JETS is to provide opportunities for students to "try out" careers while they're in high school so that they can make informed academic and career choices.

KAPLAN'S GUIDE TO NURSING AND THE NCLEX
http://www.kaplan.com/nclex/

A commercial enterprise sponsored by Kaplan Educational Centers, this site provides some interesting information for students entering the nursing field. In the careers section, for example, you'll find information about using a nursing degree as a steppingstone to advanced career paths such as nurse administrator, nurse attorney, or nurse clinician.

MONSTER BOARD
http://199.94.216.71

This job site advertises instant access to thousands of jobs in all fields and allows you to submit your resume to its database.

Career Sites on the World Wide Web

MY FUTURE
http://www.myfuture.com/

This colorful site aims to help new high school graduates "jumpstart their lives" with information about alternatives to four-year colleges, such as military opportunities, apprenticeships, and technical or vocational colleges. While the site is divided into three main sections-My Career, My Money, and My World-the majority of useful information is in the career section.

NATIONAL GERONTOLOGICAL NURSING ASSOCIATION (NGNA)
http://www.nursingcenter.com/people/nrsorgs/ngna/

This site is sponsored by the first and only specialty organization dedicated to gerontological nursing. If you are interested in improving the nursing care of the elderly, check out this site for career information.

NURSINGNET
http://www.nursingnet.org/

Could you use some advice about nursing careers or nursing school from someone who's already been there? NursingNet is the place to look. Its centerpiece is a new online mentoring program connecting nurses and nursing students from around the world to discuss their jobs and studies with one another. Just fill out an online application to become a participant.

NURSINGWORLD
http://www.nursingworld.org/

This American Nurses Association's site promises "nursing's future at your fingertips" and is devoted to member information for three affiliate organizations-the American Academy of Nursing, the American Nurses Credentialing Center, the American Nurses Foundation.

ONLINE CAREER CENTER
http://www.occ.com

This is a job and resume resource maintained by a nonprofit employer association.

OUTDOOR ACTION GUIDE TO OUTDOOR/ENVIRONMENTAL CAREERS
http://www.princeton.edu/~oa/careeroe.html#Types of Careers

If you're only beginning your search for an environmental career, this short but useful home page is a good starting place. The material was written as a resource guide for a Princeton University workshop on outdoor and environmental careers, but many people will be interested in its table of contents: finding your career, types of careers, career examples, job newsletters, books, other resources, graduate programs in environmental education, environmental job leads, basic job questionnaire, and trends in employment.

THE PRINCETON REVIEW
http://www.review.com/

This site is everything you want in a high school guidance counselor-it's friendly, well-informed, and available to you night and day. Originally a standardized test preparation company, the Princeton Review is now online, giving you frank advice on colleges, careers, and of course, SATs.

QUINTESSENTIAL CAREER AND JOB-HUNTING RESOURCES GUIDE
http://www.stetson.edu/~hansen/careers.html

In addition to the usual career links, this site focuses on information that is helpful to new college graduates seeking employment.

THE RILEY GUIDE: EMPLOYMENT OPPORTUNITIES AND JOB RESOURCES ON THE INTERNET
http://www.jobtrak.com

This is one of several comprehensive clearinghouses of job and career information on the Internet.

UBIQUITY
http://ourworld.compuserve.com/homepages/ubikk

Here's a friendly little site that was created with the sole purpose of introducing people to the environmental job market. While a bit eclectic, it's full of useful information. The most frequently visited page is the Environmental Job Descriptions Page, which provides brief job summaries for more than twenty jobs. Elsewhere in Ubiquity's site, you'll find resume and cover letter writing tips geared specifically at job seekers in environmental fields.

USDA FOREST SERVICE
http://www.fs.fed.us/

Scratch beneath the surface of this mostly text-based government site, and you'll find a useful resource for information about the Forest Service. One area labeled "Human Resources" is stuffed with relevant information on job possibilities. Here you'll find links to several job search engines, including the vast FedWorld database. There's also an overview to the kinds of Forest Service jobs there are and how to get one.

U.S. DEPARTMENT OF DEFENSE SCHOLARSHIPS AND HIGH SCHOOL APPRENTICESHIPS
http://www.acq.osd.mil/ddre/edugate/s-aindx.html

It takes some time to sort through all of the job listings on this site, but it's time well spent.

U.S. NEWS & WORLD REPORT CAREER GUIDE
http://www.usnews.com/usnews/edu/

This site, which describes the current market for engineers, hosts several great search engines. You can search the Occupational Outlook Handbook by keyword or search for information about schools.

U.S. NURSING CAREER TITLES
http://www.amideast.org/pubs/aq/aqnrsttl.htm

This web page concisely defines the various titles used in the nursing industry. Under each job title, there's information about the length of on-the-job training needed, licensing and education requirements, and a brief description of job responsibilities.

YAHOO: ENGINEERING
http://www.yahoo.com/Science/Engineering/

It might seem odd to include the popular search engine Yahoo among a list of engineering web sites, but it won't seem so after you've visited it.

YAHOO: PROFESSIONAL ASSOCIATIONS
http://www.yahoo.com/Economy/Organizations/Professional/

This is a huge collection of professional association web sites.

YAHOO: WOMEN'S CAREER RESOURCES
http://www.yahoo.com/Business_and_Economy/Employment/Womens_Career_Resources/

This Yahoo index offers links to thousands of sites related to women and careers.

SECTION V
Related Reference Books

Dates of publication are not cited because most of these books are revised annually or periodically.

Career World (periodical). General Learning Corporation, 60 Revere Drive, Northbrook, Illinois 60056.

Catalog of Federal Domestic Assistance. U.S. Government Printing Office, Washington, DC 20402.

Create Your Own School Career Information Centre. North York Career Centre, 44 Appian Way, North York, Ontario, M2J 2P9 Canada.

Developing a Career Information Centre. Canadian Career Information Association, PO Box 84, Station B, Toronto, Ontario, M5S 2S6 Canada.

Encyclopedia of Careers and Vocational Guidance. Ferguson Publishing Company, 200 West Madison Street, Chicago, Illinois 60606.

Ferguson's Guide to Apprenticeship Programs. Ferguson Publishing Company, 200 West Madison Street, Chicago, Illinois 60606.

Free Stuff from Uncle Sam. JETCO Publications, PO Box 1255K, Newark, New Jersey 07101.

Government Job Finder. Planning Communications, 7215 Oak Avenue, River Forest, Illinois 60305.

Guide to Education Advising Resources. Amideast, 1100 17th Street NW, Washington, DC 20036.

Information USA. Information USA, Inc., PO Box E, Kensington, Maryland 20895.

Internships. Peterson's Guides, Inc., Box 2123, Princeton, New Jersey 08543-2123.

The Internship Bible. Random House, Incorporated, 201 East 50th Street, New York, New York 10022.

Internships: A Directory for Career-Finders & Career-Changers. Macmillan Publishing Company, Incorporated, Division of Simon & Schuster, 201 West 103rd Street, Indianapolis, Indiana 46290.

Job Hunter's Sourcebook. Gale, 835 Penobscot Building, Detroit, Michigan 48226.

National Trade and Professional Associations of the United States. Columbia Books, 1212 New York Avenue, Suite 330, Washington, DC 20005.

Non-Profits Job Finder. Planning Communications, 7215 Oak Avenue, River Forest, Illinois 60305.

Occupational Outlook Handbook. U.S. Department of Labor, U.S. Government Printing Office, Superintendent of Documents, Washington, DC 20402.

Inexpensive Career Materials *from Ferguson*

Off to College Newsletter
A newsletter for anyone involved with college counseling

"Useful for both parents and students and belongs in high school and public libraries serving high school students…"

–Library Journal, 1997

Off to College is designed to meet the interests and needs of those concerned with guidance, college admissions, financial aid, and other phases of college counseling today.

The college admissions process is becoming more competitive and complex. This newsletter can be a valuable resource for anyone working with high school students or any high school librarian who wants to provide interesting and useful reading for students.

Off to College is published six times during the school year. Each issue contains current news articles that relate to trends, tuition rates, admission requirements and various aspects of campus life.

Request a free sample issue and take a look!

Bob Calvert, the managing editor, has been involved in career education for many years and has written the highly successful *Career Opportunities News* newsletter for the past 13 years. Bob studies over 100 periodicals each month to pull together important information for his newsletters.

GP187	1 year	$30.00
GP188	2 years	$50.00
GP189	3 years	$65.00

Career Opportunities News Newsletter

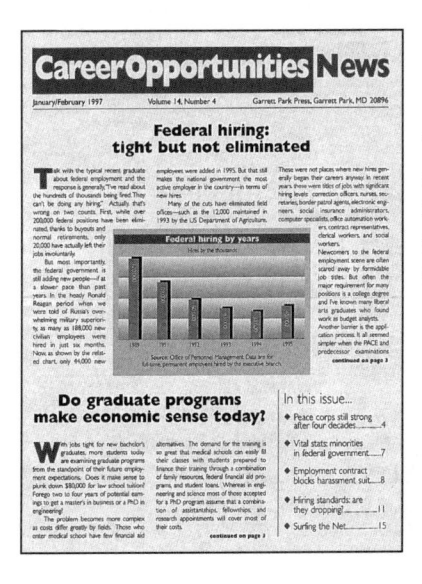

"A must read for career counselors."
–Joyce Lain Kennedy

"The best of its kind on the market."
–U.S. Department of Labor Official

This outstanding newsletter is a valuable source of information for anyone involved in career counseling or in career education. Articles cover many topics including:

- College admissions
- Financial Aid
- Occupational trends
- Free and inexpensive career materials
- Book reviews
- Articles of special interest to women and minorities
- Current information on areas of job growth and career opportunities

Subscribe now:
6 issues —plus bonuses each year!

The *Career Opportunities Newsletter* will keep you abreast of developments in the world of work. It contains practical and relevant information that will be useful in any guidance office, career center, high school or public library.

A free sample issue is available upon request!

GP161	1 year	$35.00
GP162	2 years	$55.00
GP163	3 years	$70.00

Dollars for College New for 1997!
The Quick Guide to Scholarships, Fellowships, Loans, and Other Financial Aid Programs

The *Dollars for College* series is unique in that each booklet focuses on a particular area of study. Students are able to pinpoint specific fields of interest quickly and use one booklet instead of searching through a single large directory containing information that is unrelated to the student's needs.

Each booklet contains a list of additional resources and a list of professional associations in the field. A useful index cross-references sources by state and by career field. Booklets are revised every 18 months and each cites from 300 to 400 programs and is 70–90 pages in length.

This series contains approximately 3,500 sources of financial aid. It's designed to be more user friendly than the heavy financial aid directories kept in the reserve section of the library.

Title	Code	ISBN	Year	Price
Set of all 12 booklets	GS133	0-89434-180-4	1997	$60.00
Art, Music, Drama	GP123	1-880774-19-4		$6.95
Business and Related Fields	GP124	1-880774-10-0		$6.95
The Disabled	GP186	0-84434-181-2		$6.95
Education	GP125	1-880774-12-7		$6.95
Engineering	GP126	1-880774-13-5		$6.95
Journalism and Mass Communication	GP127	1-880774-11-9		$6.95
Law	GP185	0-89434-188-X		$6.95
Liberal Arts: Humanities & Social Science	GP128	1-880774-18-6		$6.95
Medicine, Dentistry, & Related Fields	GP129	1-880774-15-1		$6.95
Nursing & Other Health Fields	GP130	1-880774-17-8		$6.95
Science	GP131	1-880774-14-3		$6.95
Women in All Fields	GP132	1-880774-20-8		$6.95

Financial Aid for Minority Students

CHOICE (American Library Association) says "this set excels in listing opportunities available through universities and private industry." Booklets are revised every 18 months and each lists around 300 programs, 60 – 80 pages each.

A six volume series which focuses on the financial aid opportunities available for minority students.

The six volumes include financial aid for students interested in:

Title	Code	ISBN
Business & Law	GP113	0-912048-88-3
Education	GP114	0-912048-99-9
Engineering and Science	GP115	0-912048-98-0
Health Fields	GP116	0-912048-96-4
Journalism & Mass Communications	GP117	0-912048-84-0
Awards Open to Students with Any Major	GP118	0-912048-93-1
Each individual title		$5.95
Set of 6 booklets	GS119	$25.00

College in Your Future
140 Questions and Answers About Getting In and Staying In

"...*Offers students and parents common sense information necessary in making a well-informed decision. Dr. Klein covers the gamut and adds additional sources available.*

With all the time, effort and expense invested in an education today, College in Your Future *is an easy to use, straight-forward guide designed to alleviate at least part of the college bound jitters.*"

–Mona Hallinan, EBR

Founder of the American College Admissions Advisory Center, Dr. Henry Klein has taken some of the guess work out of exploring the academic scene. Students learn how to get in and stay in the right school.

GP134   ISBN 1-880774-08-9   164 pages, PB
1995 $12.95

Career InfoPosters

Informational, Attractive, Motivational, and in Full Color

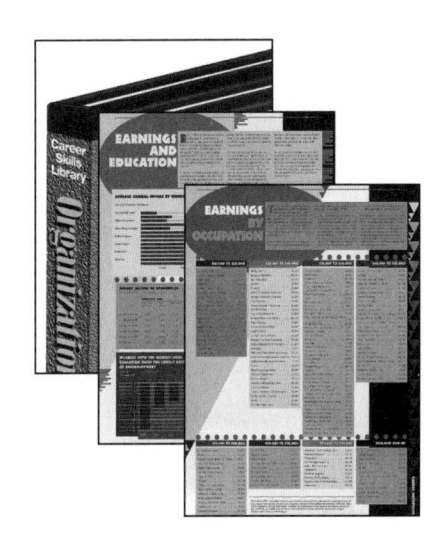

Information is presented in an appealing format. These 17" x 22" posters will enhance any wall or bulletin board and at the same time offer students valuable information on a particular aspect of career guidance.

These posters are not only attractive but they include lots of information that students can use in their career explorations.

Posters can be bought individually or as a set of six!

The set of six posters includes:

Code	Title	Year	Price
F163	Environmental Careers	1996	$3.00
F168	Earnings by Occupation	1996	$3.00
F164	Careers in Sports Fields	1996	$3.00
F166	Careers in Computer Fields	1996	$3.00
F167	Career Exploration Through School and Community Activities	1996	$3.00
F165	Earnings by Years of School	1996	$3.00
F170	Set of all six		$15.00

Ordering Information

Everything you purchase from Ferguson is returnable within 30 days if you are not satisfied. All we ask is that you include a copy of the invoice or packing list to ensure proper credit to your account.

3 Ways to Order

MAIL
Ferguson Publishing Company
200 West Madison St.
Suite 300, Chicago, IL 60606

PHONE
1-800-306-9941

FAX
1-800-306-9942

Shipping Information:

All orders are shipped UPS unless otherwise specified.
In the continental U.S., add 7% of total.
Minimum shipping charge is $4.00.